# SOAP:
## Cross Platform
## Web Service Development
## Using XML

## SCOTT SEELY

Prentice Hall PTR, *Upper Saddle River, NJ 07458*
http://www.prenhall.com

ISBN 0-13-090763-4

90000

9 780130 907639

Editorial/Production Supervision: *Kathleen M. Caren*
Acquisitions Editor: *Tim Moore*
Editorial Assistant: *Allyson Kloss*
Marketing Manager: *Debby Van Dijk*
Buyer: *Maura Zaldivar*
Cover Design: *Anthony Gemmellaro*
Cover Design Director: *Jerry Votta*
Art Director: *Gail Cocker-Bogusz*
Interior Series Design and Page Makeup: *Meg Van Arsdale*

© 2002 Prentice Hall PTR
Prentice-Hall, Inc.
Upper Saddle River, NJ 07458

The publisher offers discounts on this book when ordered in bulk quantities.
For more information, contact
Corporate Sales Department,
Prentice Hall PTR
One Lake Street
Upper Saddle River, NJ 07458
Phone: 800-382-3419; FAX: 201-236-714
Email (Internet): corpsales@prenhall.com

ISBN 0-13-090763-4

Pearson Education LTD.
Pearson Education Australia PTY, Limited
Pearson Education Singapore, Pte. Ltd.
Pearson Education North Asia Ltd.
Pearson Education Canada, Ltd.
Pearson Educación de Mexico, S.A. de C.V.
Pearson Education—Japan
Pearson Education Malaysia, Pte. Ltd.
Pearson Education, Upper Saddle River, New Jersey

*Jean, Vince, and Angelino,*
*thanks for inspiring me to do great things.*

# Contents

FOREWORD. . . . . . . . . . . . . . . . . . . . . . . . . . . . . xi

ACKNOWLEDGMENTS. . . . . . . . . . . . . . . . . . . . . xiii

## PART ONE:

### SOAP—EVERYTHING YOU WANT TO KNOW . . . 1

1   HOW WE GOT TO SOAP . . . . . . . . . . . . . . . . . . . . . 3

The Abacus      4

Early Calculatorss      6

Programmable Machines      7

Electronic Computers      9

Distributed Computing      10

Summary      20

Bibliography      21

2    XML OVERVIEW . . . . . . . . . . . . . . . . . . . . . . 23

Uniform Resource Indentifiers    24

XML Basics    26

XML Schemas    28

XML Namespaces    34

XML Attributes    37

Summary    41

3    THE SOAP SPECIFICATION . . . . . . . . . . . . . . . . 43

Things to Know    45

Rules for Encoding Types in XML    46

The SOAP Message Exchange Model    63

Structure of a SOAP Message    66

Using SOAP in HTTP    79

Using SOAP for RPC    83

Summary    85

4    BUILDING A BASIC SOAP CLIENT AND
SERVER . . . . . . . . . . . . . . . . . . . . . . . . . . . . 87

SOAP Library Design    88

In Search of One Good Socket Library    90

SimpleSOAP Library    92

SOAPNetwork Library    139

A Simple SOAP Server    146

A Simple SOAP Client    156

Summary    160

Fun Things to Try    160

*PART TWO:*

RELATED TECHNOLOGIES . . . . . . . . . . . . . . 161

5    WEB SERVICES DESCRIPTION LANGUAGE . . . . . . . 163

WSDL Overview    165

Defining a Web Service    167

SOAP Binding    182

HTTP GET and POST Binding    187

MIME Binding    191

Summary    196

6    UNIVERSAL DESCRIPTION, DISCOVERY, AND
INTEGRATION . . . . . . . . . . . . . . . . . . . . . . . . . . . 197

UDDI Basics    198

Where Does UDDI Fit In?    200

UDDI Information Types    201

The Programmer's API    204

Summary    207

7    AVAILABLE SOAP IMPLEMENTATIONS . . . . . . . . . . . 209

Apache    210

IdooXoap    211

Iona    212

Microsoft    213

pocketSOAP    215

RogueWave    215

SOAP::Lite    217

White Mesa    217

Zope    218

Summary    218


# PART THREE:
## CASE STUDY:
## A WEB-BASED ACUTION SYSTEM . . . . . . . . . . 219


## 8    AUCTION SYSTEM AND REQUIREMENTS . . . . . . . . 221

Background    221

Executive Summary    222

Bidder Enrollment and Management    223

Item Enrollment and Management    224

The Bidding System    225

Reporting    226

Summary    228


## 9    AUCTION SYSTEM DESIGN . . . . . . . . . . . . . . . . . 229

Bidder Enrollment and Management    231

Item Enrollment and Management    234

The Bidding System    238

Summary    242


## 10    BIDDER ENROLLMENT . . . . . . . . . . . . . . . . . . . . 243

The Java Environment    244

Setting Up the Java Enviroment    244

Securing Access to the Web Service    256

The VB Environment    259

Summary    280

**11   CATEGORY AND ITEM MANAGEMENT** . . . . . . . . . . 283

General Implementation Rules     284

Category Management     285

Item Management     308

Summary     317

**12   THE BIDDING SYSTEM** . . . . . . . . . . . . . . . . . . . . 319

Bidding Pages     320

Bidding Web Service     331

Summary     336

**13   CASE STUDY SUMMARY** . . . . . . . . . . . . . . . . . . 337

Client Management     338

Category Management     339

Item Management     341

Auction     342

Summary     343

**APPENDIX** . . . . . . . . . . . . . . . . . . . . . . . . . . . . . 345

**INDEX** . . . . . . . . . . . . . . . . . . . . . . . . . . . . . . . 381

# Foreword

A s long as there have been two computers, there has been difficulty getting them to communicate. Dozens, possibly hundreds, of strategies have arisen, each with their own strong and weak points. However, the end result is that still, it is difficult to get two computers to agree on a strategy for communication. Everyone wants everyone else to change to meet their strategy's needs. Thus, we end up with the "Communication Wars," CORBA vs. DCOM, DCOM vs. RMI, messaging vs. RPC, and so on.

Into this tangled mass of communication comes SOAP (Simple Object Access Protocol). SOAP does not try to solve all problems; it only defines a simple, XML-based communication format. However, with this simple goal, and a powerful extensibility mechanism, SOAP bears the promise of being a true cross-everything communication protocol–cross-programming language, cross-operating system, cross-platform. As long as a computer, operating system, or programming language can generate and process XML (that is, text), it can make use of SOAP. Since the initial release, almost every major software vendor has either produced, or announced, an implementation of SOAP. We've seen standalone SOAP, SOAP built into Web servers, application servers, communication tools and even messaging middleware using SOAP. In the future, SOAP will become even more prevalent, as companies and organizations like Microsoft, IBM, Apache, and Sun add even more SOAP support to their applications, operating systems and programming languages.

As the SOAP specification winds its way through the W3 standardization process, I'm certain that we will see changes. However, please don't let this stop you from experimenting and using SOAP in your applications. Yes, there will be changes, but these should be relatively minor, and each implementation should hide many of these details.

I first "met" Scott because of a mailing list—DevelopMentor's excellent list devoted to SOAP discussions (*http://discuss.develop.com/soap.html* if you're interested in joining). There he tirelessly helped others understand what he obviously thought as an important technology. Therefore, I was glad to hear that he was also working on this book. He has packed a great deal of practical development advice into these pages. I also love the fact that he shows a variety of the implementations available, and that they are all communicating nicely.

I hope that as you read this book, you see why Scott and I think SOAP is so important. So, whether you are a Java developer using the Apache implementation of SOAP, a VB developer using the Microsoft SOAP Toolkit, or a C# developer using .NET Web Services, or one of the many other implementations available, I hope that you join us in using SOAP in your applications. Perhaps together we can all learn to communicate.

*Kent Sharkey*
.NET Frameworks Technical Evangelist
Microsoft Corporation

# Acknowledgments

It is amazing what one little protocol can do for an individual's life. In early 2000, Tim Moore at Prentice Hall wrote to a number of technical authors, including me, and asked what we thought of the Simple Object Access Protocol (SOAP). Never having heard of it, I went out and found the v0.9 specification and joined the SOAP mailing list hosted by DevelopMentor.[1] After completing my initial survey, I could not shake the feeling that SOAP was about to become something very big and important. By May 2000, I was signed up to write the book you now hold.

Writing a book on a new technology helps you understand how experts are created. You learn to understand the various nuances of what you can do with the protocol. Other standards may emerge to handle things the early adopters deem necessary (WSDL and UDDI emerged almost in response to SOAP's existence) and you learn those as well. If you participate in a discussion group and give good answers, you get noticed. For the few of you who subscribe to the DevelopMentor list, you know what happened to me. I gave a number of good answers and I open-sourced a fairly small SOAP engine (presented in Chapter 4). These actions resulted in Microsoft approaching me and eventually hiring me. Like I said, interesting things can happen to your life.

By coming over to Microsoft, I have been able to see how they do things on the inside with respect to SOAP. Right now, they really are concerned

---

[1] You can login their various lists by browsing over to *http://discuss.develop.com*.

**xiii**

about getting interoperability to work, both between their own products and between their products and other ones. I believe that the company will do the right thing and keep this attitude of making internal and external interoperability a priority. Inside, a lot of employees care about doing the right thing for everyone, not just for Microsoft.

I wrote this book during what seems to be the busiest year of my life (so far). I finished writing *Windows Shell Programming* in May 2000. Once that was done, I started in on this SOAP book. Besides that:

- I moved four times—twice in Wisconsin, twice in Washington.
- I interviewed and got a job writing for MSDN.
- My wife and I conceived and gave birth to Angeline (born March 15, 2001).

I could not have done all this without the support and help of my family. In between the sale of my house in Hartford, Wisconsin and my move to Oak Creek, Wisconsin, my grandfather let us move in for a bit. We all enjoyed spending that time together. I also have to thank my wife Jean and my two children, Vince and Angeline. They give me the strength and support to do amazing things. I have to thank my parents and my sister for believing in me. Finally, I want to thank Tim Moore and his staff at Prentice Hall. Thanks for cutting me some slack while writing this. My schedule slipped a number of times and they just took it in stride.

# Part 1

# SOAP— EVERYTHING YOU NEED TO KNOW

*In this part of the book, we take a look at the various technologies you need to understand to use the Simple Object Access Protocol, or SOAP, in its "raw" form. We start with a condensed history of computing technology to see what SOAP gives us in added flexibility with distributed computing. An XML primer follows. The XML chapter explains the XML technologies used by SOAP. The next chapter covers the SOAP v1.1 specification and explains the document in detail. We close the section with a C++-based implementation of a SOAP library. The implementation seeks to demonstrate how simple it can be to implement a SOAP parser.*

# Chapter 1

# HOW WE
# GOT TO SOAP

To understand why we need a technology such as the Simple Object Access Protocol (SOAP) we need to spend a bit of time looking at how computing technology has evolved. SOAP itself started out as a way to make distributed computing platform agnostic. We have always had the concept of distributed computing. The idea of having people perform calculations that they are good at and then handing the work off to other mathematicians is nothing new. For example, logarithms take a long time to compute. Because of this, people wrote out and reproduced logarithmic tables for other mathematicians to use.

To review the history, I would like to take a look at the things we have done in moving from the abacus to mechanical calculators and then to distributed computing. Understanding (or simply reviewing) this history gives some perspective of where we have come from and highlights why so many people are excited about SOAP. The idea of ubiquitous computing is moving from being just a neat idea to a reality. SOAP provides a way for all those computers to talk to each other and request services of each other. Indulge me as I present a little history lesson showing where our pursuit of automated number crunching has taken us.

# The Abacus

The abacus has been used as a calculator for thousands of years, and you can still find it in use in China, Japan, and the Middle East. The most common form of the abacus can register numbers from 1 to 9,999,999,999,999.[1] The abacus does this using 13 rows of beads as shown in Figure 1–1. The user of an abacus reads the numbers from the beads touching the center bar. Each bead touching the center bar on the bottom half of the abacus equals one times the units column. Each bead touching the center bar from the top half of the abacus equals five times the units column. Figure 1–2 shows how you would represent the number 23.

The abacus shines when adding and subtracting numbers. Practiced users can usually outpace a person using a modern adding machine. As users add the second number in, they slide the beads up and down. Every time all five bottom beads touch the center bar, one bead from the same column on the top bar must come down. Then, all five beads must be returned to the bottom

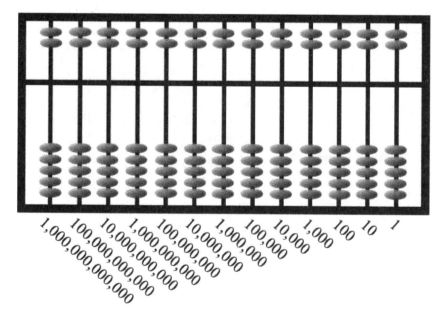

***Figure 1–1***  Thirteen–column abacus.

[1] This particular form of abacus has 13 rows. As a rule, an abacus can handle smaller or larger numbers depending on its construction. Smaller numbers need fewer rows—you could handle numbers through 9,999 with a four-row abacus. For each power of 10 that you want to handle, just add another row.

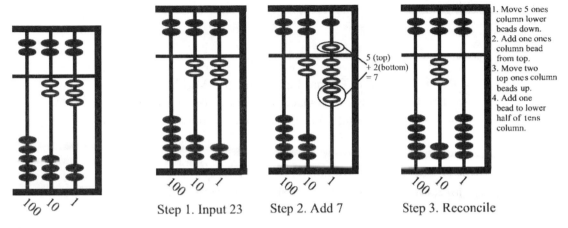

**Figure 1-3** Adding 23 and 7 using abacus.

Step 1. Input 23    Step 2. Add 7    Step 3. Reconcile

1. Move 5 ones column lower beads down.
2. Add one ones column bead from top.
3. Move two top ones column beads up.
4. Add one bead to lower half of tens column.

5 (top)
+ 2(bottom)
= 7

**Figure 1-2**
Representing 23 on the abacus (white beads).

again. Likewise, if both top beads touch the center bar these beads must moved away from the center bar and one bottom bead from the next highest rank gets moved up. Figure 1–3 shows how one would execute 7 + 23 and reconcile that to 30. To subtract 7 from 30 and get 23 you would reverse the process.

Does that all make sense to you? Here is another way to look at the abacus. For this example, we use people and their fingers instead of beads to build a human abacus. After all, the abacus is based on this same idea. The bottom five beads represent the five fingers on a hand. The top two beads represent two hands. Each "hand" equals five "fingers." We use our human abacus like this: When all the fingers on one hand fill up, we start counting on the other hand. When the person in the ones column gets to 10, that person sets their fingers to zero and the person in the tens column remembers one on their hands (by raising one finger). This counting continues through the ranks until the capabilities of the fingers in the abacus are used up.

Because of the abacus's ability to aid in addition and subtraction, the tool has endured for a long time. Due to its construction it does not handle multiplication and division very well. Multiplication essentially involves adding the numbers over and over again (25 * 4 = 25 + 25 + 25 + 25). Division is also possible but time consuming. Not surprisingly, the abacus does not help us do any serious number crunching. It does allow for distribution of computing tasks. You may ask two or more people to manipulate the same series of numbers just to verify that the results are correct. Alternatively, you can also split up large computations among many people who have an abacus. As we know now, there are faster ways to perform computations. Let's take a look at one of the first attempts to speed things up.

# Early Calculators

As we learned more and more about the world around us, we learned more about the mathematical relationships in nature. All of this math created a need for tools that could assist in performing calculations. Around 1600, Galileo began to incorporate mathematics with his observations of the physical world. For example, he noticed that objects fell to the earth at the same rate regardless of their weight. A marble will hit the ground in the same time it takes a cannon ball to travel the same distance. Figuring out the mathematics describing the various phenomena he observed created a need for new tools. For his own work, Galileo invented a number of different compasses.

Galileo was not the only person figuring out the mathematics of nature. History credits John Napier with the invention of logarithms. He published his initial work on them in 1614. Logarithms are useful for quick multiplication and division, but it takes a long time to compute logarithms manually. To save time, Napier invented a device called Napier's Bones, the predecessor of the slide rule. This tool proved to be very difficult to use and as a result, people looked for new, better ways to do the same thing. Seven years after Napier published his first paper on logarithms, William Oughtred gave us the slide rule in 1621. This tool remained a standby for students of mathematics until the calculator became affordable during the 1970s.

---

I worked with a person who has a fairly good sense of humor. On his wall, he has an engineer's emergency kit. The kit displays a good sense of where engineering and mathematics in general came from. The kit is set up in a half-inch-deep picture frame. Behind the glass are a slide rule, a pencil, and an abacus. The text above all this reads "Engineering Emergency Kit: In case of power failure, break glass" (see Figure 1–4). It's kind of funny but it also gets people thinking. Computers help us do a lot, but people also built and figured out numerous things with some very simple tools.

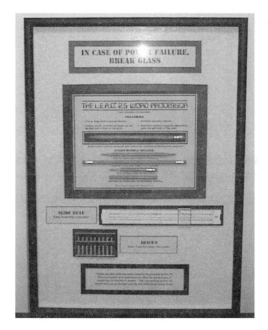

**Figure 1–4**   Engineering emergency kit.

Other people were busy inventing ways to compute faster, too. In 1623, a German astronomer named Wilhelm Schickard built a mechanical calculator that could add and subtract. With a little help from the user it could even multiply and divide. Although none of the machines that Schickard built remains, his notes did survive. Many people have built devices based on his notes and the machines worked as advertised.

Over the years, other mathematicians improved on Schickard's four-function calculator. Blaise Pascal simplified the gear mechanisms. Gottfried Wilhelm von Leibniz, co-inventor of calculus, improved the multiplication mechanisms. After 1673, only minor improvements were made to Leibniz's design. It was not until the 1970s that a better desktop calculator was invented—the electronic calculator.

# Programmable Machines

The next set of developments did not start to happen until one of the legends of computing entered the scene—Charles Babbage. In computing, Babbage is well known for three things: the Analytical Engine, the Difference Engine, and his relationship with Ada Lovelace. Before any of these things happened, he made a huge contribution to mathematics: He helped convince the

English to use the same calculus notation as the rest of the world. He and a few friends translated the works of a French mathematician, Lacroix, from French into English. England used Newton's mathematical notation, whereas, the rest of the continent used Leibniz's notation. Both mathematicians developed good systems but more people used Leibniz's notation than Newton's. This simple act of translating a leading calculus text convinced the mathematicians of England to speak the same mathematical language as the rest of Europe. This led to a great deal of information sharing among the mathematicians of Europe. Besides helping to unify the mathematical community, Babbage, devised the penny post, developed the first set of accurate life insurance actuarial tables, wrote many papers for scientific journals, and dabbled in whatever interested him.

His first major contribution to the world of computing is the Difference Engine. Babbage noticed that most equations could be solved using what he called the "method of differences." Table 1–1 shows the differences used to calculate the squares of numbers. The first column shows the values and the second column shows the square of the values. The second column shows the first differences. For example, $1^2 = 1$, $2^2 = 4$, and the first difference is $4 - 1 = 3$. The second differences are always equal to 2. Using this information, we can also figure out subsequent squares. We know that $7^2$ will be $2 + 11 + 36 = 49$ and $8^2$ is $2 + 13 + 49 = 64$. After establishing the pattern, one can carry on this process forever. You can verify the correctness of the squares by inspecting the values of the second differences. If the second difference is anything but 2, we know the calculations are incorrect. Looked at another way, the value for any given square looks like this:

```
(n + 1)² = n² + (first difference in n) + 2
```

Similar methods can be applied to polynomial expressions in general—you just need to figure out which difference repeats itself (first, second, third,

| Table 1–1 | First differences for the squares of [1, 6]. | | |
|-----------|------------------------|-------------------|--------------------|
| *Value* | *Square* | *First Difference* | *Second Difference* |
| 1 | 1 | | |
| 2 | 4 | 3 | |
| 3 | 9 | 5 | 2 |
| 4 | 16 | 7 | 2 |
| 5 | 25 | 9 | 2 |
| 6 | 36 | 11 | 2 |

etc.). Babbage rightly reasoned that a machine capable of solving any poly-nomial would have more value than one only capable of a specific polynomi-al. On June 14, 1822, Babbage proposed the construction of such a machine to the Royal Astronomical Society. Along with his proposal, he produced a miniature "proof of concept" capable of producing charts of squares, cubes, and one polynomial.[2]

The Royal Astronomical Society liked the idea and Babbage got funding to begin construction of the Difference Engine. Unfortunately for his source of funding, England, Babbage had all the ambition of an engineer. Instead of building something that worked and improving on it later, he continually improved the engine as it was built. These changes often caused work to be scrapped because of technological improvements. To compound his prob-lems, Babbage had extraordinarily poor people skills. For various reasons including funding problems and political pressure, work stopped on the Difference Engine in 1833. The incomplete machine now sits in the Science Museum in London.

Following the demise of the Difference Engine came Babbage's next idea, the Analytical Engine. He designed the engine to hold 1,000 50-digit numbers (memory) and a mill that processed these values (the central processing unit [CPU]). He used punch cards originally invented by Joseph Marie Jacquard to control a loom. These punch cards worked just as they did for the electronic computers that appeared in the 20th Century—they contained the program. He worked on the device with Ada Lovelace but never completed this machine either. His ideas for a general-purpose computing device with memory and a CPU persisted into the modern day. His ideas and designs were alarmingly close to what engineers came up with in the first electronic computers.

# Electronic Computers

The time between Babbage's work and World War II saw the invention of many more tabulating machines. By the beginning of the war, electro-mechanical computers existed. These computers resembled punch-card-fed calculators more than anything else, and they were doing a lot of work. They helped tabulate census data and process payrolls among other things. These calculators had a number of problems, however. Their two biggest shortcom-ings were their inaccuracy and lack of speed. If the calculator was not

---

[2] Yes, the computer used a teletype interface. This polynomial is $x^2 + x + 41$, a formula that produces a large number of prime numbers.

machined precisely or the gears started to wear, the machine lost accuracy. Speed was a major problem because the gears could only move so fast.[3]

World War II really got people thinking about how to make the machines faster and more accurate. People all over the globe were looking at replacing mechanical switches with electrical ones. The British produced a machine named COLOSSUS to crack German military codes by December 1943. On the other side of the Atlantic, the Americans created ENIAC to write out trajectory tables for their various projectile weapons. The mechanical machines used at the beginning of the war could write out these tables in about 30 days. These electronic computers reduced the time to 30 seconds.

Once the war was over, many of the minds that developed wartime computers looked to peacetime uses for the machines. By 1970, people had invented all sorts of things to extend computing capabilities. We had Transmission Control Protocol/Internet Protocol (TCP/IP), Ethernet, ARPANET, and a plethora of operating systems running on many computers scattered around the world. Within a single machine, programs communicated with each other via shared memory, pipes, and other devices. Even today, we distribute tasks among different programs on the same machine. You do it every time you embed a spreadsheet within a word processing document. With computing capabilities expanding all the time and connectivity getting better, the stage was set for having these tasks run in harmony across many machines.

## Distributed Computing

Thank you for indulging me in that little history of computing. I have always been fascinated at how far we have taken these tools and ideas as well as the pace at which we keep moving forward. Machines as powerful as ENIAC no longer take up rooms. Why, their keypads need more room than the machine doing the work. Simply amazing! Knowing this history, I still find it awe-inspiring that we can ask for more out of these machines and consistently get it. I guess that is what happens when a lot of bright, curious people build on each other's successes. Distributed computing has had its share of success and SOAP builds on this.

---

[3] A similar thing has been said about electrons which is why alternatives such as photonic computing are being researched.

Distributed computing has always existed in one form or another. Early on, it was more a more manual affair. Mathematicians would use computations performed for logarithmic tables to do some of the more time-consuming parts of a calculation. Any time people use work that was done by someone else (depth of a well, height of a home, distance between two points), they are using distributed computing.

When punch cards were used extensively, we still had distributed computing. The output of one job would be written to a card deck. Computer operators would then feed that card deck in as input to another program. People used feet instead of network cable to link the programs and transport the data—the card deck.

In general, distributed computing involves executing functions on connected computers as part of one overall program. This distribution allows us to manipulate the data wherever it makes the most sense. My favorite example involves meteorology.[4] Accurate weather forecasting takes lots and lots of processor power. An organization such as the U.S. National Weather Service uses meteorologists and high-powered computers to predict the weather. Because of costs, it is cheaper to give each meteorologist a workstation and a connection to one, superpowerful forecasting computer than it is to purchase several forecasting computers. In this example Beth, a meteorologist, has to write a forecast for the Dallas, Texas area. To do this, she uses a program that can output projected temperature ranges, weather maps, and other data. When Beth sits down to forecast the weather for the next three days she runs a program, enters some numbers, and creates the maps. To her, all of this appears to happen on her own workstation. What do you suppose really happens?

Probably, things worked like this:

1. Jill enters her numbers on a client application running on her workstation.
2. The client application sends a request to the forecasting computer.
3. The forecasting computer returns the requested data.
4. The client application displays the results on the workstation screen.

Why does this design make sense? A good design in distributed computing involves executing the code wherever it makes the most sense. It makes the most sense to have the user interface on Beth's computer and to interpret the weather data on the more powerful machine. Distributed computing made this possible.

---

[4] This is an example based on conjecture, not actual knowledge. I have found it useful in describing the idea to people who don't work with distributed computing.

Today, people use distributed computing all the time. For proof of this, look no further than the World Wide Web. It doesn't make sense to store the entire Web on everyone's computer, so we ask for pieces of it using Hypertext Transfer Protocol (HTTP) requests. We process the information wherever it makes the most sense. This setup makes sense because the data can be located on machines that the authors have access to. Often, these are specially configured machines with high-speed Internet connections. For my Web site, I create the content at home in Washington but pay an organization in Utah to host the content. The Web is the world's largest remote procedure call (RPC) mechanism. Through it, you request objects (typically files) via a GET command. The host computer then responds by doing something. From the requestor's standpoint, it simply serves up byte streams. Those byte streams might come from files or dynamically generated content. For example, as a user you never know what instructions create the page you are viewing when you request a Java Server Page (JSP) or Active Server Page (ASP) page. You simply requested an object from a server by name. The presentation of that page may depend on the time of day, the weather in London, England, or previous actions you made at the Web site.

Computing has learned a lot from the world of science. For example, before Babbage and company translated Lacroix's work, England spoke a mathematical language different from the rest of the world. When mathematicians began to use one notation they were able to understand each other's work and began to share ideas. The same thing has been witnessed time and again in computing. Today it is getting harder and harder to sell someone a networking solution that does not use TCP/IP. Distributed computing has its standards, too. In this section, we focus on standards related to RPC:[5] Distributed Computing Environment (DCE), Distributed Component Object Model (DCOM), and the Common Object Request Broker Architecture (CORBA).

## DCE

The Open Software Foundation (OSF), a consortium of hardware and software vendors, introduced the DCE in 1990. Distributed computing was happening long before the DCE was formalized. DCE took components from various vendors involved in the OSF and standardized the usage and services of those items. Distributed computing has been going on ever since we could get two computers to talk to each other. DCE specifies the set of

---

[5] It's important to note that SOAP does not handle only RPCs. Its usage has evolved to handle workflow processing and other forms of messaging.

services needed to make distributed computing secure and reliable. These services are:

- **Cell Directory Service:** Provides access to named resources such as users, computers, applications, and other items in a distributed computing environment. This is similar in function to Microsoft's Active Directory and Novell's Directory Service.

- **Distributed Time Service:** Keeps clocks in a DCE synchronized. This makes distributed applications more reliable because all computers in the DCE will have the same time (give or take a millisecond). Using time information, procedures can be executed in the order they were called.

- **DCE Security:** Makes sure that objects in the system (applications, users, or hardware) only access things you want them to access.

- **RPC:** Allows applications to call individual functions that are located in separate processes. The process may or may not exist on the calling machine. The Interface Definition Language (IDL) expresses the function's signature, including input, output, and input/output parameters.

- **Threads:** Implemented for the server process, threads allow that process to handle multiple requests simultaneously.

The RPC mechanism holds the most interest for programmers.[6] The interaction between client and server is illustrated in Figure 1–5. At first glance this looks pretty simple. You specify what the interface looks like using IDL, distribute a client and server stub, and write a program that calls the code. A lot of complexity exists under the covers of a DCE RPC implementation. In an attempt to be extra flexible, these RPC implementations allow developers to specify things such as the endian format of data. The "endian-ness" of a number is determined by how it is stored in memory. Different CPUs implement number storage in different ways. The implementation often has to do with optimizations the CPU engineers implemented. A big endian CPU stores the data in memory the same way we would write it. A little endian CPU stores the data with the least significant half of the word in the first half. For example, a 32-bit number representing the value 3 has two possible representations.

---

[6] I do not mean to downplay the importance of security; it is important, too. However, when I look at this kind of thing and see that it handles security, I think "Yeah! There's one less thing I need to worry about." Then, it's off to writing code.

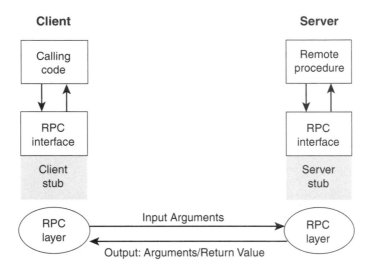

**Figure 1-5**  Basic client/server RPC block diagram.

1.  Big Endian:      0x00000003    Most significant half word: 0x0000
                                   Least significant half word: 0x0003

2.  Little Endian:   0x00030000    Most significant half word: 0x0003
                                   Least significant half word: 0x0000

This flexibility comes at a cost. If a little endian machine fails to recognize that a number came across in big endian format, it may interpret the 3 as 196608 (196608 looks like 0x00000003 in little endian format). Failure to recognize this fact typically comes from a poor understanding of RPC conventions by the programmer. Initial implementations may assume that the same platform (operating system and CPU) is being used on the client and server. To keep things fast, the developer may write his or her own code (known as a custom marshaler) to send the data over the wire. Consider the following C-style structure:

```
typedef struct
{
  char szFirstName[20];
  char szMiddleName[20];
  char szLastName[40];
  int nBirthMonth;
  int nBirthDay;
  int nBirthYear;
} Person;
```

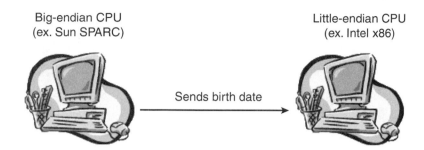

Big-endian CPU
(ex. Sun SPARC)

Little-endian CPU
(ex. Intel x86)

Sends birth date

Thinks it is sending April 5, 1972

In memory, the bytes appear like this:
```
nBirthMonth = 0x00000004
nBirthDay   = 0x00000005
nBirthYear  = 0x000007B4
```
The big-endian machine just sends
the twelve bytes as they sit in memory
without sending the corresponding
type information.

This machine receives the data and
copies the same bit patterns into
memory. Because the "endian-ness"
is off, this machine interprets the date as:
        Month = 262144 (invalid!)
        Day  = 327680
        Year = 129236992 (valid, but does
                    not happen for a long time)

Valid data (for this CPU) would have been:
```
nBirthMonth = 0x00040000
nBirthDay   = 0x00050000
nBirthYear  = 0x07B40000
```

**Figure 1–6**   Problems with sending memory-only copies of data when
"endian-ness" of participants differs.

When sending this fixed-size structure the programmer can opt to send the
structure as its exact binary representation on both ends of the RPC (think
memcpy style conversions). This has good speed because the custom marshaler does not worry about data type and shows no problems. Down the
road, a new platform comes in with a different endian scheme.[7] The developer builds the client stub for the new machine and gets the application up
and running. Immediately, bugs begin to show up with the Person structure.
The name looks wrong and numbers are all mixed up. Figure 1–6 shows the
differences that occur in the birthdate half of the structure (nBirthMonth,
nBirthDay, nBirthYear) when transmitting the data by just sending the
bits and nothing else.

Debugging an RPC can take a lot of time. To do this, the developer must
have some way to see what the data looks like before it hits the wire as well
as a solid understanding of what each byte in each location represents. Then,
the developer has to watch to make sure that the data comes over the wire
correctly with a correct interpretation by the RPC layer. Why invest all this

---

[7] As an example, think of a SPARC-based implementation later involving an Intel-based x86 processor.

effort? Binary RPCs work well from a speed perspective. The program and remote procedure communicate using the data as it is meant to be used without any time wasted on interpretation. As a result, some applications will always require binary RPC mechanisms because of the speed issues.

## DCOM and CORBA

Two other popular ways of performing distributed computing are DCOM and CORBA. Both systems have the same goal in mind: Enable developers to use component-based software in a networked environment. Object-oriented software has taken hold in the industry. Component-based software, through DCOM and CORBA, also gives us language neutrality. These architectures define how programs access components and how those components communicate with their users (other executables). Armed with this information, developers can create software in one language (such as C) that talks to components written in another (like COBOL).[8] Both DCOM and CORBA have the same goal in mind: providing an object-based RPC mechanism. Both systems provide us with location transparency, the ability to write programs without being concerned about the physical location of the component. The component gives the object request broker (ORB) information about how to find the component. Programs needing a component ask the ORB for a specific component or component type. The ORB then hands over an appropriate reference that has meaning within the component architecture. If you are using CORBA, your ORB was probably purchased from someone like Iona, RogueWave, or IBM. If you are using DCOM then the ORB is provided by Microsoft or one of the firms contracted to put DCOM on other platforms. How about an example?

A good place to look would be the weather forecasting system used by our meteorologist, Beth. As stated earlier, distributed computing is all about running parts of the program where it makes the most sense. The fictitious forecasting system has registered a few components with the ORB:

- **Forecast:** Given a region and a date and time range it gives temperature data and weather information for that region based on current weather data.
- **WeatherMap:** Takes data generated by the Forecast object and turns it into a weather map for the region.

---

[8] If you do not like these languages, substitute two others. Ada, C++, Pascal, Assembler, and others can all work with DCOM and CORBA.

- **Cartographer:** A component that overlays the outlines of
  countries, states, or smaller units on a picture. Simply supply
  the rectangle of the view represented by the top right and bottom left corners in their latitude and longitude pairs.

When Beth submits her request, her user interface asks the ORB to instantiate a Forecast object. When the Forecast object returns the data, the
executable hands the data over to the WeatherMap object. This object takes
the weather information and returns a series of images representing the
weather patterns at various intervals. Finally, the images are handed to the
Cartographer component and told to overlay a map on the image.
Cartographer takes the map and overlays an outline of the counties sur-
rounding the Dallas, Texas, area. A second call then tells Cartographer to
place the names of any cities with a population greater than 100,000 on the
map. The client application never worried about where these objects were
located. From its perspective, these objects were located on Beth's machine.

Both DCOM and CORBA could be used to handle the previous scenario.
From a distance, these two technologies look very much alike. They both handle security. They both allow you to do your computing on the machine that
makes the most sense. They also share many of the same problems.

## Problems With Current RPC Methods

Like DCE RPC, a developer will have a hard time simply reading and
debugging DCOM and CORBA messages in their wire format. If objects use
custom marshaling, they run into the same problems DCE RPC applications
see when the communicating platforms use different endian architectures or
standard word sizes.

Another problem arises with implementation. Many computing platforms
do not have the horsepower to handle a full DCOM or CORBA implementation. Many embedded devices run on TCP/IP-based networks. Even
though PCs typically have 32 or more megabytes (MB), an embedded device
may be limited to 64 kilobytes[9](KB) or less. Windows CE, typically touted as
an embedded solution, cannot be stripped to such a small footprint. The RPC
mechanisms presented in this chapter have problems operating in this type of
environment. In small memory environments the RPC mechanisms are
homegrown and they change from one application to another. The device

---

[9] And that's 64 KB if you are lucky. Lots of specifications call for a network-able device that costs
under $10 U.S. to manufacture. The device's housing and constituent parts often eat up a lot of that bud-
get, leaving precious little for memory or processor power.

probably only has a few functions that it performs, making a full-scale DCOM, DCE RPC, or CORBA implementation fairly useless. A number of these homegrown protocols use plain ASCII for transmission to make debugging easier. Unfortunately, this also means that a new protocol is invented for each application.

---

If you think that HTTP and Web servers can only exist on big computers, think again. In 1999, a graduate student named Hariharasubrahmanian Shrikumar made news with a $1 U.S. Web server (see Figure 1–7). Shrikumar was a PhD candidate at the University of Massachusetts. After seeing claims on the Web from many people building tinier and tinier Web servers, he decided to join the race. "For a long time I have been reading about people claiming that they had created the smallest Web server," Shrikumar said. "So I told myself that I would create a Web server much smaller than theirs." The computer uses an 8-bit PIC processor. It uses a fully functional TCP/IP stack written using only 256 bytes. On top of that, it handles HTTP requests like a champ. The processor itself connects to the Internet via a serial connection. At the time of this writing, a functional version could be found at
http://www-ccs.cs.umass.edu/~shri/iPic.html.

---

**Figure 1-7**   Picture one of the world's smallest Web servers. This one was actually on the Internet at http://www-ccs.cs.umass.edu/~shri/iPic.html.

Another problem lies in complexity. The Component Object Model (COM) takes quite a while to grasp. Layering that on top of a distributed application development, Microsoft Transaction Server (MTS) or COM+, and security results in a fairly difficult learning curve for any developer. CORBA is no picnic either.

These problems are not insurmountable. Developers worldwide have built applications that successfully run within a heterogeneous environment. Any problems we do have exist because DCOM, DCE RPC, and CORBA all represent early attempts at formalizing a distributed environment. Distributed computing has many inherent challenges:

- Only authorized individuals or processes should be given access to another machine's functionality.
- You need a method to communicate between different endian architectures. (If you use standard marshaling the underlying implementation will handle any differences transparently.)
- You need to be functional across multiple platforms (or be so ubiquitous that it's a moot point).
- You need to handle network outages.
- You need to handle situations in which a server or client might disappear during program execution.

For all the challenges, the first pass at distributed computing was wildly successful. Corporations launch ambitious projects utilizing this technology all the time. We now need to address any mistakes that have been discovered. The architectures presented so far all came into being before the explosion of the Internet happened. Before Tim Berners-Lee created the World Wide Web, the Internet was only known to a small percentage of the planet. Since then, Web servers have been implemented in programs smaller than 512 bytes. We know that any device out there can be attached to the Web. This connectivity highlights another problem with the presented RPC mechanisms. They typically use dynamically assigned ports for both the client and the server. Administrators of machines on the public Internet have trouble securing multiple ports against all sorts of trouble. Solutions exist that allow RPC traffic to be directed over a controlled port. Due to the binary nature of these protocols, the administrator cannot easily block certain messages and allow others. Most network administrators do not have extensive programming experience, just like most developers have little or no network design and maintenance experience. Because uninterpretable traffic runs over their ports, they feel safer blocking anything they do not understand.

All these distributed solutions also use their own protocols. DCOM is really an extension to DCE RPC. CORBA uses the Internet Inter-ORB Protocol (IIOP). Neither of these chose to take advantage of existing protocols. For example, you cannot email or File Transfer Protocol (FTP) function calls. Doing this may make little sense until you think about the small memory device. It may already have a Web server on board, meaning that it already handles HTTP traffic. Wouldn't it be great if a developer could reuse that protocol to handle RPC calls? Even better, what if that program used a formalized RPC mechanism that just happened to ride on any protocol you gave it? We investigate just such a mechanism in this book: SOAP. SOAP can do this because of its small set of requirements. SOAP works well because when a limitation of the given protocol inhibits you from doing some things with SOAP, you can use another one. For example, HTTP does not work well as a one-way mechanism or single-sender/multiple-recipient mechanism but others, such as Simple Mail Transport Protocol (SMTP, or email) do.

SOAP only requires basic text processing capabilities. You do not need a full-featured security model, component model, or Extensive Markup Language (XML) implementation. If your device only supports a few RPCs, you can use SOAP. In an embedded device, the set of calls you support will probably have limited variability, meaning that your parser will only need to validate the SOAP call and handle named arguments. How is this better than the custom, simple protocol many shops develop? You can now get a person familiar with SOAP, show them the method signatures, and that person can be productive immediately. Why? The new team member does not have to learn any new inventions.

## Summary

The pursuit of automated computing has brought us from wanting to speed up the calculation process to running personnel programs over networks. As networked programs became more common, the RPC mechanism was formalized. This process assumed that every procedure or component needed security of some form. These mechanisms also forced the developer to use a specific protocol instead of the one that made the most sense for the transport medium. Fortunately, the Internet became pervasive and opened up some options that were not practical when DCE RPC[10] or CORBA were initially formalized. Even IIOP is a specialized protocol. These items also ignore something that has been done in the small memory space for years: easy to read RPC communications.

In Chapter 2, we cover all the XML you will need to understand SOAP. The rest of the book focuses on SOAP: the specification, a super-simple SOAP client and server, and a large-scale SOAP application running on UNIX and Windows. Many of the chapters include exercises for you to perform. These exercises should help you solidify your knowledge of the various topics. By the end, you should be a first-rate SOAP developer. Let's move on and take a look at XML, one of SOAP's building blocks.

# Bibliography

CLARKE, Donald. *The Encyclopedia of How It Works: From Abacus to Zoom Lens*. A&W Publishers, Inc. New York. 1977. pgs. 7–8.

SHENOY, J. M. A. "Graduate Student Builds World's Tiniest Web-Server." http://www.rediff.com/news/1999/aug/12us2.htm

SHURKIN, Joel. *Engines of the Mind: A History of the Computer*. W. W. Norton & Company. New York. 1984. pgs. 19–172.

[10] Remember that DCOM rides on top of DCE RPC.

# Chapter 2

# XML OVERVIEW

When looking for a way to express the SOAP payload, the authors of the specification had a number of ways they could have gone. They could have invented their own protocol, declared that CORBA or DCOM would now be known as SOAP, or invented something new by combining existing technologies. In the end, they chose to minimize the amount of required invention by combining existing technologies. To express the content of a SOAP message, the authors chose the *eXtensible Markup Language*, XML.

XML contains a large number of features—far more than SOAP uses or needs. For example, the SOAP specification states, "A SOAP message MUST NOT contain a Document Type Declaration. A SOAP message MUST NOT contain Processing Instructions."[1] Of the XML standards that SOAP has adopted, it specifies how that feature will be used. You will see this in Chapter 3 when looking at SOAP serialization. As we will see later, this decision makes it fairly easy to implement solutions using SOAP because developers do not need to have a full-fledged XML parser to use SOAP. To understand SOAP, we need to understand the following items first:

---

[1] SOAP 1.1 specification, section 3, "Relation to XML."

- Uniform Resource Identifiers (URIs)
- XML basics
- XML schemas
- XML namespaces
- XML attributes

# Uniform Resource Identifiers

To access a unique item over the Internet, you need to know how to identify that one object among everything else out there. URIs provide a way of uniquely identifying those many different items. Described in detail by Request for Comments (RFC) 1630, this specification spells out the rules used to use many different protocols within the URI framework. A URI has the form

```
<scheme>:<scheme-specific-part>
```

When the `scheme-specific-part` contains slashes (/), those slashes indicate some hierarchical structure within the path.

## *Uniform Resource Locators*

The best-known type of URI is the Uniform Resource Locator, or URL. Like all URIs, a URL follows the <scheme>:<scheme-specific-part> method of addressing. Table 2–1 identifies the schemes named by RFC 1738 and RFC 1808.[2] Using these schemes, we can connect to various places on the Web using nothing but a URL translator such as Microsoft Internet Explorer or Netscape Navigator. URLs define this layout for the `scheme-specific-part`:

```
//<user>:<password>@<host>:<port>/<url-path>
```

If you are at all familiar with URLs, you know that a good number of the items in this layout are optional. More often than not, you type in URLs such as:

---

[2] You can obtain these and other RFCs from *ftp://ftp.ietf.org/rfc.*

| Table 2–1   Currently available URL Schemes. | |
| --- | --- |
| *Scheme Name* | *Description* |
| ftp | File Transfer Protocol |
| http | Hypertext Transfer Protocol |
| gopher | The Gopher Protocol |
| mailto | Electronic mail address |
| news | USENET news |
| nntp | USENET news using NNTP access |
| telnet | Reference to interactive sessions |
| wais | Wide Area Information Servers |
| prospero | Prospero Directory Service |

http://www.scottseely.com (my Web site) or
ftp://ftp.scottseely.com (my FTP site)

The various parts of the scheme syntax identify the following elements:

- **user:** User name at the target location (optional).
- **password:** The password assigned to user (optional).
- **host:** The Internet Protocol (IP) address or fully qualified domain name of a network host (required).
- **port:** Identifies the port to use when establishing a connection. Most protocols identify a default port number. For example, HTTP uses port 80 by default (optional).
- **url-path:** Contains details of how to access the specified resource. The / immediately after the host or port is not a part of the url-path.

## Uniform Resource Names

Uniform Resource Names (URNs) are much less familiar to the average Web user than the ubiquitous URL. Unlike a URL, a URN does not resolve to a unique, physical location. URNs serve as persistent resource identifiers.

They allow other collections of identifiers from one namespace to be mapped into URN space. Because of this requirement, the URN syntax provides the ability to pass and encode character data using existing protocols. RFC 2141 defines how to create and use a URN. The production for a URN follows the general rules for a URI. In general, it looks like this:

```
<URN> ::= "urn:" <NID> ":" <NSS>
```

A URN uses the string "urn:" to identify the scheme. NID specifies the Namespace ID and NSS specifies the Namespace-Specific String. When interpreting URNs we look to the NID to tell us how to interpret the NSS. When reading or creating a URN, the initial construct "urn:" <NID> is case-insensitive.

URLs and URNs represent two common uses for a URI. In the next section we see yet another use of URIs: XML Namespaces.

# XML Basics

When XML first hit and the trade press began reviewing it in the 1996–1997 time frame, I dug around looking for examples of what XML looked like. I was surprised at how many industry wonks were saying that it was the next big thing but then would not (or could not) show what this markup language looked like. Given the hype and lack of examples, I imagined it to be a fairly complex, ornery beast. After a few months of hype, developers began writing articles on the topic, giving out the details I wanted. Some of these articles described it as a descendent of Standard Generalized Markup Language (SGML), only better suited for development. How was it made to work better in the program development area? SGML offers extraordinary levels of flexibility but makes it very difficult to implement a full-featured SGML parser. XML more or less defines a concrete set of rules that readers and writers of XML data must follow. Because the language definition for XML is more rigid, it is easier to create conforming documents and parsers. Do not get the wrong idea—XML is a subset of SGML. Anyhow, after the digerati calmed down and the developers got their chance to speak up I got really excited. Why? I finally saw some practical applications of XML. It works as a data language that both machines and people can easily understand. If you have ever read or written Hypertext Markup Language (HTML), you will find XML fairly easy to understand and use. Like HTML, it contains begin tags and end tags. Unlike HTML, every begin tag must have a matching end tag. End tags look like their matching begin tag with a leading /. Let's jump in and take a look at what XML can look like.

The following XML shows one way of encoding the contents of a library:

```
<?xml version="1.0">
<Library>
  <Book>
    <Title>Green Eggs and Ham</Title>
    <Author>Dr. Seuss</Author>
  </Book>
  <Book>
    <Title>Windows Shell Programming</Title>
    <Author>Scott Seely</Author>
  </Book>
  <Picture>
    <Title>American Gothic</Title>
    <Artist>Grant Wood</Artist>
  </Picture>
</Library>
```

Even if you have never read XML in your life, this example makes a fair amount of sense. The document demonstrates a number of the rules found in an XML document. The first line in the sample is a processing instruction declaring the version of XML used by the document. Documents do not have to include this element, but normally you should include it. All XML documents must have one enclosing element (the version information does not count as an enclosing element). The `Library` element wraps the entire document in this case. It contains three subelements: two books and a picture. As you may guess, not one word in the XML document shown is an XML keyword. If you want to be a free-wheeling XML author, all you need to do is watch the spelling in your tag names and make sure that every begin tag has an end tag. Writing XML documents this way can cause problems. For example, you could accidentally write this:

```
<Library>
  <Book>
    <Title>Green Eggs and Ham</Title>
    <Author>Dr. Seuss</Author>
  </Book>
  <Bokk>
    <Title>Windows Shell Programming</Title>
    <Author>Scott Seely</Author>
  </Bokk>
  <Picture>
```

```
      <Title>American Gothic</Title>
      <Artist>Grant Wood</Artist>
  </Picture>
</Library>
```

As a human reader, you recognize that the author of the document mis-spelled "Book" for the book *Windows Shell Programming*. Likewise, the pars-er will accept the document but it will not realize that you have two books in the library list. Instead, it will think you have one `Book`, one `Bokk`, and one `Picture`. If you want the XML parser to do some checking for you and only read valid constructs, you can use something called a Document Type Declaration (DTD) or an XML Schema. DTDs are not covered in this book because Section 3 of the SOAP specification specifies that a SOAP message "MUST NOT contain a Document Type Declaration." If you really must know how to use DTDs, see the recommended reading list at the end of the chapter. With a few exceptions (i.e., publishing, document management, etc.), you should always use an XML Schema to describe data.

# XML Schemas

An XML Schema provides a superset of the capabilities found in a DTD. They both provide a method for specifying the structure of an XML ele-ment. Whereas both schemas and DTDs allow for element definitions, only schemas allow you to specify type information. All XML data is character based. It will specify a four as the character 4, rarely as the binary repre-sentation 0100.[3] We can enhance the library example to demonstrate the benefits of schemas over DTDs, adding copyright date to the book information.

A simple DTD has elements that contain other elements or character data. The simplest element declaration would declare the element name and the contents as character data:

```
<!ELEMENT element-name (#PCDATA)>
```

An element may also consist of other elements. If an element contains exactly one instance of a given element, we would have the following DTD:

---

[3] Yes, XML does allow for encoding binary data within the message. This method allows us to send things such as image data inside of an XML message.

```
<!ELEMENT parentElement (childElement)>
<!ELEMENT childElement (#PCDATA)>
```

Alternatively, the `parentElement` might contain zero or more `childElements`. We indicate this using an asterisk, *:

```
<!ELEMENT parentElement (childElement*)>
<!ELEMENT childElement (#PCDATA)>
```

Finally, you can also indicate composition of elements in a DTD. For example, `parentElement` might contain two different pieces of data:

```
<!ELEMENT parentElement (childElem1, childElem2)>
<!ELEMENT childElem1 (#PCDATA)>
<!ELEMENT childElem2 (#PCDATA)>
```

If we wanted to generate a DTD for a library of books, it might look like this:

```
<!ELEMENT Library (Book*)>
<!ELEMENT Book ( Title, Author*, Copyright )>
<!ELEMENT Title (#PCDATA)>
<!ELEMENT Author (#PCDATA)>
<!ELEMENT Copyright (#PCDATA)>
```

The `Library` consists of zero or more elements of type `Book`. Each `Book` has a `Title`, zero or more elements of type `Author`, and a `Copyright`. The `Title`, `Author`, and `Copyright` elements all contain character data. Rewriting the library example to use the DTD, we have the following XML document:

```
<?xml version="1.0" ?>
<!DOCTYPE Library PUBLIC "." "Library.dtd" >
<Library>
  <Book>
    <Title>Green Eggs and Ham</Title>
    <Author>Dr. Seuss</Author>
    <Copyright>1957</Copyright>
  </Book>
  <Book>
    <Title>Windows Shell Programming</Title>
    <Author>Scott Seely</Author>
    <Copyright>2000</Copyright>
  </Book>
</Library>
```

A validating parser will load `Library.dtd` and use it to validate the contents of the document. This is all well and good, but wouldn't it be nice if we could specify more information than "this element contains character data"? You see, DTDs come from SGML. SGML primarily concerned itself with document publishing. As such, the print industry has been using it for years, because SGML provided ways to reproduce the same document in many different forms. Now that computing has embraced XML, programmer types (i.e., you and me) wanted a way to express the characteristics of the data. A DTD can specify the number of instances of a piece of data and what a particular structure looks like. By extending an SGML dialect, I could even specify the characteristics of the data. The problem here is that every developer may come up with a different naming system. I also have a gripe with DTDs—they do not look like XML. For these and other reasons, the World Wide Web Consortium (W3C) (www.w3c.org) eventually published the XML Schema recommendation. Here is the `Library` DTD defined as a schema:

```
<Schema xmlns:xsd
  "http://www.w3.org/2001/XMLSchema"
  xmlns:xsi=
    "http://www.w3.org/2001/XMLSchema-instance">
  <complexType name="Book" content="mixed">
    <element type="Title"></element>
    <element type="Author"></element>
    <element type="Copyright"></element>
  </complexType>
  <simpleType name="Title" content="textOnly"
    xsi:type="string">
  </simpleType>
  <simpleType name="Author" content="textOnly"
    xsi:type="string">
  </simpleType>
  <simpleType name="Copyright"
    content="textOnly" xsi:type="integer">
  </simpleType>
</Schema>
```

You would save this as an XML file. To use the schema, simply reference it in your document like so:

```
<myLibrary:Library xmlns:myLibrary=
  "x-schema:http://www.scottseely.com/LibrarySchema.xml">
  <myLibrary:Book>
```

```
      <myLibrary:Title>Green Eggs and Ham
      </myLibrary:Title>
      <myLibrary:Author>Dr. Seuss
      </myLibrary:Author>
      <myLibrary:Copyright>1957
      </myLibrary:Copyright>
   </myLibrary:Book>
   <myLibrary:Book>
      <myLibrary:Title>Windows Shell Programming
      </myLibrary:Title>
      <myLibrary:Author>Scott Seely
      </myLibrary:Author>
      <myLibrary:Copyright>2000
      </myLibrary:Copyright>
   </myLibrary:Book>
</myLibrary:Library>
```

Both the schema and the document use the text xmlns. This string tells the parser to use the set of names specified by the namespace identified by the indicated URI. If the scheme of the URI is x-schema then the parser must load the schema at the specified address. All elements inside the tag using the xmlns declaration are part of the enclosing namespace unless otherwise specified.

## Facets

To aid with the definition and validation of data, an XML Schema uses facets to define characteristics of a specific datatype. A *facet* defines an aspect of a value space. A *value space* is the set of all valid values for a given datatype. You use a facet to distinguish what makes one datatype different from another. The XML schema document specifies two types of facets: fundamental and nonfundamental facets.

A fundamental facet is an abstract property that characterizes the values of a value space. These include the following facets:

- **Equal:** Defines the notion of two values of the same datatype being equal. The following rules apply to this concept:
  1. For any two values (a, b), a is equal to b (denoted a=b) or a is not equal to b (a!=b).

  2. No pair of values (a, b) exists such that a=b and a!=b.

3.  For every valid value a, a=a.

4.  For any two values (a, b) in the value space, a=b if and only if b=a.

5.  For any three valid values (a, b, c), if a=b and b=c then a=c.

- **Order:** This specifies a mathematical relation to set the total order of members in the value space. For every pair of values **(a, b)**, their relationship is either a<b, b<a, or a=b. For every triple (a, b, c), if a<b and b<c then a<c.

- **Bounds:** This simply states that a given value space may be **bounded above** or **bounded below**. If a value U exists such that for all values v in the value space the statement v<=U is true, U represents the upper bound of the value space (bounded above). If a value L exists such that for all values v in the value space the statement v>=L is true, L represents the lower bound of the value space (bounded below). If the datatype has both an upper and lower bound, then that datatype is bounded.

- **Cardinality:** Some value spaces have a finite set of values. Others have an unlimited set of values. A datatype has the cardinality of the value space, which is either "finite" or "countable infinite."

- **Numeric:** If the values of the datatype are quantities in any mathematical number system, then the datatype is numeric. Everything else is nonnumeric.

The nonfundamental or constraining facets are optional properties that you can apply to a datatype to constrain its value space. The following facets do this for you:

- **length:** This facet has a different meaning depending on the base type. If the type derives from string, length measures units of Unicode code points (i.e., characters). For binary datatypes this facet is measured in octets (8 bits) of binary data. List datatypes (e.g.,. NMTOKENS, IDREFS, etc.) use this facet to indicate the number of list items.

- **minLength:** Sets the minimum number of units of length. The value of the facet must be a `nonNegativeInteger`.
- **maxLength:** Sets the maximum number of units of length. The value of the facet must be a `nonNegativeInteger`.
- **pattern:** This constrains the value space to values that match a regular expression defined by the `pattern` facet.
- **enumeration:** Specifies a value space by setting a set of values. This does not impose order on the created value space. Order is imposed on the enumeration's base type.
- **maxInclusive:** States the upper bound for an ordered datatype. Inclusive means that the upper bound is also in the value space. For an upper bound $U$, all values $v$ must be $v<=U$.
- **maxExclusive:** States the upper bound for an ordered datatype. Exclusive means that the upper bound is not in the value space. For an upper bound $U$, all values $v$ must be $v<U$.
- **minInclusive:** States the lower bound for an ordered datatype. Inclusive means that the lower bound is also in the value space. For a lower bound $L$, all values $v$ must be $v>=L$.
- **minExclusive:** States the lower bound for an ordered datatype. Exclusive means that the lower bound is not in the value space. For a lower bound $L$, all values $v$ must be $v>L$.
- **precision:** Used for value types derived from `decimal`, this facet defines the maximum number of decimal digits. Its value must be a `positiveInteger`.
- **scale:** Used for value types derived from `decimal`, this facet defines the maximum number of decimal digits in the fractional part of the value. Its value must be a `positiveInteger`.
- **encoding:** Used to form the lexical space for datatypes derived from binary. Its value must be either `hex` or `base64`. If the value is `hex`, the value consists of the two hexadecimal digits needed to represent the octet code. For example, "20" is the hex value for the US-ASCII space character. If the value is `base64`, the binary stream must use the Base64 Content-TransferEncoding defined in Section 6.8 of RFC 2045.
- **duration:** Set of values for datatypes derived from `recurringDuration`. Its value must be a `timeDuration`.

- **period:** Set of values for datatypes used to define the period for datatypes derived from `recurringDuration`. Its value must be a `timeDuration`.

Using all of these facets you can constrain existing datatypes. This helps perform tasks such as data validation and verifying the overall "correctness" of an XML document.

## Datatypes

Combined with facets, the XML Schema datatypes can help you give meaning to the items contained by your schema. For a complete listing of the datatypes specified by http://www.w3.org/2001/XMLSchema, go to http://www.w3.org/TR/XMLSchema–2.

# XML Namespaces

We already saw these in use in the last section on XML Schemas. Simply put, namespaces define a set of unique names within a given context. A namespace can use any URN as long as that URN is unique. For example, the preceding schema defined the namespace `myLibrary`. The schema contained in the file `LibrarySchema.xml` is in the same directory as the source page and uniquely identifies the namespace.

What does a namespace *do* for us? It allows us to create multiple elements with the same name (e.g., `postOffice:address` and `memory:address`). Putting these similar structures into unique namespaces helps prevent the concepts from clashing with each other and allows the computer to unequivocally determine which structure is being referenced. This same practice exists in C++, Java, C#, and a number of other languages. A number of arguments exist both for and against namespaces. Many of the arguments against namespaces boil down to the idea that namespaces are a solution in search of a problem. The arguments for them state that developers are better off when they do not have to rearchitect an application because someone else used a function with the same name. With regards to the C language and pre-standardized C++, people avoided collisions with things such as standard library functions all the time. For better or worse, these same people also had to avoid collisions with names of functions supplied by various vendors.

Often, the code supplied by these vendors would clash with functions written by the developer. In Java, the location of the package often defines the namespace. For example, you can create two classes named Foo and differentiate them by putting them in different packages (`com.scottseely.foo` is different from `com.prenticehall.foo`). This is a bit off the topic, but here is an example of how namespaces work in C++.

Developer code:

```
#include "someVendorHeader.h"

void someFunc()
{
  // Code to do something
}
```

Inside of the vendor's header file, they have a function with the same signature as `someFunc()`, which means that the code will not compile. To fix this, the programmer can write this:

```
#include "someVendorHeader.h"

namespace myFuncs
{
  void someFunc()
  {
    // Code to do something, even call the
    // vendor's function!- :: says to use the
    // function in the global namespace.
    ::someFunc();
  }
}
```

Problem solved! With the various DTDs and schemas being created, the creators of XML namespaces figured that they could learn from others and include similar functionality. Let's look back at the schema example and the lines that define the namespace:

```
<Library xmlns:myLibrary=
  "x-schema:LibrarySchema.xml">
```

Regardless of the name of the schema in `LibrarySchema.xml`, the enclosing namespace is named `myLibrary`. The namespace could have easily been called x, `Bob`, or `yth443`. By using a namespace, we make it possible to use many different schemas that define Book. Imagine that you are an online bookseller. All of your vendors ship you their catalogs via XML. Each vendor defines the Book element slightly differently. Because there is no standardization, you have to read in the various catalogs and normalize the data for your database. Namespaces can help you do this by putting each Book definition into a uniquely identified namespace.[4]

Namespaces also come in handy for creating self-documenting XML. If you are using schema from many different sources, using namespaces will help the human reader know where the various bits of data came from. Within an XML document, a namespace remains active for the element declaring it and all elements contained by the declarer. Likewise, if an inner element declares a different namespace, then all of its inner elements use the new namespace. To see this, consider the following example. Elements in the outer namespace are displayed using regular characters and the inner namespace is in *italics*.

```
<outer:library xmlns:outer=
  "http://www.scottseely.com/library">
  <book>
    <title>The XML Handbook</title>
    <author>Charles F. Goldfarb</author>
    <author>Paul Prescod</author>
  </book>
  <inner:book
    xmlns:inner="http://www.phptr.com/book">
    <title>Windows Shell Programming</title>
    <writer>Scott Seely</writer>
  </inner:book>
</outer:library>
```

These scoping rules help by reducing the verbosity of the XML document. An XML document may also mix and match namespaces within a single element. The scoping rules just outlined still apply—they just seem to get a bit more complex. Consider this example that matches up a book with some Library of Congress information:

```
<lib:library xmlns:lib=
  "http://www.scottseely.com/lib"
  xmlns:LOC=
    "http://www.libraryofcongress.gov/book>
```

[4] Other examples abound. You could use namespaces to aggregate job databases, stock market data, or cooking recipes.

```
<book>
  <title>The XML Handbook</title>
  <author>Charles F. Goldfarb</author>
  <author>Paul Prescod</author>
  <LOC:ISBN>0-13-014714-1</LOC:ISBN>
</book>
</lib:library>
```

In the preceding example, the elements `book`, `author`, and `library` are all part of the `lib` namespace. `ISBN` exists as a part of the `LOC` namespace. The actual URNs used in the `xmlns` attribute declaration do not necessarily have to exist unless the URN specifies a schema:

```
<LIB:Library xmlns:LIB=
  "x-schema:www.scottseely.com/lib/lib.xml">
```

Namespaces combined with schemas provide some great opportunities for document validation and ease of readability. They can point to a schema definition if one exists, but they do not have to. A namespace can be used to simply make the named element unique within the XML document.

# XML Attributes

All of the XML documents presented in this chapter have used elements to present data. XML also supports attributes. We saw these used as facets within the description of XML Schema. As stated earlier, elements require begin and end tags. Attributes do not. Instead, they are contained by the begin tag of an element. A given element can have one or more elements of the same type. It can only have one attribute of any given type. The following XML is legal:

```
<Library>
  <Book title="Windows Shell Programming">
    <Author>Scott Seely</Author>
  </Book>
</Library>
```

The `Book` element has an attribute, `title`, which gives the title of the book. The XML expresses `Author` as a subelement. This could have easily been expressed as another attribute and been 100% valid.

```
<Library>
  <Book title="Windows Shell Programming"
    author="Scott Seely" />
</Library>
```

How would you express a book with more than one author? You could try this:

```
<Library>
  <Book title="The XML Handbook"
      author="Charles F. Goldfarb"
      author="Paul Prescod">
  </Book>
</Library>
```

As I mentioned already, this fragment is invalid. You cannot have two attributes with the same name. You could achieve a similar effect by writing this:

```
<Library>
  <Book title="The XML Handbook">
    <author name="Charles F. Goldfarb" />
    <author name="Paul Prescod" />
  </Book>
</Library>
```

The author element uses a name attribute to contain the names of any writers associated with the Book. Because these are empty elements, the fragment uses the empty element notation: "/>". Attributes can be declared in three different ways:

1. Well-formed XML with no DTD or schema
2. Well-formed XML using a DTD
3. Well-formed XML using schema

The preceding examples use Option 1. This works well for learning but poorly for production environments. As mentioned earlier, SOAP forbids the use of DTDs, so we will not investigate that option. This leaves us with Option 3, schema. When creating attributes for an XML Schema, you use the attributeType and attribute keywords. These words only have meaning within the schema namespace. You use attributeType to define characteristics of the type. attribute includes the item within an element type definition. To create the book example using attributes, the schema would look something like this:

```
<Schema xmlns:xsd
  "http://www.w3.org/2001/XMLSchema"
  xmlns:xsi=
    "http://www.w3.org/2001/XMLSchema-instance">
  <attributeType name="title"
    xsi:type="string" />
  <attributeType name="name" xsi:type="string" />
  <complexType name="Author" content="empty">
    <attribute type="name" />
  </complexType>
  <complexType name="Book" content="eltOnly">
    <attribute type="title" />
    <element type="Author" />
  </complexType>
</Schema>
```

Looking at the `title` `attributeType` definition, we see that it specifies the datatype (`string`) and the name of the element. Fairly easy, right? The full syntax for an `attributeType` is:

```
<attributeType
  default="default value"
  xsi:type="type"
  xsi:values="enumerated values"
  name="idref"
  required="{yes | no }" >
```

- **default:** The default value for the attribute. This value must be legal. For example, enumerations can only use elements in the enumeration as the default value.
- **xsi:type:** The data type for the attribute. If enumeration is selected, `xsi:values` must be filled in.
- **name:** Identifies the attribute type. The `attributeType` must have a name to be valid.
- **required:** Indicates if the attribute must be present for any elements including the `attributeType`.

For an example using all the fields, let's add a new attribute to the `myBook` schema, `format`.

```
<Schema xmlns:xsd
  "http://www.w3.org/2001/XMLSchema"
  xmlns:xsi=
    "http://www.w3.org/2001/XMLSchema-instance">
```

```
      <attributeType name="title"
        xsi:type="string" />
      <attributeType name="name" xsi:type="string" />
      <attributeType name="format"
        default="soft-cover" nullable="0">
        <enumeration value="soft-cover" />
        <enumeration value="hard-cover" />
      </attributeType>
      <complexType name="Author" content="empty">
        <attribute type="name" />
      </complexType>
      <complexType name="Book" content="eltOnly">
        <attribute type="title" />
        <attribute type="format" />
        <element type="Author" />
      </complexType>
    </Schema>
```

Using this schema for one title, we would have the following XML:

```
<lib:Book xmlns:lib=
  "x-schema:www.scottseely.com/BookSchema.xml"
  title="The XML Handbook">
  <author name="Charles F. Goldfarb" />
  <author name="Paul Prescod" />
</lib:Book>
```

If a program requested the format attribute from the Book element, it should get back the value soft-cover. Viewing this XML document in Internet Explorer (IE) 5.5 yields the data shown in Figure 2–1. IE does not

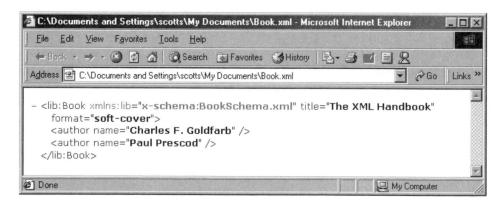

***Figure 2–1*** Using Microsoft Internet Explorer to view XML documents.

flag invalid data, but it does flag properly (and improperly) structured data. For example, you could set the format attribute to "stone-tablet" and IE would still display the document.

# Summary

This chapter presented just enough information to make SOAP accessible to you. Many Internet technologies use URIs to express locations and other concepts. You must understand how these are formed and what they mean to appreciate their usefulness when used by other markup languages and protocols. After discussing the basics, we took a quick look at XML. Since this language came onto the scene in late 1997, many new ideas have been layered on top of it. Besides XML Schemas and Namespaces we have also seen other technologies layered on top of XML. Among the proposals winding their way through the W3C approval process are the following:

- **XML Style Language (XSL):** Specifies a way of converting documents from one format to another. XSL lets you convert documents between various schemas, generate text files, or create an HTML view of the data.
- **XML Schema:** An improvement over DTDs that allows the author to specify data types, maximum and minimum values, enumerations, and other items.
- **XPointer:** An extension and customization of XPath.[5]
- **XLink:** Allows XML authors the ability to establish relations within documents as well as between them. For example, XPath is used within XSL to specify which element to transform.
- **XML Query Language:** Allows an external entity to query an XML document for specific data.

At the request of my reviewers, I have to point out that these synopses are very limited descriptions of all you can do with the various W3C recommendations and their related implementations. Many of the specifications are

---

[5] XPath is already a W3C recommendation. In W3C jargon, "recommendation" refers to the accepted, ratified standard.

fairly long. I would recommend visiting www.w3c.org to read the current overviews of the various technologies if one looks interesting to you.

Of course, there are many other ideas related to XML winding their way through the standards process, such as SOAP. While working with SOAP, you will find it handy to have XML reference material handy. I went through much effort to make sure this book stands on its own. Still, it is hard to cover all of XML in a chapter. Fortunately, a lot of good books exist. The best all-around book on the market that I have found is *The XML Handbook* by Charles F. Goldfarb and Paul Prescod. Goldfarb has been involved with SGML (and consequently XML) since its inception. If you have the financial resources you should also purchase the *XML Developers Toolkit*, which contains three books at a reduced price. These truly are the best books I own regarding XML and I went through several before I found these.

At this point you should understand enough about XML to make the SOAP specification readable. Let's get moving and cover the specification!

# Chapter 3

# THE SOAP
# SPECIFICATION

SOAP, the Simple Object Access Protocol, is an interapplication communication mechanism. SOAP specifies three different items:

1. A packaging model (the SOAP envelope).
2. A serialization mechanism (the SOAP encoding rules).
3. An RPC mechanism (the SOAP RPC representation).

The group that specified SOAP designed these three pieces to work together but nothing prevents a developer from using only one of the items. For example, a program may use the SOAP encoding rules to save configuration files. An instant messaging system could use the packaging model to send data between the parties involved in a conversation. With RPC, one could ignore the envelope and just use the encoding rules and RPC representation to make the function calls. Why did the designers of SOAP do such a thing? They did so for modularity. Modular designs work well because the various parts are not dependent on one another. If the envelope does not work well for your application you can create a different envelope and still use SOAP for encoding and RPC.

This chapter explains the SOAP v1.1 protocol. One of the things that made this protocol possible is the wholesale adoption of Internet protocols and languages by the computing world. In particular, XML, HTTP, and an abundance of Web servers made the whole concept behind SOAP palatable. Besides all this, high-powered machines have become affordable. This is crucial because many computers now have spare computing cycles. Don't believe me? Just look at all the time spent drawing fancy backgrounds, monitoring your progress (auto-complete), and developing helper applications (the Microsoft Office paper clip and family). Most RPC mechanisms are designed to squeeze every bit of performance out of the protocol. To do this they transmit data in binary form giving the computers involved in the communication as much time as possible to run the requested functions. Thanks to faster computers we can afford to sacrifice some of that speed for more elegant solutions.

Since 1994,[1] the Internet and its protocols have become a part of all of our lives. Not everyone knows how the Internet's protocols work, but most developers know that these protocols are, for the most part, text-based. Working with them we have learned three very important things:

1.  As a general rule, text-based protocols are easy to implement and debug.

2.  Translating a request from human-readable text to an action on a computer can be done quickly and efficiently.

3.  When a protocol gains acceptance, its users have a large support group.[2]

With these items in mind, a major design goal for SOAP is "simplicity and extensibility."[3] As a result it does not contain a lot of features one might find in traditional distributed systems such as COM/COM+ and CORBA. The most prominent unspecified features include:

-   **Distributed garbage collection.** This means that if a SOAP client creates an object on the server and that client disappears before releasing the object on the server, SOAP does not tell you what to do.

-   **Batching of messages.** If you want to send multiple messages, you have to create multiple messages.

---

[1] I know the Internet appeared in the form of DARPA long before this. I'm thinking more in terms of when the tools for the Web were being first released to the public: HTTP, HTML, Mosaic—that stuff.

[2] As a side note, SOAP seemed to gain immediate acceptance. A lot of very smart people did a lot of work very quickly with the protocol.

[3] SOAP v1.1 Specification, Section 1.1.

- **Object-by-reference.** SOAP does not state that you cannot return a reference to an object in a SOAP response. It just means that if you do return a reference, then you also need to figure out how to handle distributed garbage collection.
- **Activation.** This requires object-by-reference. SOAP does not specify how one would obtain a reference to the function or object contained by the SOAP request. This reduces the requirements for any system that wants to use SOAP.

As this chapter moves through the specification, you may wonder exactly when each individual feature may be used. The creators of the specification had big things in mind. They are currently documenting the applications that require things like transactions and authentication. In this chapter, I often use section headings that are very similar to the section headings in the SOAP specification. This is no accident. I did it to help those of you who have this book in one hand and the specification in the other.

# Things to Know

The SOAP v1.1 specification states how to use SOAP with HTTP. This simply standardizes how to implement SOAP over one delivery mechanism. As the protocol evolves, expect to see standards for other delivery mechanisms including SMTP and even straight TCP/IP.

Many people who are using SOAP see a need to attach binary data to the SOAP payload. BizTalk incorporates a Multipurpose Internet Mail Extensions (MIME) to handle this task. IBM and Microsoft have introduced a standard for "SOAP with attachments" that is being considered for part of the XML programming standards work. A number of issues show up when attempting this operation including properly encoding and decoding the XML data. Properly escaping and encoding the XML data becomes an onerous task. Many of the possible solutions just generate new situations where the proposed solution falls down. A MIME attachment of type `text/xml` is one solution that has few (if any) drawbacks.

SOAP v1.1 defines two namespace prefixes:

- `SOAP-ENV:` Associated with the URI http://schemas.xmlsoap.org/soap/envelope/.

- SOAP-ENC: Associated with the URI
  http://schemas.xmlsoap.org/soap/encoding/.

The specification (and consequently, this book) also uses two existing namespaces fairly heavily. These namespaces are:

- xsd: Associated with the URI
  http://www.w3.org/2001/XMLSchema/.
- xsi: Associated with the URI
  http://www.w3.org/2001/XMLSchema-instance/.

These could have had any prefix. The specification chooses to map these two prefixes to those specific namespaces to avoid the need to provide a complete SOAP message every time the document requires an example. In other words, the SOAP specification uses fragments a lot.

# Rules for Encoding Types in XML

As a programmer, you probably have seen a number of different type systems in different languages. Languages that support typed, structured data usually have the following things in common:

- They have simple (scalar) types such as integer, string, and float.
- They allow custom types built out of scalar types and other custom types.
- They support arrays.

Instead of letting programmers encode data any way we choose, the SOAP specification reins us in and defines how to encode these common items. These rules help in two areas. First, an XML grammar can be constructed for any schema that follows the SOAP type system. Second, an application can create an XML instance of the particular item using this schema and an element in the SOAP Body. You can also reverse this process and create the correct XML given a copy of the schema and a data instance.

SOAP applications do not have to use SOAP encoding even though the specification encourages developers to use it. You can use other data models and encoding styles and still have a valid SOAP message. To let a SOAP application know that you are using the common encoding rules, specify the "`http://schemas.xmlsoap.org/soap/encoding/`" as the encoding URI.

As we saw in Chapter 2, XML allows us to encode data in many different ways. You can create tags without any concern for datatypes, put in claims that a document uses a specific DTD or schema, or encode type information within your document. To make SOAP applications easier to implement, the specification defines a smaller set of options. The specification defines some terminology related to these encoding rules. These terms are:

- **Value:** This is a string, number, date, enumeration, or similar item. It may also be a composite of many primitive values. All values have a specific type.

- **Simple value:** This type of value has no named parts. A simple value is a single element that has meaning on its own. In most programming languages, this is called a primitive type (int, float, string, etc.). In Step 3 of the order-processing example, `customerID` is a simple value.

- **Compound value:** A compound value has named parts and is typically composed of other simple values or compound values. In the order-processing example, `customer` is a compound value.

- **Accessor:** Within a compound value you can distinguish each related value using a role name, ordinal, or both. The role name and ordinal are the accessors. You can have compound values that have several accessors all using the same name.

- **Array:** A compound value where the ordinal position of the element is the only distinguishing characteristic between member values.

- **Struct:** In a struct, the accessor name is used to distinguish between member values. No accessor has the same name as any other.

- **Simple type:** Simple values are made up of simple types. These include classes named string, integer, enumerations, among others. Basically, you can express a simple type using a single element.

- **Compound type:** Compound values are made up of compound types. To define a compound type you would use XML schema or an array.

- **Locally scoped:** You use this term with respect to a name in a compound type. A locally scoped name is unique within the compound type but not necessarily within the SOAP message. This uniqueness may be based on its ordinal position within the message.
- **Universally scoped:** If the name is based on a URI in a way that the URI can uniquely identify the accessor within a SOAP message regardless of the type, then the name is universally scoped.
- **Independent element:** This element appears at the top level of the serialization.
- **Embedded element:** If the element is not independent, it is embedded.

We will see examples of all of these items as we move through this section on serialization. Looking at the information here you might have figured out that you can serialize messages just by using the `xsi:type` attribute on all the elements. After all, this would describe the type and structure of the elements without requiring anything else. The serialization rules state that the type of value is determinate only by reference to a schema. What does this mean? Suppose we have a compound value that looks like this:

```
<product kind="utensil">
  <productName>fork</productName>
  <price>1.25</price>
</product>
```

Is `kind` an enumeration or string? How about `productName`? Is `price` a string or float? You cannot tell without a schema. Now, if you had a schema in a file named `schema.xml` that looked like this:

```
<xsd:schema xmlns:xsd="http://www.w3.org/2001/XMLSchema"
  xsd:targetNamespace="http://www.scottseely.com/product">
  <simpleType name="kind" base="xsd:string">
    <enumeration value="utensil" />
    <enumeration value="flatware" />
    <enumeration value="china" />
```

```
    </simpleType>
    <complexType name="product" content="mixed">
      <element type="kind" />
      <element type="productName" />
      <element type="price" />
    </complexType>
    <element name="productName" type="xsd:string">
    </element>
    <element name="price" type="xsd:float">
    </element>
</xsd:schema>
```

and encoded the data like this:

```
<x:product xmlns:x="http://www.scottseely.com/product"
   xmlns:xsi="http://www.w3.org/2001/XMLSchema-instance"

xsi:schemaLocation="http://www.scottseely.com/product.xsd">
   <x:productName>fork</x:productName>
   <x:price>1.25</x:price>
   <x:kind>flatware</x:kind>
</x:product>
```

then the value types would be determinate.

The schemas do not have to follow the notation specified by the XML schema specification. The SOAP specification does state that you can use a different notation if it suits your product better. Be warned that if you choose to go ahead and use a different notation, odds are fairly good that you will run into problems if any people use your SOAP server outside of your organization. From reviewing the capabilities of XML schema, I personally cannot see a situation where it will fail you. For example, if you have a field that must follow a certain pattern, you will be better off defining that item as a string. Use the `pattern` facet to describe what the field looks like.

The SOAP specification spends quite a bit of time explaining exactly how to serialize data. These rules help keep everything standardized and minimize the amount of invention required to transmit a message. As developers we spend enough time solving problems. Why add to the list? In reviewing these rules, we look at what the specification spells and then apply the rules on a few examples.

## Value Representation

You must use element content to represent any values. If a multireference value exists in the document, that element must be represented as an independent element. A single reference value should not be represented as an independent element, but it is acceptable if it is.

## Determining Value Type

Any element that contains a value must provide some way to determine the value's type. To do this, you have three options:

1. The element instance (or schema) contains an `xsi:type` attribute according to the XML schema specification.
2. The containing element is contained by an element using a `SOAP-ENC:arrayType` attribute.
3. The name of the element clearly indicates a relation to the type and that type can be determined from a schema.

## Simple Value Representation

Simple values are represented as character data. Every simple value has to use a valid XML schema datatype or a custom datatype derived from that set of datatypes. This sounds simple, right? It is. If you needed to pass two distinct values, a string and integer, you would do so using the following schema (contained in a file named `exSchema.xml`) and instance data. The instance data is represented as a fragment.

```
<Schema xmlns:xsd="http://www.w3.org/2001/XMLSchema"
   xmlns:xsi="http://www.w3.org/2001/XMLSchema-instance"
   targetNamespace="http://scottseely.com/title" >
   <ElementType name="title"
     xsi:type="xsd:string" />
   <ElementType name="numPages"
     xsi:type="positiveInteger" />
</Schema>

<fragmentXML
```

```
   xmlns:xsi="http://www.w3.org/2001/XMLSchema-instance"
   xmlns:ex="http://scottseely.com/title"
   xsi:schemaLocation="http://www.scottseely.com/title.xsd">
   <ex:title>Horton Hears a Who</ex:title>
   <ex:numPages>45</ex:numPages>
</fragmentXML>
```

## Strings

The specification goes out of its way and defines a string datatype. The specific type is SOAP-ENC:string and is identical to the type specified in the XML schema Part 2: datatypes specification. Why would the specification do this? Convenience. Strings get used a lot in XML documents and having a shortcut to encoding a string will be helpful. Most SOAP documents reference the SOAP-ENC namespace.

## Enumerations

Enumerations have been in use for a long time in programming. The thing I have always liked about them is the ability to create a new datatype whose values are meaningful to the task at hand. For example, you could encode the days of the week as Monday=1, Tuesday=2, Wednesday=3,... or you could create an enumerated type, dayOfWeek, that does the same task. It could look something like this:

```
<element name="dayOfWeek" type="tns:dayOfWeek">
<simpleType name="dayOfWeek" base="xsd:string">
   <enumeration value="Sunday" />
   <enumeration value="Monday" />
   <enumeration value="Tuesday" />
   <enumeration value="Wednesday" />
   <enumeration value="Thursday" />
   <enumeration value="Friday" />
   <enumeration value="Saturday" />
</simpleType>
```

Of course, this is just a fragment of the complete schema definition you might declare. It is fairly easy to use the item. Just declare a dayOfWeek element in a SOAP message that uses the schema. The one line looks like this:

```
<dayOfWeek>Monday</dayOfWeek>
```

## Array of Bytes

The ability to encode an array of bytes allows a SOAP message to carry data that does not lend itself to a straight string representation. Using this capability, you can send images, sounds, movies, and similar data. Like the `string` datatype, the SOAP-ENC namespace brings this datatype in from XML to make it easily accessible to SOAP messages. If you have ever used base64 encoding for MIME types (e.g., encoding email attachments), you had to worry about line length restrictions. Section 5.2.3 of the specification explicitly states that these restrictions do not apply to SOAP. If you were to pass some base64-encoded data as an element in your SOAP message, that picture might look something like this:[4]

```
<picture xsi:type="SOAP-ENC:base64">
  Ag93ig5VdYbICM73BIbJB3CnCG==
</picture>
```

You can also abuse this feature. How? When encoding a structure you normally would serialize its data member by member. You could also recreate one of the problems associated with other RPC mechanisms. In Chapter 1, we looked at the problem of writing a custom marshaler that takes the block of memory used by a structure and just sends that block over the wire. Doing this causes the receiver to need to know an awful lot about the client's architecture: endian representation of those data, byte alignments of those data, and other items. Well, with base64 encoding, you can create the exact same problem in SOAP. Do everyone a favor and take the extra time to serialize your data properly. Binary encoding should only be used for data such as binaries, pictures, video, and sound.

## Polymorphic Accessor

Several languages allow accessors to access values of several types where the various types are available at run type. We call this a polymorphic type. For this to work in a SOAP message, the accessor instance must contain an `xsi:type` attribute describing the type of the actual value. The following item shows a polymorphic accessor named `answer`.

```
<answer xsi:type="xsd:float">145.443</answer>
```

```
<answer xsi:type="SOAP-ENC:string">
  George Washington
</answer>
```

---

[4] This example comes straight out of the specification.

Contrast this with an accessor also named `answer` in which the value's type is invariant:

```
<answer>INF<answer>
```

In that example, we really do not know what value the element wants to get across. We could interpret this as the XML datatype `number`. In that case, `answer`'s value is the mathematical value infinity. If we interpret this as a `string`, the value is simply INF.

Why do we call this a polymorphic accessor? If anything, looking at this item seems to indicate that we have a fixed, nondynamic type. So how is the accessor polymorphic? The lines with `answer` indicating both a `float` and a `string` demonstrate some of this dynamic capability. If we use this example with a test-taking system, we can begin to see some of the benefits. Our fictitious system stores answers based on test name and problem number. The generic scoring system works as follows:

1.  Math tests give half credit for a question if the decimal portion is right, full credit if the decimal and fractional portion is correct.

2.  Other tests only give credit if the strings match. Variations in capitalization and spacing do not count against the person (i.e., `"George Washington"` = `"GEORGE WASHINGTON"` = `"George Washington "`).

The answer will be part of a larger element. The full item may look like this:

```
<testAnswers>
   <testID xsi:type="xsd:string">math101</testID>
   <question>
     <number xsi:type="xsd:integer">1</number>
     <answer xsi:type="xsd:float">145.443</answer>
   </question>
   <question>
     <number xsi:type="xsd:integer">2</number>
     <answer xsi:type="xsd:float">-6.0938</answer>
   </question>
</testAnswers>
```

The answers themselves might be stored in a text file named `[testID].txt`. When receiving the given information in the `SOAP:Body`, the SOAP application knows to load the file named `math101.txt`. This file has the following contents:

```
1,  145.743
2,  -6.0938
```

Using the accessor information, we know to load the values into floats, not strings. Looking at the answers provided by the user and the file, we see that the user gets half credit on Question 1 and full credit on Question 2 (75% of all possible points). If the answers were values in a multiple-choice test, the type for answer would be xsd:string.

## Null Values

You have three options to use when representing a null value. First, the accessor element may be omitted from the message. Another option is to include the element and set the attribute xsi:null to "1". Finally, you can use some other application dependent attributes and values. If the only real options are to omit the element or set the xsi:null attribute, then set the attribute. Doing so will make the message more readable.

Most of us have used a null value at one time or another. As a function argument for a caller or client, they come in handy to indicate things such as "I don't need all the information this function provides" or "I am not providing that piece of information." On the other side of a call, they come in handy to say things like "That information is not available." What would this look like as XML? The fragment looks like this:

```
<someElement xsi:null="1" />
```

Of course, the xsi namespace must be declared appropriately somewhere before the appearance of this fragment.

## Compound Value Representation

Compound values are encoded as a sequence of elements. Each embedded element represents an accessor with a name that is the same as the name of the accessor. If the accessor has a name that is unique within the scope of the containing element, then that element does not have to be namespace qualified. All others must be namespace qualified. We have already seen a number of examples of compound values. Most recently, we saw this in the section on polymorphic accessors.

```
<question>
  <number xsi:type="xsd:integer">1</number>
  <answer xsi:type="xsd:float">145.443</answer>
</question>
```

If the question element name is unique within the message Body, the previous element is legal—even without an associated schema. We go over the rules for this later in the chapter. For now, it's enough to know that you can publish type information within the SOAP message.

Assuming that the following is not contained by an array, this is not legal in the SOAP Body:

```
<question>
  <number xsi:type="xsd:integer">1</number>
  <answer xsi:type="xsd:float">145.443</answer>
</question>
<question>
  <content xsi:type="SOAP-ENC:string">
    How many heads does Zaphod Beeblebrox have?
  </content>
  <answer xsi:type="xsd:integer">2</answer>
</question>
```

With this, the question becomes "How do we make this a legal message?" To do this, we have to namespace one of these elements, preferably by using XML Schema. Let's do the schema for the first question element.

```
<xsd:Schema xmlns:xsd=
  "http://www.w3.org/2001/XMLSchema"
  xmlns:xsi="http://www.w3.org/2001/XMLSchema-instance"
  targetNamespace="http://scottseely.com/testing">
  <ElementType name="number" content="textOnly"
    xsi:type="xsd:integer" />
  <ElementType name="answer" content="textOnly"
    xsi:type="xsd:float" />
  <complexType name="question" content="mixed">
    <element xsi:type="number" />
    <element xsi:type="answer" />
  </complexType>
</xsd:Schema>
```

We'll place this schema into a file called question.xml and store it at the URI http://www.scottseely.com/question.xml. Then, the full message becomes:

```
<ques:question
  xmlns:xsi="http://www.w3.org/2001/XMLSchema-instance"

xsi:schemaLocation="http://www.scottseely.com/question.xsd">
  xmlns:ques="http://scottseely.com/testing">
  <ans:number xsi:type="xsd:integer">1</number>
  <answer xsi:type="xsd:float">145.443</answer>
</ques:question>
<question>
  <content xsi:type="SOAP-ENC:string">
    How many heads does Zaphod Beeblebrox have?
  </content>
  <answer xsi:type="xsd:integer">2</answer>
</question>
```

Using the schema and namespace we have made the two elements valid
again.

## Multireference Values

If the message contains any multireference values, those values must be
encoded as an independent element. That element must have a local, unqualified attribute named `id` of type ID. To use this value, encode accessors as
empty elements that have a local, unqualified attribute named `href` of type
`uri-reference`. Encode the `href` attribute value as a URI fragment iden-
tifier that references the independent element. You can encode several references to a value as though they were references to several distinct values,
but only when the context indicates that the meaning of the XML has not
been altered.

So, what would all of this look like? We have two things we want to see.
First we need to know what the schema looks like. Second, we want to see an
example using a "normal" reference and a reference in which the encoding
appears to be a distinct reference. Here is the schema we would expect for an
employee:

```
<schema xmlns="http://www.w3.org/2001/XMLSchema"
  targetNamespace="http://scottseely.com/book" >
  <complexType name="employee">
    <group minOccurs="0" maxOccurs="1">
      <element name="title" type="string" />
```

```
      <element name="fullName" type="string" />
    </group>
    <attribute name="href" type="uriReference" />
    <attribute name="id" type="ID" />
    <anyAttribute namespace="##other" />
  </complexType>
  <complexType name="speaker">
    <element name="individual" type="employee" />
    <element name="topic" type="string" />
  </complexType>
</schema>
```

This XML indicates that the employee element may contain either a title, fullName, and id or it may simply reference another item. When using this type of encoding, you should only use uriReference types if the item gets referenced more than once. You can encode single references if necessary. This flexibility in the specification acknowledges the fact that most SOAP messages will be written by code, not humans. If you know that you will always have one or more items referencing a given element in a message, encoding the first item as a reference will probably make it easier to avoid odd permutations and special cases in a program generating a SOAP message. A fragment using the preceding schema would look like this:

```
<e:employee id="employee-1">
  <title>Software Developer</title>
  <fullName>Barbara Jones</fullName>
</e:employee>
<e:speaker>
  <individual href="#employee-1" />
  <topic>Coding Standards</topic>
</e:speaker>
<e:speaker>
  <!--Showing as a different type of href, still the same
element-->
  <individual href="../employee-1" />
  <topic>Programming for the Web</topic>
</e:speaker>
```

The first pass references the element directly using its ID. The second time we reference the item using the relative path to the item. In each instance we can tell that it refers to the same item even though the value of href changes.

## *Arrays*

As stated earlier, arrays are compound values. When encoding an array, define the type as `SOAP-ENC:Array` or as a type derived from it. Arrays can have one or more dimensions. You distinguish array members by their ordinal position. Always arrange them in ascending ordinal sequence. For a multidimensional array, the right-most dimension changes the "fastest." Looking at a C-style array, if you declare an integer array as `int a[2][2][3]`, then the elements would be encoded in the following order:

```
a[0][0][0], a[0][0][1], a[0][0][2]
a[0][1][0], a[0][1][1], a[0][1][2]
a[1][0][0], a[1][0][1], a[1][0][2]
a[1][1][0], a[1][1][1], a[1][1][2]
```

Because arrays are compound values, they can also be employed as multireference and single reference values. When encoding arrays, the array must contain a SOAP-ENC:arrayType specifying the type of element contained by the array. The encoded value must also indicate the dimension(s) of the array. To encode the previous array, we would declare the SOAP-ENC:arrayType attribute as SOAP-ENC:arrayType="int[2,2,3]".

To analyze how this works, we take a look at how to encode the following items:

- Single-dimensional arrays
- Multidimensional arrays
- Partially transmitted arrays
- Sparse arrays

For each of these, we only look at how to encode integers. The semantics do not change for other simple or complex types.

A single-dimensional array contains a simple sequence. To encode a three-element array of integers, you would do something like this:

```
<SOAP-ENC:Array SOAP-ENC:arrayType="xsd:int[3]">
   <number>12</number>
   <number>45</number>
   <number>92</number>
</SOAP-ENC:Array>
```

I demonstrate multidimensional arrays using strings. The main reason is that I can give the strings names that help you read the example better. Encoding a two-dimensional array of strings would look like this:

```
<SOAP-ENC:Array
   SOAP-ENC:arrayType="xsd:string[3,2]">
   <item>row1col1</item>
   <item>row1col2</item>
   <item>row1col3</item>
   <item>row2col1</item>
   <item>row2col2</item>
   <item>row2col3</item>
</SOAP-ENC:Array>
```

At times you may want to partially transmit arrays. This functionality comes in handy when your application needs to return a large dataset and you need to start displaying output quickly. A partially transmitted array allows your code to pump data while retrieving even more. If the application were returning a 10,000-row set of strings at five rows per message, the message sending rows 995 to 999 would have the following content:

```
<SOAP-ENC:Array
   SOAP-ENC:arrayType="xsd:string[10000]"
   <!- Counting starts at 0, so element 994
       equates to the 995th element in the array. ->
   SOAP-ENC:offset="994">
   <item>elem995</item>
   <item>elem996</item>
   <item>elem997</item>
   <item>elem998</item>
   <item>elem999</item>
</SOAP-ENC:Array>
```

When sending only select elements, you may send a sparse array as well. For many reasons, an application may only need to transmit a subset of all the elements in an array. Typically, it would do this if the majority of the elements did not contain "interesting information." They may be zero, null, or simply of no interest to the request or response. SOAP has the `SOAP-ENC:posi-tion` attribute defined to indicate exactly what element is represented by the sparse array. For example, the application may only want to get the values in a 6 x 6 array where both the column and row indices are prime.

```
<SOAP-ENC:Array
   SOAP-ENC:arrayType="xsd:string[6,6]">
   <item SOAP-ENC:position="[1,5]">row2col6</item>
   <item SOAP-ENC:position="[2,3]">row3col4</item>
   <item SOAP-ENC:position="[3,2]">row4col3</item>
   <item SOAP-ENC:position="[5,1]">row6col2</item>
</SOAP-ENC:Array>
```

Using a sparse array, we only had to transmit 4 elements out of the potential 36 to satisfy the request of only using prime indices.

Finally, arrays may also have mixed elements in them.

```
<someElement id="elem-1">Bizarre</someElement>
<SOAP-ENC:Array
   SOAP-ENC:arrayType="SOAP-ENC:ur-type[3]">
   <!- Simple types ->
   <SOAP-ENC:int>12</SOAP-ENC:int>
   <xsd:string>Hello world!</xsd:string>
   <product>car</product>
   <!- Reference type ->
   <someElement href="#elem-1" />
   <!- Complex type ->
   <owner>
      <firstName>Bob</firstName>
      <lastName>Smith</lastName>
   </owner>
</SOAP-ENC:Array>
```

## *Generic Compound Types*

By recognizing that not all SOAP applications will have pre-existing schema before sending or receiving a message, the specification tries to be as flexible as possible. Computers with Internet connections should have no problems finding and loading schema as long as the machine can find that document on another connected machine. Many more systems do not have this type of connection. When the computer lives inside of a car and is communicating with another 15 in that same car, Internet connections will not exist and space for schema documents will be scarce. The encoding rules for generic compound types still allow SOAP to work.

All stated encoding rules still apply when a schema does not exist. The accessor still needs to be encoded as an element with a name that is the same as the name of the accessor. The accessor needs to either contain or reference its value. If the type cannot be determined in advance, each accessor must contain an appropriate `xsi:type` attribute that indicates the type of the value. We take a look at what this means in a moment.

By encoding the document properly, an application should be able to manufacture a corresponding XML syntactic schema and instance if that information is not known ahead of time. When serializing the values, accessor names must be unique. They obtain uniqueness using one of two methods:

1. They have the only accessor at the given scope with that particular element name.

2. The document creator encoded that element as a part of an array. The element is then unique based on ordinal position.

So, what type of latitude do you get with this? If you have no interest in getting some usability out of polymorphic accessors, you can encode an element like this:

```
<boxContents>
   <item>
     <description>DVD player</description>
     <count>1</count>
   </item>
   <item>
     <description>Remote control</description>
     <count>1</count>
   </item>
   <item>
     <description>Cable</description>
     <count>3</count>
   </item>
</boxContents>
```

This contains three elements with the exact same layout. Because it structurally resembles an array, we can treat the compound value as an array anyhow.

## Default Values

In a SOAP message, an element that is present in the schema might not show up. This absence implies a default value or that the value was not known at the time of transmission. The interpretation depends on a few different things:

- If the accessor defines a default value in the schema, then that value is assumed.

- If the message is calling some RPC, the default value for that argument is assumed.

- If the previous two do not help, then the context helps determine the interpretation of the missing, expected item.

## SOAP *root* Attribute

You will find this attribute marked as SOAP-ENC:root. The rules allow it to appear on any subelement within the SOAP Header and Body elements. This attribute helps a SOAP application deserialize an object graph by indicating which elements are and are not true serialization roots. The attribute can contain one of two values, 1 and 0. Usage of the attribute is not exactly intuitive.

All elements have this attribute implicitly defined. True roots of an object graph implicitly define this value as 1. Everything else is a 0. For example, look at a SOAP Body with the following contents:

```
<someElem>
   <memberData1>someData1</memberData1>
   <memberData2>someData3</memberData2>
   <memberData3>someData3</memberData3>
</someElem>
```

The someElem element implicitly defines the SOAP-ENC:root attribute as 1.

Alternatively, you can tell the processor where the serialization root exists. You do this by placing the SOAP-ENC:root attribute within the serialization root. Let's look at the contents of another SOAP Body:

```
<name id="name-1" SOAP-ENC:root="0">
   <first>Scott</first>
   <last>Seely</last>
</name>
<phoneNumber id="phone-1" SOAP-ENC:root="0">
   <areaCode>414</areaCode>
   <prefix>555</prefix>
   <suffix>1212</suffix>
```

```
</phoneNumber>
<contact SOAP-ENC:root="1">
  <name href="#name-1" />
  <phoneNumber href="#phone-1" />
</contact>
```

The serialization root initially appears to be the `name` element. We can avoid any confusion by explicitly making the `contact` element the root.

# The SOAP Message Exchange Model

A SOAP message is a one-way transmission from the sender to the receiver. This setup has permitted things such as SOAP over SMTP.[5] One-way transmissions do not do much to handle remote RPCs when the caller expects a response of some sort. Most of the time, SOAP messages are combined to implement a request and response pattern. The SOAP specification contains an example of this in Section 1.3, "Examples of SOAP Messages."

Request:

```
POST /StockQuote HTTP/1.1
Host: www.stockquoteserver.com
Content-type: text/xml
charset="utf-8"
Content-Length: nnnn
SOAPAction: "Some-URI"

<SOAP-ENV:Envelope
  xmlns:SOAP-ENV=
    "http://schemas.xmlsoap.org/soap/envelope/"
  SOAP-ENV:encodingStyle=
    "http://schemas.xmlsoap.org/soap/encoding/">
  <SOAP-ENV:Body>
    <m:GetLastTradePrice xmlns:m="Some-URI">
      <symbol>DIS</symbol>
    </m:GetLastTradePrice>
  </SOAP-ENV:Body>
</SOAP-ENV:Envelope>
```

---

[5] IBM implemented this in their SOAP for Java product available at their alphaWorks Web site.

Response:

```
HTTP/1.1 200 OK
Content-type: text/xml;
Content-Length: nnnn
charset="utf-8"

<SOAP-ENV:Envelope
 xmlns:SOAP-ENV=
   "http://schemas.xmlsoap.org/soap/envelope/"
 SOAP-ENV:encodingStyle=
   "http://schemas.xmlsoap.org/soap/encoding/">
   <SOAP-ENV:Body>
     <m:GetLastTradePriceResponse
       xmlns:m="Some-URI">
       <Price>34.5</Price>
     </m:GetLastTradePriceResponse>
   </SOAP-ENV:Body>
</SOAP-ENV:Envelope>
```

The Some-URI declaration just indicates a generic URI. In your applications you need a specific URI—these are standard XML namespaces after all. In the preceding request and response pair, the SOAP-ENV:Envelope begin and end tags contain the entire message. You will see the SOAP-ENV used as the namespace name for most SOAP examples. This does not mean that you have to follow suit. You could use MY-SOAP-NAMESPACE, MARS, or any other valid namespace string as the name of the SOAP namespace.

You can optimize SOAP for whatever delivery mechanism you use. For example, a SOAP request over HTTP can issue the response using the same connection as the inbound request. This also eliminates the need to communicate to whom the response needs to go. If you look at the above preceding example, you will note that nothing indicates where to send the response. It just goes to the right spot. You can implement the same type of thing using SMTP. The example would look the same except that the HTTP header would be replaced with an email header. So where would the response go? It goes to the sender. If the network protocol does not provide data about how to respond to the sender, what do you do? You invent something.

One protocol that does not provide sender information is FTP. To accomplish this you would most likely package the SOAP envelope within a larger XML document. The end result might look something like this:

Request:

```
<SOAP-ENV:Envelope
 xmlns:SOAP-ENV=
   "http://schemas.xmlsoap.org/soap/envelope/"
 SOAP-ENV:encodingStyle=
   "http://schemas.xmlsoap.org/soap/encoding/">
  <SOAP-ENV:Header>
    <ftpNS:soapFTPRequest xmlns:ftpNS=
       "http://www.scottseely.com/ftpNS"
       SOAP-ENV:mustUnderstand="1">
       <responseLocation>
         <ftpSite>ftp://mysite.com</ftpSite>
         <ftpDir>soapResponse/myApp</ftpDir>
         <userName>myAppSOAP</userName>
         <password>somePassword</password>
         <respFileName>
           UUID.soap
         </respFileName>
         <ttl>00:15:00</ttl>
       </responseLocation>
    </ftpNS:soapFTPRequest>
  </SOAP-ENV:Header>
  <SOAP-ENV:Body>
    <m:GetLastTradePrice xmlns:m="Some-URI">
      <symbol>DIS</symbol>
    </m:GetLastTradePrice>
  </SOAP-ENV:Body>
</SOAP-ENV:Envelope>
```

Response (posted to *ftp://mysite.com/soapResponse/UUID.soap*):

```
<SOAP-ENV:Envelope
 xmlns:SOAP-ENV=
   "http://schemas.xmlsoap.org/soap/envelope/"
 SOAP-ENV:encodingStyle=
   "http://schemas.xmlsoap.org/soap/encoding/">
  <SOAP-ENV:Body>
    <m:GetLastTradePriceResponse
       xmlns:m="Some-URI">
       <Price>34.5</Price>
    </m:GetLastTradePriceResponse>
  </SOAP-ENV:Body>
</SOAP-ENV:Envelope>
```

The UUID uniquely identifies the response to the caller. The caller has to set this field because only it knows the match for the call or response pair. The `ttl` field is for the time-to-live. If the SOAP engine at the server does not process the request within 15 minutes of the file time, the server can ignore the SOAP message. A similar technique could be used for any implementation with a network mechanism that does not include a path back to the sender. The actual response from this item may or may not be posted to *ftp://mysite.com/soapResponse/myApp/UUID.soap*. The server will store the result in the `soapResponse/myApp` directory off of the `myAppSOAP` home directory. Finally, note that the returned message looks almost exactly the same as the HTTP response. It is simply missing the HTTP header text.

The preceding examples show that SOAP uses XML fairly heavily. Guess what? You have to encode SOAP messages using XML. This relationship does not mean that SOAP gets to use all elements of XML. In particular, SOAP messages cannot use a DTD. You also cannot use Processing Instructions (PIs) within SOAP messages.

# Structure of a SOAP Message

All SOAP messages are XML documents. They always contain a SOAP envelope and body. They may contain an optional SOAP header. Figure 3–1 contains a block diagram of a SOAP message. Each element has a special set of rules.

## SOAP Envelope

The envelope is the enclosing element in a SOAP message. It has the following grammar rules:

- The element is always named `Envelope`.
- Every SOAP message must contain this element as the enclosing XML element.
- The element may contain namespace declarations and additional attributes. All attributes contained within the element must be namespace qualified. The `Envelope` element can also contain subelements. Like the additional attributes, these elements must be namespace qualified and they must follow the SOAP `Body` element.

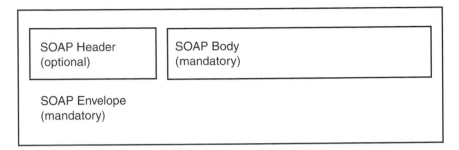

**Figure 3-1** Block diagram of a SOAP message.

Like all of the elements in a SOAP message, the `Envelope` might specify the encoding style via the `encodingStyle` attribute. You could find this attribute used in any of the three SOAP elements (`Envelope`, `Header`, `Body`). We look at this attribute later in the chapter.

For compatibility reasons, SOAP contains a versioning mechanism. Versioning mechanisms traditionally allow for backward compatibility within the application domain. Most of these use a model of major and minor version numbers. For example, this book uses SOAP major version 1 (**1**.1), minor version 1 (1.**1**). SOAP does **not** handle versioning by using numbers. Instead, it must have an `Envelope` element associated with the `http://schemas.xmlsoap.org/soap/envelope/` namespace. A message that specifies any other namespace for the envelope must be treated as a version mismatch. When possible, the SOAP application must respond to the caller with a `VersionMismatch` faultcode message. Of course, the fault message must use the *http://schemas.xmlsoap.org/soap/envelope/* namespace.

## SOAP Header

A SOAP message may or may not include a SOAP `Header`. This optional piece of the SOAP message provides a mechanism for adding information about the message *to* the message. When included, this must be the first child element of the SOAP `Envelope` element. When would you use a `Header`? Most likely, you would use the `Header` to authenticate the caller or provide transaction management. For protocols that do not provide a return path (like FTP),[6] the `Header` can also communicate the return path for the response.

---

[6] To the best of my knowledge, an ftp server cannot initiate a `get` request.

Any immediate children of the `Header` must use a fully qualified element name. This name consists of the namespace URI and the local name. Following the XML rules, the application assumes that any elements contained by the immediate child of the `Header` are in the same namespace. The FTP example presented earlier in the chapter utilized the `Header` element to provide response delivery information. The following two items are equivalent:

With namespace used throughout:

```
<SOAP-ENV:Header>
<ftpNS:soapFTPRequest
xmlns:ftpNS="http://www.scottseely.com/ftpNS"
    SOAP-ENV:mustUnderstand="1">
    <ftpNS:responseLocation>
      <ftpNS:ftpSite>
         ftp://mysite.com
      </ftpNS:ftpSite>
      <ftpNS:ftpDir>
         soapResponse/myApp
      </ftpNS:ftpDir>
      <ftpNS:userName>
         myAppSOAP
      </ftpNS:userName>
      <ftpNS:password>
         somePassword
      </ftpNS:password>
      <ftpNS:respFileName>
         UUID.soap
      </ftpNS:respFileName>
      <ftpNS:ttl>00:15:00</ftpNS:ttl>
    </ftpNS:responseLocation>
  </ftpNS:soapFTPRequest>
</SOAP-ENV:Header>
```

With namespace only used on immediate child element:

```
<SOAP-ENV:Header>
  <ftpNS:soapFTPRequest
xmlns:ftpNS="http://www.scottseely.com/ftpNS"
    SOAP-ENV:mustUnderstand="1">
    <responseLocation>
      <ftpSite>ftp://mysite.com</ftpSite>
      <ftpDir>soapResponse/myApp</ftpDir>
      <userName>myAppSOAP</userName>
      <password>somePassword</password>
```

```
      <respFileName>
        UUID.soap
      </respFileName>
      <ttl>00:15:00</ttl>
    </responseLocation>
  </ftpNS:soapFTPRequest>
</SOAP-ENV:Header>
```

Besides the encodingStyle attribute, immediate subelements may also use the mustUnderstand or actor attribute. If these elements show up on any other element within the Header, the recipient of the message must ignore those attributes. Because examples speak fairly loudly, here is another one. A SOAP application has to process these two messages the same way:

Must ignore SOAP-ENV:mustUnderstand because it does not appear on an immediate child element:

```
<SOAP-ENV:Header>
  <t:immediateChild xmlns:t="Some-URI">
    <t:childElem SOAP-ENV:mustUnderstand="1">
      data
    </t:childElem>
  </t:immediateChild>
</SOAP-ENV:Header>
```

This message means the same thing as the previous to the SOAP application:

```
<SOAP-ENV:Header>
  <t:immediateChild xmlns:t="Some-URI">
    <t:childElem>
      data
    </t:childElem>
  </t:immediateChild>
</SOAP-ENV:Header>
```

# SOAP-ENV:mustUnderstand

This attribute can have a value of 0 (can skip this element if it does not make sense) or 1 (must fail if it does not make sense). If the Header child element does not contain this element, the receiving application processes it as if the attribute exists and is set to 0. This element allows a particular usage of SOAP to change without adversely affecting the client or server. Why would this be important?

When `mustUnderstand` is 0, this allows servers that do not know what to do with the header to ignore it and still provide a response. For example, the header may provide some basic client information as in:

```
<SOAP-ENV:Header>
  <t:client xmlns:t="Some-URI"
    SOAP-ENV:mustUnderstand="0">
    scott@scottseely.com
  </t:client>
</SOAP-ENV:Header>
```

You could use this type of item to log activity between a SOAP client and server combination. The server that understands this header can gather data on the clients that use the server. When this item is missing in the header, the server logs the client ID as unknown. From the client's perspective, the `client` element does add meaning to the message. If the server does not understand the element, the server can still process and respond to the message.

The FTP SOAP mechanism presented earlier in the chapter sets `mustUnderstand` to 1. If the SOAP application processing the message does not understand the header it cannot return the response. As a rule, you should only set `mustUnderstand` to 1 when the message cannot be processed unless the server understands the `Header` element.

## SOAP-ENV:actor

A SOAP message may need to travel through several intermediaries on its way to the final destination. An intermediary is nothing more than an additional SOAP application along the path of the message. It can both receive and forward a SOAP message. At each stop, the SOAP application receiving the message will look to the header to see which pieces are intended for it as well as to see who gets the message next. Both the intermediaries and the ultimate destination are identified by a URI. As the header passes from one actor to another, each follows a certain set of rules.

First off, as the message travels along, each application needs to remove its processing information after acting on the message and before forwarding the message to the next processor. The recipient of the message can figure out which header element it needs to process by looking for the `actor` attribute with the URI *http://schemas.xmlsoap.org/soap/actor/next/*. You always use a URI as the value for the `actor` attribute. An application could use this mechanism to handle any process that may need to be acted on by several SOAP services. For example, you could use the `Header` to process an order. Our hypothetical client knows how the order needs to be processed, but it does not need a response until the complete order has been placed. Let's walk through this scenario.

1.  Original client request:

```
<SOAP-ENV:Envelope xmlns:SOAP-ENV=
   "http://schemas.xmlsoap.org/soap/envelope/">
  <SOAP-ENV:Header>
    <t:fillInID xmlns:t=
      "http://www.scottseely.com/customer"
       SOAP-ENV:mustUnderstand="1"
       SOAP-ENV:actor="http://schemas.xmlsoap.org/soap/actor/next">
       <t:bodyID>cust</t:bodyID>
    </t:fillInID>
    <u:placeOrder xmlns:u=
      "http://www.scottseely.com/po"
       SOAP-ENV:mustUnderstand="1"
       SOAP-ENV:actor=
      "http://www.scottseely.com/placeOrder">
       <u:bodyID>lineItems</u:bodyID>
    </u:placeOrder>
    <v:shipOrder xmlns:v=
      "http://www.scottseely.com/po"
       SOAP-ENV:mustUnderstand="1"
       SOAP-ENV:actor=
      "http://www.scottseely.com/shipOrder">
       <v:bodyID>shipper</v:bodyID>
    </v:shipOrder>
  </SOAP-ENV:Header>
  <SOAP-ENV:Body>
    <customer ID="cust">
      <name ID="custName" first="Joe" last="Smith"/>
      <address id="custAddress">
        <street>
          123 Main St.
        </street>
        <city>Milwaukee</city>
        <state>WI</state>
        <zip>53219</zip>
      </address>
    </customer>
```

```
    <order ID="lineItems">
      <item>bat</item>
      <item>glove</item>
      <item>baseball</item>
    </order>
    <ship ID="shipper">
       <shipBy>UPS Ground</shipBy>
       <shipTo>
         <name href="#custName"/>
         <address href="#custAddress"/>
       </shipTo>
    </ship>
  </SOAP-ENV:Body>
</SOAP-ENV:Envelope>
```

In the first step, the SOAP application reads the message. On encountering the header, it sees that it only needs to process the first item because it uses the correct URI. The other two headers have mustUnderstand set to 1. Because they do not use *http://schemas.xmlsoap.org/soap/actor/next/*, the first application must ignore the headers. Still, it also needs to understand the first header. This first header tells the first receiver that it needs to fill in the customer ID based on the information found in the body element whose ID is cust. Once done processing the message, the header and body change a bit.

2.    Message gets passed to the order system (*http://www.scottseely.com/placeOrder*):

```
<SOAP-ENV:Envelope xmlns:SOAP-ENV=
  "http://schemas.xmlsoap.org/soap/envelope/">
  <SOAP-ENV:Header>
    <u:placeOrder xmlns:u="http://www.scottseely.com/po"
      SOAP-ENV:mustUnderstand="1"
      SOAP-ENV:actor="http://schemas.xmlsoap.org/soap/actor/next">
       <u:bodyID>lineItems</u:bodyID>
    </u:placeOrder>
    <v:shipOrder xmlns:v="http://www.scottseely.com/po"
       SOAP-ENV:mustUnderstand="1"
       SOAP-ENV:actor="http://www.scottseely.com/shipOrder">
       <v:bodyID>shipper</v:bodyID>
    </v:shipOrder>
  </SOAP-ENV:Header>
```

```
<SOAP-ENV:Body>
  <customerID ID="10233"/>
  <customer ID="cust">
    <name ID="custName" first="Joe" last="Smith"/>
    <address id="custAddress">
      <street>123 Main St.</street>
      <city>Milwaukee</city>
      <state>WI</state>
      <zip>53219</zip>
    </address>
  </customer>
  <order ID="lineItems">
    <item>bat</item>
    <item>glove</item>
    <item>baseball</item>
  </order>
  <ship ID="shipper">
    <shipBy>UPS Ground</shipBy>
    <shipTo>
      <name href="#custName"/>
      <address href="#custAddress"/>
    </shipTo>
  </ship>
</SOAP-ENV:Body>
</SOAP-ENV:Envelope>
```

You should notice a few things about the preceding message.

- The first header field has been removed. This is mandatory because each forwarded message creates a new contract between the sender and receiver.
- The second header element has become the first item. The URI has changed to indicate that it must be processed.
- A customerID element has been added to the body.

The new customerID element allows the order processing system to tie the customer and the purchase together. With this information in hand, the system can create a new purchase order in Step 2. In the process, it also creates a new order number for that customer.

3. Message gets passed to the shipping system (*http://www.scottseely.com/placeOrder*):

```
<SOAP-ENV:Envelope xmlns:SOAP-ENV=
  "http://schemas.xmlsoap.org/soap/envelope/">
  <SOAP-ENV:Header>
    <v:shipOrder xmlns:v="http://www.scottseely.com/po"
        SOAP-ENV:mustUnderstand="1"
        SOAP-ENV:actor="http://schemas.xmlsoap.org/soap/actor/next">
        <v:bodyID>shipper</v:bodyID>
    </v:shipOrder>
  </SOAP-ENV:Header>
  <SOAP-ENV:Body>
    <customerID ID="10233"/>
    <customer ID="cust">
      <name ID="custName" first="Joe"
        last="Smith"/>
      <address id="custAddress">
        <street>
          123 Main St.
        </street>
        <city>Milwaukee</city>
        <state>WI</state>
        <zip>53219</zip>
      </address>
    </customer>
    <order ID="lineItems">
      <item>bat</item>
      <item>glove</item>
      <item>baseball</item>
    </order>
    <ship ID="shipper">
      <shipBy>UPS Ground</shipBy>
      <shipTo>
        <name href="#custName"/>
        <address href="#custAddress"/>
      </shipTo>
    </ship>
  </SOAP-ENV:Body>
</SOAP-ENV:Envelope>
```

The final message went to *http://www.scottseely.com/shipOrder* for processing. Here, it creates a shipping request for UPS Ground and completes the order. At this point, we can tell the original requester that the order was successfully processed as the calls unravel back toward the client. The `actor` attribute provides a means to route a document and process individual elements in separate stages.

## SOAP Body

Think of the `Body` as the SOAP payload. It contains the information intended for recipient (or recipients) of the message. This piece was initially designed for marshaling RPC calls and returning error information (SOAP `Faults`). Since then, people have begun using it to pass around other types of data. The purchase activity in the section describing the SOAP `Header` shows one example of this change. In the example, the `Header` pieces communicated which piece of the `Body` each stage should act on. Of course, you can also use the `Body` element to execute RPCs.

Any data you place in the `Body` should use the SOAP encoding rules. This is a fairly substantial item that is covered later in the chapter.

## SOAP Fault

Of the three main child elements of `Envelope`, only `Body` has a predefined child: `Fault`. A SOAP application can use the `Fault` element to carry error and status information in a message. You should only use this element in a message response. Whenever this element appears in a message, it must be in the `Body` and can only appear one time. `Fault` defines the following four child elements:

- **faultcode:** Software should use this code to provide some way to programmatically figure out what happened. All `Fault` elements must include a `faultcode`.

- **faultstring:** This element expresses what went wrong using human-readable text. All `Fault` elements must include a `faultstring`. Text such as "You broke it" technically fulfills the obligation but violates the spirit of the rules.

- **faultactor:** Tells which of the SOAP applications along the message path wrote the `Fault`. When writing a `Fault`, an application only needs to include this element if the application is an intermediary and not the final destination of the message. The application at the end of the line has the option of writing or not writing this item out. When set, it must always be a URI identifying the source of the `Fault`.

- **detail:** This element carries application-specific error information related to the `Body` element. A SOAP application has to add this element to the `Fault` if it could not process the contents of the `Body`. If the `Fault` describes a problem with processing a `Header` entry, the SOAP application cannot fill this item in. Using these rules, we know that presence of the element means that the problem happened in the `Body` and its absence means the problem happened elsewhere.

Like the other SOAP elements, a SOAP application always has to specify the `Fault` using its fully qualified name: `SOAP-ENV:Fault`. A `Fault` may contain subelements so long as those elements are namespace qualified.

SOAP messages can fail for a number of reasons. The specification attempts to label common failures so that all SOAP implementations can understand why a call did not succeed when it fails. For example, in distributed applications the most common reason for failure is that the caller did not have permission to access the resource (database, RPC, object, etc.).[7] You will find this true on Windows, UNIX, or any other operating system. Of course, other common reasons exist. The SOAP specification defines fault codes in a non-traditional manner. Typically, fault codes are numeric: 101, 3404, and so on. Instead of using integers, SOAP uses XML-qualified names. They all use the dot character (".") to separate the generic fault code from the more specific one. For example, if the call failed due to inadequate permissions, the fault code should be `Client.Authentication`. The specification defines four generic fault codes:

- **VersionMismatch:** The processing SOAP application found an invalid namespace for the SOAP `Envelope`. Recall that the SOAP message indicates the version by using the URI *http://schemas.xmlsoap.org/soap/envelope/*.

- **MustUnderstand:** A processing SOAP application did not understand a `header` element that had the `mustUnderstand` attribute set to `1` and was intended for that application as indicated by the `actor` URI value.

- **Client:** This class indicates that a problem existed somewhere within the original SOAP message. These errors occur in incorrectly formed messages as well as messages that do not contain enough information to succeed. For example,

---

[7] I have no statistics for this. My experience in debugging distributed systems in a production environment has been that if something works on my machine in the office and not in the field, the field machine has permissions set up incorrectly.

authentication errors, missing transaction data, and payment information could cause this error. On receiving this type of fault, the client should not resend the message without modifying it first.

- **Server:** These errors relate to the processing of the message, not the message itself. The machine may have run out of disk space, an upstream processor may have failed to respond, or some other problem may have occurred. A message that receives this fault code as a response might succeed at a later time.

If the customer lookup from the preceding purchase order failed because the customer did not exist and could not be created, what should the Fault look like? Because the example uses actors and the customer lookup happens as the first stage of a three-stage message, we know that all four elements are mandatory. Let's look at each element in turn, then construct the full `Fault` message.

First, we know that the `faultcode` and `faultstring` will have some sort of `Server` class fault. Because the specification does not define anything for the secondary part of the message, we can invent the second part. For the `faultcode`, we can put something in like `Server.customerCreate Failed`. The `faultstring` element needs to be more descriptive and should help in troubleshooting what went wrong. How about "The customer Joe Smith did not exist. The server failed to create a new customer."?

The next item, `faultactor` is pretty simple to fill in. We know it happened at the URI `http://www.scottseely.com/customer`. Finally, we need to fill in the `detail` element. Now, the error did not occur because of an issue with the `header`. Here, we should include the complete customer element. This will help us and the operators of the SOAP server understand what went wrong. Using this information we can see if the customer did get created, already existed, or the record contained information the server or related component may have had a problem understanding. The complete message winds up looking like this:

```
<SOAP-ENV:Envelope xmlns:SOAP-ENV=
  "http://schemas.xmlsoap.org/soap/envelope/">
  <SOAP-ENV:Body>
    <SOAP-ENV:Fault>
      <SOAP-ENV:faultcode>
        Server.customerCreateFailed
      </SOAP-ENV:faultcode>
```

```
<SOAP-ENV:faultstring>
  The customer Joe Smith did not
  exist. The server failed to create
  a new customer.
</SOAP-ENV:faultstring>
<SOAP-ENV:faultactor>
  http://www.scottseely.com/customer
</SOAP-ENV:faultactor>
<SOAP-ENV:detail>
  <customer ID="cust">
    <name ID="custName" first="Joe" last="Smith"/>
    <address id="custAddress">
      <street>123 Main St.</street>
      <city>Milwaukee</city>
      <state>WI</state>
      <zip>53219</zip>
    </address>
  </customer>
</SOAP-ENV:detail>
    </SOAP-ENV:Fault>
  </SOAP-ENV:Body>
</SOAP-ENV:Envelope>
```

## Processing Requirements

A SOAP application has to process a SOAP message using a specific order of actions. This ordering standardizes the behavior of a SOAP system regardless of the implementation. Section 2 of the SOAP specification states the order as:

1. Identify all parts of the SOAP message intended for the application.

2. Verify that all mandatory parts identified in Step 1 are supported by the application for this message and process them accordingly. If this is not the case, then discard the message. The processor may ignore optional parts identified in Step 1 without affecting the outcome of the processing.

3. If the SOAP application is not the ultimate destination of the message, remove all parts identified in Step 1 before forwarding the message.

Processing a message or part of a message requires the SOAP application to understand the following items:

- The exchange pattern being used
- The role of the recipient in that exchange pattern
- The RPC mechanisms in use—if any
- The encoding of the data
- Any other semantics needed to correctly process the message.

Potential exchange patterns include one-way, request and response, multicast, and others. In a one-way exchange, the message goes out and the only potential response is a SOAP `Fault`. Request and response follows one of the best-known patterns from traditional RPC programming, in which you call a function and wait for the results. You might use the multicast pattern when for implementing something like the COM+ publisher and subscriber model. Many SOAP applications (the subscribers) may be interested in learning about the occurrence of one event. When that event happens, the coordinating application (the publisher) lets all the subscribers know what happened. You can also use the multicast pattern in a push type application.

Besides the aforementioned exchange patterns, you may have some others that you like to use. No matter. As long as all parties understand what is expected of them everything should work fine.

# Using SOAP in HTTP

You may be wondering why the SOAP specification singles out HTTP over all the available carrier protocols out there. Why not POP3, FTP, NNTP, or something else?[8] The first few versions of the protocol (those prior to 1.1) only addressed RPCs over HTTP. It appears that the authors of the specification first tackled the usage they were most interested in: RPCs over HTTP. Once that problem had an answer they released the specification so that more people could take a look at it. This change in flexibility between 0.9 and 1.1 also shows another change—IBM and Lotus joined the SOAP party as

---

[8] In order, these are Post Office Protocol 3 (email), File Transfer Protocol, and Network News Transport Protocol (Usenet).

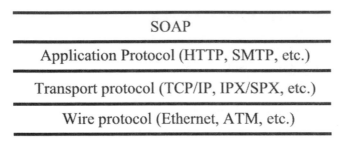

***Figure 3–2*** Typical protocol layering for SOAP.

co-authors. IBM released the first implementation of SOAP over a protocol other than HTTP. They implemented SOAP over SMTP, showing that SOAP can be used over other protocols.

This section on SOAP over HTTP provides a good example of how to implement SOAP over protocols that provide a request and response message model. While reading how this works, also look at how the semantics of SOAP naturally map to those of HTTP. Essentially, SOAP is an application protocol that rides on top of other application protocols. Typically, the network layering will look something like Figure 3–2. This figure shows the four layers you see in any "typical" Internet application. I think that is enough time spent on generalities. How did they do it with HTTP?

The first thing to understand is that SOAP does not override the semantics of HTTP. HTTP already has rules for carrying various types of data. HTTP can already carry images, text, and sounds.[9] HTTP does have some functionality that appears to parallel that of SOAP. Both SOAP and HTTP have the concept of intermediaries. These are not the same. SOAP uses actors to handle this functionality. An HTTP intermediary should be expected to do HTTP activities: authentication, translation, or whatever. HTTP-based SOAP applications must indicate that the data being shipped is "text/xml".

## SOAP HTTP Request

You can use SOAP with HTTP using different HTTP request methods. The specification only defines a binding in relation to HTTP POST requests. My suggestion to you: unless you are doing so as an academic exercise, do not waste your time creating a new way to do SOAP over HTTP. Why? The only vendor that would support your new solution would be you.

---

[9] Even though HTTP can handle SOAP, the HTTP server still will need modifications to handle the requests.

Using the HTTP `Header` field we can indicate the intent of the SOAP request via a new field item named `SOAPAction`. The value of this field, a URI, does not need to be in a specific format and it does not have to be resolvable. This new field, in the presence of a SOAP request, can tell us one of three things:

1. If present and filled in, the value gives us the intent. For example, `SOAPAction:` `"http://scottseely.com/val#msg"`

2. If present but empty, the intent needs to be provided by the HTTP Request URI. For example, `SOAPAction:` `""`

3. No value means that no indication of the message's intent exists.

## SOAP HTTP Response

SOAP over HTTP follows the semantics of HTTP `Status` codes. If the response comes back with a 2xx status code, the message was understood, received, and processed. If an error occurs while processing the request the SOAP application must return an HTTP 500 "Internal Server Error" response. The SOAP `Body` on this response must contain a SOAP `Fault` element that indicates the nature of the error.

This whole piece of the specification caused a lot of discussion on the SOAP mailing list.[10] Discussion concentrated fairly heavily on whether or not other HTTP error codes should be used; things like, "Why not use 400 level error codes when indicating that the error exists in the client request?" We rely on a 500 error code because SOAP is an application layer sitting on top of HTTP (yet another application layer). According to the HTTP specification, 500 has the following meaning:

> *"500 Internal Server Error*
>
> The server encountered an unexpected condition which prevented it from fulfilling the request."

Because the error did not happen within the HTTP layer but the SOAP layer, the HTTP portion really should only report that something happened inside the machine. HTTP status codes do provide for things such as indicating that a gateway could not be found or that a server is unavailable. Still, these codes indicate things about HTTP, not SOAP. After a lot of discussion, it seems that only two HTTP status codes made sense, assuming that the

---

[10] At the time of this writing, the mailing list and its archives are located at http://discuss.develop.com.

SOAP message was successfully passed on to a SOAP recipient: 200 (success) or 500 (failure). If any part of a SOAP message fails, the whole message fails.[11] Otherwise it succeeds.

## The HTTP Extension Framework

The HTTP extension framework allows many different things. SOAP uses it to identify the presence of a SOAP request within a message as well as the intent of that request. A SOAP application and client only use this mechanism when both entities know how to use it. As mentioned, SOAP only defines how to use an HTTP Post. If a client wants to use the extension framework it sends the message as an "M-POST" and a mandatory extension declaration. If a server does not handle this it will return the 510 "Not extended" HTTP status code. If this initial post fails the message can regress to not using the framework. The 510 error value indicates that the server does not support the request and has nothing to do with the validity of the SOAP message.

For those of us who are not literate with HTTP-speak, the M-POST method allows a requestor to discover what HTTP extensions are supported by a given HTTP server. To discover if the server supports SOAP, you use the URI for the SOAP envelope:

*http://schemas.xmlsoap.org/soap/envelope*

The specification contains two excellent examples of SOAP over HTTP.

SOAP HTTP Using POST:
(request)

```
POST /StockQuote HTTP/1.1
Content-Type: text/xml; charset="utf-8"
Content-Length: nnnn
SOAPAction:
  "http://electrocommerce.org.abc#MyMessage"

<SOAP-ENV:Envelope...
```

(response)

```
HTTP/1.1 200 OK
Content-Type: text/xml; charset="utf-8"
Content-Length: nnnn

<SOAP-ENV:Envelope...
```

---

[11] The failure conditions are discussed in the section "SOAP Fault."

SOAP HTTP Using `M-POST`:
(request)
```
M-POST /StockQuote HTTP/1.1
Man: "http://schemas.xmlsoap.org/soap/envelope";
  ns=nnnn
Content-Type: text/xml; charset="utf-8"
Content-Length: nnnn
NNNN-SOAPAction:
  "http://electrocommerce.org.abc#MyMessage"

<SOAP-ENV:Envelope...
```

(response)
```
HTTP/1.1 200 OK
Ext:
Content-Type: text/xml; charset="utf-8"
Content-Length: nnnn

<SOAP-ENV:Envelope...
```

There you have it. Both methods will work to execute a method over HTTP. If something had gone wrong, the response would have contained a first line reading "`HTTP/1.1 500 Internal Server Error.`"

# Using SOAP for RPC

"Necessity is the mother of invention." Microsoft, DevelopMentor, and UserLand saw a need to execute RPCs over the Internet.[12] Current methods had a number of problems:

- RPCs use a lot of different ports and network administrators cannot easily secure their networks if too many ports are open.
- RPCs can be hard to debug because these often use semantics that make it easy for the computer to read but difficult for the programmer to read.
- Network administrators did not have a way to audit what RPCs were called over their networks.

[12] Yes, other people did too. That's what Internet Inter ORB Protocol (IIOP), Common Gateway Interface (CGI), and others are all about. This group included the original authors of SOAP.

After the standardization of XML, many cross-platform projects used it to execute RPCs on the various platforms. XML gives us easy-to-read, convenient packaging. Given an XML parser, it is fairly trivial to send a message to another machine specifying a function name along with any related parameters. The other machine then generates the return value, if any, and returns it using XML too. SOAP simply standardizes the way this conversation happens.

Because SOAP is a messaging protocol, an RPC is just another class of message transmitted using SOAP. With respect to HTTP, RPC calls map to the HTTP request and response exchange model. When making a method call, you need the following information:

- The URI of the target object
- A valid method name for that object
- The method signature (*optional*)
- The method parameters
- Header data (*optional*)

SOAP typically relies on the protocol binding to map the message to the URI. In HTTP, the request URI tells the SOAP application the target object to use when executing the call. If the protocol binding does not provide a way to give these mappings, you can use `Header` elements to provide some direction. You can also use a `Header` element to provide things like transaction IDs and security information. These and other infrastructure pieces reside outside of the actual RPC call and should not be an intrinsic part of it.

## *RPC and SOAP Body*

The SOAP `Body` carries both the method call and the response. The specification details how you should encode RPC. The request should model the method call as a struct. The accessor for the struct must be the same name as the method being called. Each [in] and [in/out] parameter must appear as a separate element contained by the method element. Like the method, you must name the accessors for these elements using the names of the parameters. These should appear in the same order as in the method signature.[13]

---

[13] The 1.1 specification hints that the ordering is a requirement. I suspect that the W3C XML Protocol Working Group will make the ordering optional. This group is using SOAP as a starting point. If the element names match up, why should the order matter?

Not surprisingly, the response has a similar set of rules. The specification encourages a convention of setting the name of the return value struct to `[method name]Response`. Likewise, the return value will encode all of the [out] and [in/out] parameters. If a fault occurred, the response will contain it. As stated earlier, the response can only contain return values or a fault. If it contains both, you have an invalid response.

When encoding data, I encourage you to use the methods described in this chapter. You can do so using other encoding methods, but you will find that you are only making it harder for your system to interoperate with others.

# Summary

XML has done a lot for the computer industry. Because it does not require us to buy into a specific toolset or operating system, it has become a flexible tool for a number of problems. SOAP uses it to tackle two very tough problems: "How do I call RPCs on any system?" and "How do I encode data?"

If you read the book starting at page 1, you know all there is about how SOAP is built and the XML standards it employs. From this point forward, we concentrate on how to use this protocol to solve real problems. We see how to use the protocol with and without support tools.

# Chapter 4

# BUILDING A BASIC
# SOAP CLIENT AND
# SERVER

The name of the protocol, SOAP, expands to Simple Object Access Protocol. How simple is it really? The answer depends on your perspective. If your job involves using one of the many tools out there that use SOAP transparently, life should be problem free. On one machine, set up a server that can handle SOAP messages. On a client, install whatever libraries are needed to speak SOAP to the server. If things do not work, contact the vendors and find out why the two endpoints will not play nicely with each other. Chapter 7 takes a look at a number of these tools.

Your perspective changes quite a bit if you have to actually implement the SOAP part of a client or server. For one thing, you have to really *learn* the protocol inside and out. You also have to decide how much of the protocol you will implement. If you do not intend to use a feature, is there any benefit in implementing it? Here are just some of the decisions you will have to make:

- *What types of usage will the library permit?* You will make different decisions based on how you see the library being used. You will make different decisions based on how general purpose your implementation will get. For example, if you support only a handful of methods, your implementation can forego implementing the ability to serialize and deserialize object graphs.

- *What are your space requirements?* If you have to worry about space, you will have to decide which features you do or do not need.
- *What language will you use?* The language you choose dictates the facilities available to you. For example, a Java, Perl, or Python implementation will give you plenty of ready-to-use and well-documented network packages/protocols and XML parsers.
- *Who is your audience?* Your choice of language will often define your audience, too ("I want to help language X programmers write SOAP code").
- *How will you receive, send, and process requests?* SOAP can ride on top of other application protocols. Implementations exist for HTTP and SMTP as well as other protocols. To use HTTP or SMTP you need to use something that also understands the other protocol.

In this chapter, we actually write a SOAP library. If you have little or no interest in how to write the internals of a SOAP client and server, I suggest that you skip this chapter. This chapter's main value comes from its explanation of one primitive server. If you do choose to slog through this, you should emerge from it appreciating what the really full-featured libraries can do for you. This library will support SOAP clients and servers. For better or worse, I chose to implement the library using C++. For those of you who do not have a lot of C++ experience, I explain things as best I can.

# SOAP Library Design

I thought it would be nice to have a SOAP implementation that did not rely on a given Web server or XML parser. DevelopMentor[1] hosts a number of mailing lists, one of them for SOAP users. From reading the SOAP list it seemed that a number of people had some difficulty getting the Microsoft and IBM/Apache SOAP implementations up and running. Whether it was getting the Xerces parser set up correctly or establishing the right set of permissions on Internet Information Server, the correct solution often eluded many of the early adopters. This made me start to think about what I would like to see in a SOAP implementation. The following requirements seemed to make sense:

---

[1] You can sign up for any of these at *http://discuss.develop.com/*.

- Sit on top of HTTP because SOAP's behavior on that protocol has been defined.

- Only use HTTP for its headers. I reasoned that I could find a decent TCP library on the Internet and use it to tack on the appropriate HTTP headers without much difficulty.

- Separate the protocol-specific parts from others so that more protocols could be added as desired.

- Be able to parse well-formed XML documents. As long as all the begin tags had matching end tags, I could make sense of the rest.

- Allow for delegation of the SOAP objects and methods based on information clients would send in the messages. This type of structure should not preclude someone else from using the code as the basis of a SOAP-based messaging system.

- Make it so that once I figured out most of the SOAP particulars, I could implement a client or server without worrying about them anymore.

- Needs to interoperate with other SOAP implementations (at least Microsoft and Apache).

- Needs to be written using portable code. To me, this means that the code should be released once it can be built on Linux and Windows. To avoid the inevitable issues of the code not running on any other platform I figured that I could open source the code using the Lesser GNU Public License.

- Use a language I really like: C++. I could have used others that I like, but Perl, Java, and Python already had implementations when I started my project. I wanted to at least feel like I was doing something new.

---

The Lesser GNU Public License allows others to use the library in commercial products and to charge for those products. If these same vendors make improvements to the library, they are legally obligated to return those improvements to me for incorporation into the main distribution. That's the legal stuff reduced. Why would I (or anyone else) do this? I hope that this code will be of help to someone. Maybe they will repay me by reporting and fixing any bugs they find.

Once I had these goals set down, I had to go about accomplishing them. The first thing I did was to try and create a simple Web server capable of returning the following document to any client:

```
HTTP/1.1 200 OK
Content-Length: nnnn

<html>
  <body>
    Hello World!
  </body>
</html>
```

This simple test checked a number of things. If I could get "Hello World!" to display in a Web browser, I could confirm that I had figured out how to accept a client socket, read the request contents (if I echoed the request to my local console), and write a response back to the client. Once this task was complete I could write the SOAP bits.

# In Search of One Good Socket Library

A lot of people have published cross-platform C/C++ code for making connections over sockets. After downloading and failing with my sixth or seventh sockets library, I asked the denizens of the SOAP discussion list for help. In my quest I did not run into a lot of bad code. Instead, I ran into a lot of incompatible code. Many of the libraries I ran into prefer themselves as clients and eschew all other couplings. Others have fairly complicated interactions and poor documentation. One example of this is libwww, supported by the World Wide Web Consortium. The libwww mailing list helps out quite a bit when you have problems with the library itself. If you want to find something that supports the latest in standard Web tools and protocols, libwww is for you. But, if you want to get something done in a weekend, libwww will eat hours before paying you back. With all its capabilities it looked like my best bet.

While waiting for a response on something easier, I started work on the SOAP parser. I drew up pictures, wrote a first cut at the implementation, and started calling methods within one application using SOAP. Like I said, libwww eats up time and an individual gets tired of failure after a while. Just as I wrapped up the first cut at the SOAP code, a programmer with the same goal in mind, Jasen Plietz, responded to my plea. Jasen had a complete-enough socket library that sounded like what I was looking for. Within an hour of the code exchange (my SOAP bits for his socket bits), I had "Hello World!" working. I threw out my libwww code and spent the rest of that weekend working on what would become the SimpleSOAP library.

## TcpServer

To understand how these connections work, you need to understand a little bit about how to use Jasen's library. Figure 4–1 shows the basic architecture of the library. The library defines its own `main` that does any initialization. It then calls an external function that the user of the library must write: `networkAppMain( int argc, char* argv[])`. With this infrastructure, writing the simple, single-response Web server took just a few lines of code:

```
int networkAppMain(int argc, char* argv[])
{
  // Create connection server with well-known
  // port on local host.
  TcpConnectionServer server( SocketAddress( 5043 ) );

  TcpSocket socket;
  std::string szHelloWorld =
```

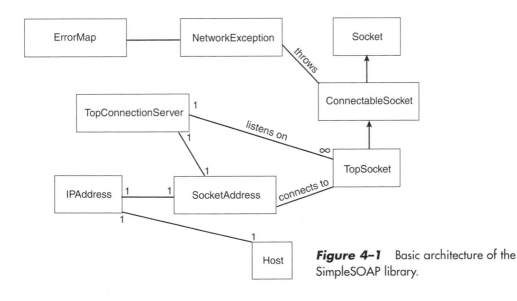

**Figure 4–1**　Basic architecture of the SimpleSOAP library.

```
        "HTTP/1.1 200 OK\r\nContent-Length: 38\r\n\r\n"
        "<html><body>Hello World!</body></html>";

    char* buffer = NULL;
    while (true)
    {
        // Accept incoming connection.
        server.accept( socket );
        buffer = new char[socket.receive_buffer_size()];
        memset( buffer, 0, socket.receive_buffer_size() );
        socket.read( buffer, socket.receive_buffer_size() );

        // Print out whatever we read.
        std::cout << buffer << std::endl;

        // Send the default back to the caller.
        socket.write( szHelloWorld.c_str(),
            szHelloWorld.length() );

        // Close the connection.
        socket.close();
        delete[] buffer;
    }

    return 0;
}
```

This program listens for connections on port 5043. It could have listened on the standard HTTP port, 80, but my development machine also has a Web server running on it. For any connections on this port, it reads in all the bytes in the receive buffer and returns the "Hello World!" response. The code here would probably not work if the number of bytes sent exceeds the size of the receive buffer. Still, it proved to me that I could use this to read SOAP requests and write a response.

# SimpleSOAP Library

With the ability to send and receive simple messages over HTTP, I had a mechanism for testing out SOAP methods. According to the requirements for this library, it needs to make things as easy as possible for the user. This means that the library ought to do a lot of things for server and client applications. It should be able to handle the creation of SOAP messages. It should also be able to take a SOAP message and create some structure that a program can use to make sense out of the message. The library needs to work without a protocol to send the messages (i.e., the protocol part must be independent of the parser part). You should be able to swap out one protocol for another and still have the SOAP bits work—assuming you factored your solution correctly.

To keep everything simple for the user, the library needs to do the following things:

- Provide a method to encode objects as SOAP objects.
- Allow objects to register their capabilities with the message processor.
- Check to make sure that any incoming SOAP messages are valid. They ought to have proper begin and end tag matches and use the same version of SOAP as the library. Clients should only be able to invoke objects and methods available on the server.
- Make it easy to create a fault-tolerant SOAP server.

The end result of trying to implement these requirements resulted in the SimpleSOAP library. Figure 4–2 has an illustration of the classes and their relationships in a server implementation. Servers finish off this piece by

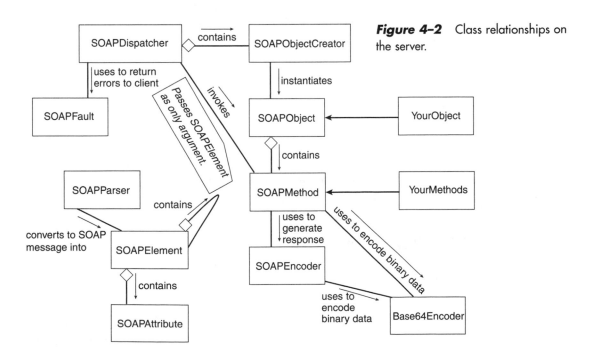

**Figure 4–2**  Class relationships on the server.

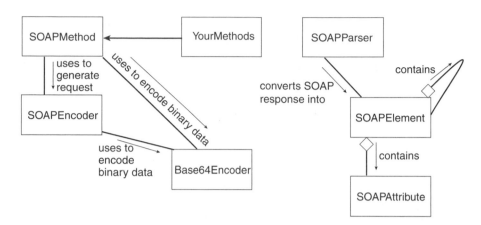

**Figure 4–3**   Class relationships on the client.

implementing something that can receive a message and extract the SOAP message from the rest of the data. This message ought to contain something that specifies the target object outside of the SOAP message. This then takes that information and has it parsed via SOAPParser. Assuming no faults were generated due to a version mismatch or the construction of the message, the user of the library ships the SOAPElement off to the SOAPDispatcher for processing. If all goes well, the SOAPDispatcher returns a SOAP response, ready to be packaged and shipped to the client using whatever protocol the server chose.

Figure 4–3 shows the relationships for clients that use the library. Because this is a client, I did not worry about the object side of things. If the client wants to call an object on the server it will likely do so on an individual basis. On the server side, SOAPObject only exists to act as a container for related SOAPMethod objects. Using this container, the SOAPDispatcher can locate and call the required SOAPMethod. The client explicitly calls the method, making a lookup scheme unnecessary. We now take an in-depth look at the library and then create a sample client and server.

## SOAPElement

The biggest benefit of the library is its ability to create a SOAPElement from an arbitrary, valid SOAP message. A SOAPElement can contain zero or more SOAPElements and zero or more SOAPAttributes. In other words, it is a recursively defined class. Besides this, the class also knows its accessor name as well as its namespace name and value. The following SOAP message contains a number of elements, attributes, and values:

```
<SOAP-ENV:Envelope
   xmlns:SOAP-ENV="http://schemas.xmlsoap.org/soap/enve-
lope/"
   xmlns:xsd="http://www.w3.org/2001/XMLSchema"
   xmlns:xsi="http://www.w3.org/2001/XMLSchema-instance"
   SOAP-
ENV:encodingStyle="http://schemas.xmlsoap.org/soap/encod-
ing/">
   <SOAP-ENV:Body>
     <add>
       <a xsi:type="xsd:int">10</a>
       <b xsi:type="xsd:int">20</b>
     </add>
   </SOAP-ENV:Body>
</SOAP-ENV:Envelope>
```

The class that contains all this information has the following declaration:

---

The SimpleSOAP library uses a number of items available from the Standard C++ library. This library provides a number of generic container classes. The library uses three of these:

1. **std::list:** Implements a doubly linked list—you can traverse it forward and backward. These come in handy when there is no need for random access of the contained elements.

2. **std::vector:** Implements a dynamic array. These come in handy when code primarily accesses the contained elements by ordinal position.

3. **std::map:** Provides a dictionary container. Use this when lookups are performed on something other than ordinal number (as is done in **std::vector**). For small collections of elements a map often contains too much overhead to be of any benefit.

The library also uses a type called std::auto_ptr for managing pointers. This template class acts as a stack variable for dynamically allocated memory. When the variable goes out of scope, its destructor gets called. In its destructor, it calls delete on the contained pointer, making sure that the memory is returned to the heap. I like to think of it as deterministic garbage collection.

---

```
class SOAPElement
{
public:
  // Constructor/ Destructor
  SOAPElement();
  virtual ~SOAPElement();

  // accessorName
  // Description:
  //   Returns the string used to access the SOAPElement.
  // Arguments:
  //   N/A
  // Return Value:
  //   Reference to the actual accessor name. Since I have no
  //   intention of guarding the getting and setting of the accessor
  //   name, I return a reference to the internal element.
  std::string& accessorName();

  // namespaceName
  // Description:
  //   Returns the string used as the SOAPElement namespace.
  // Arguments:
  //   N/A
  // Return Value:
  //   Reference to the actual namespace name. Since I have no
  //   intention of guarding the getting and setting of the
  //   namespace name, I return a reference to the internal element.
  std::string& namespaceName();

  // value
  // Description:
  //   Gets the value inside the element (between the
  //   begin and end tags). It's up to you to decide
  //   how to interpret it.
  // Arguments:
  //   N/A
  // Return Value:
  //   Reference to the actual value. Since I have no intention
  //   of guarding the getting and setting of the value,
  //   I return a reference to the internal element.
  std::string& value();

  // addAttribute
  // Description:
  //   Adds an attribute to the element.
  // Arguments:
```

```
//   theAttribute: The attribute to add.
// Return Value:
//   true: Successfully added.
//   false: Didn't add.
bool addAttribute( SOAPAttribute theAttribute );

// getAttribute
// Description:
//   Given an attribute name, this finds the named attribute.
//   If you are looking for a fully qualified attribute (namespace
//   plus base name), just pass it in. I'll find the colon (':').
// Arguments:
//   szAttributeName: Name of the attribute to find.
//   szValue: On return, contains a copy of the internal
//   attribute.
// Return Value:
//   true: Found it.
//   false: Didn't find it.
bool getAttribute( const std::string& szAttributeName,
   SOAPAttribute& szValue );

// addElement
// Description:
//   Adds an element beneath the current element.
// Arguments:
// pElement: Pointer to the element. This object
//      expects to assume ownership of the element and
//      will destroy it when this element is deleted or
//      goes out of scope. Don't call, this method if you
//      want to control the object's lifespan.
// Return Value:
//   true: Successfully added.
//   false: Didn't add.
bool addElement( SOAPElement* pElement );

// getElement
// Description:
//   Given an element name, this finds the named element.
//   If you are looking for a fully qualified element (namespace
//   plus base name), just pass it in. I'll find the colon (':').
// Arguments:
//   szElementName: Name of the element to find.
//   pValue: Pointer to a SOAPElement pointer. You don't need to
//    delete this pointer when you are done— this class still
//    owns the memory.
// Return Value:
```

```
//   true: Found it.
//   false: Didn't find it.
bool getElement( const std::string& szElementName,
  SOAPElement** pValue );

// numElements
// Description:
//   Tells the caller how many immediate subelements
//   are contained by this SOAPElement. This does
//   not return the total number of nodes in the tree.
// Arguments:
//   N/A
// Return Value:
//   Number of immediate child nodes.
long numElements() const;

// numAttributes
// Description:
//   Tells the caller how many attributes this element contains.
// Arguments:
//   N/A
// Return Value:
//   See description.
long numAttributes();

// elementAt
// Description:
//   Returns the SOAPElement at a specific index.
// Arguments:
//   index: Zero-based index of the SOAPElement you
//      want to retrieve.
// Return Value:
//   Reference to the requested SOAPElement.
SOAPElement& elementAt( long index );

// attributeAt
// Description:
//   Returns the SOAPAttribute at a specific index.
// Arguments:
//   index: Zero-based index of the SOAPAttribute you
//      want to retrieve.
// Return Value:
//   Reference to the requested SOAPAttribute.
SOAPAttribute& attributeAt( long index );

private:
```

```
// m_szAccessorName
// Description: Name of the element (minus namespace name).
std::string m_szAccessorName;

// m_szNamespace
// Description: Name of the namespace (minus accessor name).
std::string m_szNamespace;

// m_szValue
// Description: Value contained between the start and stop tags.
std::string m_szValue;

// Retrieve attributes using attribute name.
typedef std::vector< SOAPAttribute > AttributeContainer;

// m_attributes
// Description: List of attributes.
AttributeContainer m_attributes;

// ElementContainer
// Description: Container of SOAPElements.
typedef std::vector< std::auto_ptr<SOAPElement> >
  ElementContainer;

// m_internalElements
// Description: The SOAPElements owned by this SOAPElement.
ElementContainer m_internalElements;

// Disable the copy constructor and operator=.
// Deep copy needs to be implemented by hand
// and I haven't needed it yet. I'll let the
// compiler warn me if and when I start to use it.
SOAPElement( const SOAPElement& rhs );
SOAPElement& operator=( const SOAPElement& rhs );
};
```

Using this class, you can retrieve elements and attributes by ordinal position or by argument name. For calls such as the add message, you would probably grab the Body and add elements by name. As for the arguments to add it would be just as easy to get the arguments by position as by name. Because (a + b) = (b + a), the order in which you use these elements does not matter. SOAPElement uses a vector to store subelements and attributes. This allows the elementAt and attributeAt methods to be very efficient but requires the name lookups to iterate over all elements and attributes.

```
bool SOAPElement::getElement( const std::string&
szElementName,
  SOAPElement** pValue )
{
  bool retval = false;
  *pValue = NULL;

  std::string szAccessor;
  std::string szNamespace;
  splitNamespaceAndName( szElementName, szNamespace, szAccessor );

  // I don't expect most SOAP messages to have large numbers of
  // elements. If I did, I would have used a map as well as a
  // vector.
  for( ElementContainer::iterator itElement =
      m_internalElements.begin();
    itElement != m_internalElements.end();
    ++itElement )
  {
    if ( (*itElement)->accessorName() == szElementName )
    {
      if ( szNamespace.empty() ||
        ( (*itElement)->namespaceName() == szNamespace ) )
      {
        // We found the element.
        *pValue = (*itElement).get();
        retval = true;
        break;
      }
    }
  }

  return retval;
}
```

As the comments indicate, this should be fine most of the time. I do not expect to see any messages that contain thousands of elements where only one is needed by the method being called. If a message returned that much data, it would probably be for display reasons, not for looking at one unique piece of information (meaning that the user would display everything and get elements by ordinal position, not by accessor).

The other item you will use a lot is SOAPAttribute. What does this class look like?

## *SOAPAttribute*

SOAPAttribute does not do as much as SOAPElement. It just acts as a repository for the value, name, and namespace of any attributes attached to the element. It has this declaration:

```
class SOAPAttribute
{
public:
   SOAPAttribute();
   virtual ~SOAPAttribute();

   // namespaceName
   // Description:
   // Returns a reference to the internal namespace name.
   // Arguments:
   // N/A
   // Return Value:
   // See description.
   std::string& namespaceName();

   // accessor
   // Description:
   // Returns a reference to the internal accessor.
   // Arguments:
   // N/A
   // Return Value:
   // See description.
   std::string& accessor();

   // value
   // Description:
   // Returns a reference to the internal value.
   // Arguments:
   // N/A
   // Return Value:
   // See description.
   std::string& value();
private:

   // m_szNamespaceName
   // Description: Stores the name of the namespace associated
   // with the attribute.
```

```
std::string m_szNamespaceName;

// m_szAccessor
// Description: Stores the name of the attribute's acces-
sor.
std::string m_szAccessor;

// m_szValue
// Description: Value of the attribute.
std::string m_szValue;
};
```

As you can see, SOAPAttribute just holds the attribute data: name, namespace, and value. It never exists without a SOAPElement.

## *SOAPObjectCreator*

As we will see in a moment, the library uses one of the creational patterns, Factory,[2] to create objects capable of handling requests. To do this, you typically need a Singleton that manages other Singletons who in turn create the new objects for your Factory. Functionally, a Factory works just like its real-world counterpart. You design the Factory to manufacture various specific items. The Factory may house several manufacturing lines (the other Singletons). To get things from the manufacturing lines, you put in your orders at one point within the Factory (maybe embodied by a sales slip in the real world) and get the requested items out the back. In the framework, SOAPDispatcher takes the Factory role, whereas SOAPObjectCreator exists as a machine within the Factory. It has one and only one responsibility: Create an object that implements the SOAPObject interface. First, let's take a look at the class itself:

```
class SOAPObjectCreator
{
public:
  // Constructor/ Destructor
  SOAPObjectCreator();
  virtual ~SOAPObjectCreator();
```

[2] Gamma, Erich, Helm, Richard, Johnson, Ralph, and Vlissides, John, *Design Patterns*. Addison-Wesley, Reading, MA. 1995. If you program and do not own this book, you should go buy it and read it now.  If you own it but have not read it, start in on it now.  This may be an opinion, but it is one I share with a lot of people.

```
// newSOAPObject
// Description:
// Creates a new SOAP object that can hopefully do something
// worthwhile for us.
// Arguments:
// N/A
// Return Value:
// Returns a pointer to a newly allocated SOAP object.
virtual SOAPObject* newSOAPObject() = 0;

// createdObjectName
// Description:
// Used to tell the subsystem the name of the
// object this creator makes. This is used by
// a server to create the correct object in response
// to a SOAP request.
// Arguments:
// N/A
// Return Value:
// Returns the name of the created object.
virtual std::string createdObjectName() = 0;
};
```

Pretty simple, right? The comments tell the whole story. Both overrides should be one-liners. One returns the result of a call to new; the other returns a string. For example, a class that creates a SOAPObject-derived class named WeatherData would look like this:

```
class WeatherDataCreator: public SOAPObjectCreator
{
public:
  virtual SOAPObject* newSOAPObject() { return new WeatherData; }
  virtual std::string createdObjectName()
    { return std::string( "WeatherData" ) ; }
};
```

This means that this class does not do anything but make an abstraction work. The derived object achieves Singleton behavior via the SOAPObjectDispatcher class. Essentially, SOAPObjectDispatcher contains a map of all registered SOAPObjectCreators. It knows these by their response to the createdObjectName method. Only one object may create an object known by a given name. The call to newSOAPObject might also return a reference to yet another Singleton. For this reason, I did not make the base class a template class. However, if all you want to do is make the simple creator, the library has a header file with this template:

```
template <class T>
class TSOAPObjectCreator : public SOAPObjectCreator
{
public:
  TSOAPObjectCreator( std::string& szObjectName ) :
    m_szObjectName( szObjectName ) {}
  virtual SOAPObject* newSOAPObject() { return new T; }
  virtual std::string createdObjectName()
    { return m_szObjectName; }

private:
  std::string m_szObjectName;
};
```

Then, to declare and add a class capable of creating a WeatherData handler, just use the following line:

```
SOAPDispatcher::Instance().registerObject(
  new TSOAPObjectCreator< WeatherData >(
    std::string("WeatherData") ) );
```

Not much more can be said of the type of object it creates: SOAPObject.

## SOAPObject

A SOAPObject acts as a container for a set of methods. Objects derived from it may have to do with incoming requests: save persistence information, perform logging, or whatever else is needed. As a user of the class, you may also decide to just have the object hold stateless methods. In its simplest form, an object derived from SOAPObject may just act as repository for a functional group. SOAPObject looks like this:

```
class SOAPObject
{
public:
  // Constructor/ Destructor
  SOAPObject();
  virtual ~SOAPObject();

  // Contains an array of soap methods.
  typedef std::list< SOAPMethod* > MethodList;
```

```
  // getMethodList
  // Description:
  // Returns the SOAPMethods that this object implements.
  // This is a member of the base class because
  // this information should be constant across implementations.
  // Arguments:
  // N/A
  // Return Value:
  // Returns a reference to the m_methodList parameter.
  MethodList& getMethodList();

protected:

  // insertMethod
  // Description:
  // Meant to be called by classes derived from SOAPObject.
  // This method inserts a method into the method list.
  // Arguments:
  // pMethod: Pointer to one of the SOAPMethods contained
  //   by the SOAPObject.
  // Return Value:
  // N/A
  void insertMethod( SOAPMethod* pMethod );

  // m_methodList
  // Description: List of all the methods implemented
  // by the derived object.
  MethodList m_methodList;
};
```

The typical derived object contains a number of SOAPMethod objects. Within its constructor, it calls insertMethod for each SOAPMethod. The derived object is responsible for the lifetime of SOAPMethod objects. Normally, this does not cause any problems because these are simply members of the derived instance.

## SOAPDispatcher

Before we take a look at what SOAPMethod looks like, we should really look at the engine behind any SOAP server that uses this library: SOAPDispatcher. As mentioned earlier, SOAPDispatcher is a Singleton. This means that within the program, one and only one instance of the object may exist.

I wrote a class called Singleton a while ago. It comes in very handy for implementing the Singleton pattern. It uses lazy initialization (i.e., it does not get created until someone actually needs it). Also, it avoids many of the tricks I have seen employed to make Singleton behavior work. Using my template, you can code your class as you would any other. The only caveat is that you must privately inherit from the template and you must implement a function preferably named Instance. Why? The class is a template. On all compilers I have used, they generate multiple instances of the pointer to derived type.

```cpp
template <class T>
class Singleton
{
private:
  // Pointer to the one and only instance.
  // As an auto_ptr, we won't get memory leaks
  // because it will be destroyed when the program
  // shuts down and before memory leak detection kicks in.
  static std::auto_ptr<T> m_ptheSingleton;

protected:
  // Constructor
  // Allows derived classes access to the constructor.
  Singleton(){}

  // Allows access to the instance.
  // Derived classes should make this public by naming the method
  // in the derived class's public section. This gives only one
  // path to one instance of m_ptheSingleton, making the Singleton
  // behavior work.
  static T& Instance();

public:
  // Destructor
  virtual ~Singleton(){}
};

template <class T>
std::auto_ptr<T> Singleton<T>::m_ptheSingleton;

template <class T>
T& Singleton<T>::Instance()
```

```
{
  // All auto_ptrs are initalized to NULL.
  // Only create the object if needed.
  if ( NULL == m_ptheSingleton.get() )
  {
    m_ptheSingleton = std::auto_ptr<T>( new T() );
  }
  if ( NULL == m_ptheSingleton.get() )
  {
    throw std::bad_alloc();
  }
  return *m_ptheSingleton;
}
```

Singletons are rarely polymorphic. If polymorphism is required, my template will not help you. To see a typical derived class, see the declaration of SOAPDispatcher in this chapter.

Before a SOAPObject can be used, an application must register a SOAPObjectCreator with the SOAPDispatcher instance. Then, when the component handling client requests receives a message, that component tells the SOAPDispatcher to process the request. SOAPDispatcher assumes that all requests are well-formed SOAP messages. On return, the external component gets the SOAP response. This string may contain the result of the method or message or it may contain a Fault. In either case, this string should be able to be sent to the caller for it to handle. In SOAPDispatcher's class declaration, notice that it privately inherits from Singleton< SOAPDispatcher >. This allows it to inherit the Singleton behavior without exposing the Singleton interface.

```
class SOAPDispatcher : private Singleton< SOAPDispatcher >
{
public:
  // Instance
  // Description:
  // Returns the single instance of this object within the
  // program.
  // Arguments:
  // N/A
  // Return Value:
  // Reference to the SOAPDispatcher instance.
```

```
static SOAPDispatcher& Instance();

// processMessage
// Description:
// Given a SOAPElement, object name, and method name, this calls
// the appropriate SOAPMethod on the appropriate SOAPObject.
// If this fails, ask for a SOAPFault.
// Arguments:
// KszObjectName: Name of the SOAPObject
//    (SOAPObjectCreator.createdObjectName()).
// KszMethodName: Name of the SOAPMethod
//    (SOAPMethod.methodName()).
// theCall: Pre-parsed message.
// bContainsFault: Indicates if the returned string
//    contains a fault.
// Return Value:
// Returns a SOAP. send-ready response.
std::string processMessage( const std::string&
  KszObjectName,
  const std::string& KszMethodName,
  SOAPElement& theCall,
  bool& bContainsFault );

// registerObject
// Description:
// Adds an object creator to the list of objects the dispatcher
// can call.
// Arguments:
// pCreator: Pointer to an allocated SOAPObjectCreator. The
//    object assumes ownership of the object and will destroy
//    it at program termination.
// Return Value:
// true: Object successfully registered.
// false: Object already in registry. You need to delete
//    the memory yourself in this case (the dispatcher didn't
//    take ownership of the object).
bool registerObject( SOAPObjectCreator* pCreator );

private:
  // Allow these two to create and destroy this class.
  // The file singleton.h explains why this is necessary.
  friend Singleton< SOAPDispatcher >;
  friend std::auto_ptr<SOAPDispatcher>;
  // Constructor/ Destructor
  SOAPDispatcher();
  virtual ~SOAPDispatcher();
```

```
  // SOAPObjectCreaterPtr
  // Description: Makes typing easier for the auto-destroy pointer.
  typedef std::auto_ptr<SOAPObjectCreator> SOAPObjectCreaterPtr;

  // CreatorContainer
  // Description: Makes typing easier for the container.
  typedef std::map<std::string, SOAPObjectCreaterPtr>
    CreatorContainer;

  // m_creatorContainer
  // Description: The dispatcher's registry.
  CreatorContainer m_creatorContainer;
};
```

Calls to SOAPDispatcher::Instance() simply call into the parent class:

```
SOAPDispatcher& SOAPDispatcher::Instance()
{
  return Singleton<SOAPDispatcher>::Instance();
}
```

The truly interesting pieces are in SOAPDispatcher::registerObject and SOAPDispatcher::processMessage. You should probably call SOAPDispatcher::registerObject at application initialization for each and every object that you want to handle incoming requests. This method only allows you to register on SOAPObjectCreator for each named object. It will not add an item with the same name twice.

```
bool SOAPDispatcher::registerObject( SOAPObjectCreator* pCreator )
{
  // Check to see if the item is in the map.
  CreatorContainer::iterator it = m_creatorContainer.find(
    pCreator->createdObjectName() );
  bool retval = false;
  if ( it == m_creatorContainer.end() )
  {
    // The item was not found. Indicate success
    // and take ownership of the memory.
    retval = true;
    m_creatorContainer[pCreator->createdObjectName()] =
      std::auto_ptr<SOAPObjectCreator>(pCreator);
  }
  return retval;
}
```

Later on, a client will request to execute a method on a particular object. To handle this, you call `SOAPDispatcher::processMessage`. At the time of the call your program will need to know the name of the object and the method being called. Normally, you would find the method name as the one and only subelement inside the `Body`. If I assumed this in the library I would have precluded the ability to use the code for handling messages as well. So, I force the user to pull this item out after parsing the incoming message. This does slow down the many to benefit the few, but not by much.

```
std::string SOAPDispatcher::processMessage(
  const std::string& KszObjectName,
  const std::string& KszMethodName,
  SOAPElement& theCall,
  bool& bContainsFault)
{
  std::string retval;
  SOAPEncoder theEncoder;
  SOAPFault soapFault;
  CreatorContainer::iterator it = m_creatorContainer.find(
    KszObjectName );
  if ( it != m_creatorContainer.end() )
  {
    std::auto_ptr<SOAPObject> pObject =
      std::auto_ptr<SOAPObject>( it->second->newSOAPObject()
);
    if ( NULL != pObject.get() )
    {
      // Iterate over the list of methods
      SOAPObject::MethodList& methodList =
        pObject->getMethodList();
      bool bFoundMethod = false;
      for ( SOAPObject::MethodList::iterator it =
          methodList.begin();
        it != methodList.end(); ++it )
      {
        if ( (*it)->methodName() == KszMethodName )
        {
          bFoundMethod = true;
          if ( (*it)->execute( theCall ) )
          {
            retval =
              theEncoder.encodeMethodResponse( **it );
          }
          else
```

```
          {
            retval = theEncoder.encodeFault(
              *((*it)->getFault()) );
            bContainsFault = true;
          }
            break;
        }
      }
      if ( !bFoundMethod )
      {
        // Return SOAP error. Class: Client.
        soapFault.setSpecificFault( "CouldNotLocateMethod",
          SOAPFault::Client );
        soapFault.faultString() =
          std::string( "Requested object exists but does not "
          "implement the requested method: " ) +
          KszObjectName + std::string(".") +
          KszMethodName;
        retval = theEncoder.encodeFault( soapFault );
        bContainsFault = true;
      }
    }
    else
    {
      // Return SOAP error. Class: Server.
      soapFault.setSpecificFault( "CouldNotCreateObject",
        SOAPFault::Server );
      soapFault.faultString() =
        "Requested object exists but could not be created.";
      retval = theEncoder.encodeFault( soapFault );
      bContainsFault = true;
    }
  }
  else
  {
    // Return object not found error. This would be a
    // Client fault.
    soapFault.setSpecificFault( "ObjectNotFound" );
    soapFault.faultString() =
      "The requested object does not exist on this server.";
    retval = theEncoder.encodeFault( soapFault );
    bContainsFault = true;
  }
  return retval;
}
```

This code uses a number of classes we have not hit yet: SOAPMethod, SOAPEncoder, and SOAPFault. We cover these next. Looking at the code, you see the basic program flow:

1.   See if we know anything about the requested object.
2.   If we know about the object, see if it supports the requested method.
3.   If the requested method exists, execute it.
4.   Encode the method response.
5.   Return the method response.

At any of these steps the code might detect an error. When this happens it sets the fault information and writes the fault to the response string. Regardless of success or failure, SOAPEncoder translates the objects into a SOAP string.

## *SOAPEncoder*

SOAPEncoder helps out by allowing you to transform your structures and other messages into ready-to-transmit SOAP calls. The class has a number of functions to encode strings, binary data, or various types of integers, or to perform custom encoding. The class has a number of functions that are overloaded on basic datatypes:

```
// encodeArgument
// Description:
// This set of overloads encodes the argument using
// the xsd:[type] data as <szArgName>value</szArgName>.
// To avoid spelling errors, I recommend using the
// encodeArg macro, which can produce the argument name
// and value.
// Arguments:
// szArgName: Name of the argument.
// value: Value to encode.
// Return Value:
// Returns a string representing the value when encoded.
virtual std::string encodeArgument( const std::string& szArgName,
   const std::string& value );
virtual std::string encodeArgument( const std::string& szArgName,
   const int& value );
virtual std::string encodeArgument( const std::string& szArgName,
```

```
         const __int64& value );
   virtual std::string encodeArgument( const std::string& szArgName,
      const short& value );
   virtual std::string encodeArgument( const std::string& szArgName,
      const char& value );
   virtual std::string encodeArgument( const std::string& szArgName,
      const unsigned int& value );
   virtual std::string encodeArgument( const std::string& szArgName,
      const unsigned __int64& value );
   virtual std::string encodeArgument( const std::string& szArgName,
      const unsigned short& value );
   virtual std::string encodeArgument( const std::string& szArgName,
      const unsigned char& value );
   virtual std::string encodeArgument( const std::string& szArgName,
      const float& value );
   virtual std::string encodeArgument( const std::string& szArgName,
      const double& value );
   virtual std::string encodeArgument( const std::string& szArgName,
      const bool& value );
```

Each of these functions does the same thing: encode the argument along with type information. Here's a typical example:

```
std::string SOAPEncoder::encodeArgument( const std::string& szArgName,
   const float& value )
{
   std::ostringstream szStream;

   // Set the begin tag for the argument element.
   szStream << "<" << szArgName << " xsi:type=\"xsd:float\">"
<< value;

   // Set the end tag for the argument element.
   szStream << "</" << szArgName << ">" << std::endl;
   m_encodedValue += szStream.str();
   return szStream.str();
}
```

Calling this function with a float named `myFloat` with a value of 28.906 generates the following string:

```
<myFloat xsi:type="xsd:float">28.906</myFloat>
```

You typically do not code this function directly. Instead, I recommend that you name your variables as they appear in the SOAP message and use the following macro to encode your calls:

```
#define encodeArg(a) encodeArgument( "" #a "" , a )
```

To encode myFloat, you would write

```
SOAPEncoder aSoapEncoder;
float myFloat = 28.906;
aSoapEncoder.encodeArg(myFloat);
```

Using this macro helps prevent XML generation errors as long as you name your data items correctly. If the message recipient expects a given item to be named someArgument, then name your program variable someArgument. When it comes time to send the data, everything ought to work fine.[3]

Here is the full class declaration:

```
class SOAPEncoder
{
public:
    // Constructor/ Destructor
    SOAPEncoder();
    virtual ~SOAPEncoder();

    // Encoding functions

    // encodeMethodCall
    // Description:
    // Given a method, turns it into a SOAP message.
    // Arguments:
    // aMethod: The method to encode.
    // Return Value:
    // aMethod as a SOAP compliant string.
    virtual std::string encodeMethodCall( SOAPMethod& aMethod
        );

    // encodeMethodResponse
    // Description:
    // Pretty much the same thing as encodeMethodCall,
    // except this one sets the aMethod name to the following:
    // [aMethod.methodName()]Response. You will see this called
    // in response to a call to SOAPMethod.execute().
    // Arguments:
    // aMethod: The method to encode.
    // Return Value:
```

---

[3] Of course, if you mistype the name, you're still in trouble.

```cpp
// aMethod as a SOAP compliant string.
virtual std::string encodeMethodResponse( SOAPMethod& aMethod );

// encodeArgument
// Description:
//  This set of overloads encodes the argument using
// the xsd:[type] data as <szArgName>value</szArgName>.
// To avoid spelling errors, I recommend using the
// encodeArg macro, which can produce the argument name
// and value.
// Arguments:
//  szArgName: Name of the argument.
// value: Value to encode.
// Return Value:
//  Returns a string representing the value when encoded.
virtual std::string encodeArgument( const std::string& szArgName,
  const std::string& value );
virtual std::string encodeArgument( const std::string& szArgName,
  const int& value );
virtual std::string encodeArgument( const std::string& szArgName,
  const __int64& value );
virtual std::string encodeArgument( const std::string& szArgName,
  const short& value );
virtual std::string encodeArgument( const std::string& szArgName,
  const char& value );
virtual std::string encodeArgument(
      const std::string& szArgName,
  const unsigned int& value );
virtual std::string encodeArgument(
  const std::string& szArgName,
  const unsigned __int64& value );
virtual std::string encodeArgument(
  const std::string& szArgName,
  const unsigned short& value );
virtual std::string encodeArgument(
  const std::string& szArgName,
  const unsigned char& value );
virtual std::string encodeArgument(
  const std::string& szArgName,
  const float& value );
virtual std::string encodeArgument(
  const std::string& szArgName,
  const double& value );
virtual std::string encodeArgument(
  const std::string& szArgName,
  const bool& value );
```

```cpp
// encodeBase64
// Description:
// This one is a bit special. It takes a pointer and the
// length
// of the data to encode from that pointer in bytes, then
// base64
// encodes the data.
// Arguments:
// szArgName: Name of the argument.
// value: Pointer to the start of the bytestream.
// ulSizeofValue: Length of the stream, in bytes.
// Return Value:
// Returns a string representing the encoded value.
virtual std::string encodeBase64 ( const std::string&
szArgName,
    void* value, unsigned long ulSizeofValue );

// clientFaultClass
// Description:
//  For this encoder, returns a string that represents
// the
// Client fault class.
// Arguments:
// N/A
// Return Value:
// See description.
virtual std::string clientFaultClass();

// serverFaultClass
// Description:
//  For this encoder, returns a string that represents
// the
// Client fault class.
// Arguments:
// N/A
// Return Value:
// See description.
virtual std::string serverFaultClass();

// versionMismatchFaultClass
// Description:
//  For this encoder, returns a string that represents
// the
// Client fault class.
// Arguments:
```

```
// N/A
// Return Value:
// See description.
virtual std::string versionMismatchFaultClass();

// mustUnderstandFaultClass
// Description:
//   For this encoder, returns a string that represents
// the
// Client fault class.
// Arguments:
// N/A
// Return Value:
// See description.
virtual std::string mustUnderstandFaultClass();

// addBeginTag
// Description:
//   For this encoder, adds a begin tag to the stream. You
// must not provide anything other than the name.
// Ex. give the method "startTag", not "<startTag>"
// Arguments:
// szValue: Name of the tag.
// Return Value:
// The string as encoded to this point.
virtual std::string addBeginTag( const std::string& szValue );

// addEndTag
// Description:
//   For this encoder, adds an end tag to the stream. You
// must not provide anything other than the name.
// Ex. give the method "endTag", not "</endTag>"
// Arguments:
// szValue: Name of the tag.
// Return Value:
// The string as encoded to this point.
virtual std::string addEndTag( const std::string& szValue );

// encodeFault
// Description:
//   For this encoder, encodes the SOAPFault.
// Must be used apart from other SOAPEncoder methods.
// Arguments:
// soapFault: Name of the tag.
// Return Value:
```

```
      // Encodes the complete fault into a complete SOAP Envelope.
      virtual std::string encodeFault( SOAPFault& soapFault );

protected:

      // encodeMethod
      // Description:
      // Called by the encodeMethodResponse
      // and encodeMethodCall members to finish
      // encoding the method. As you may guess, the
      // two methods share a lot, and this item holds
      // that common code.
      // Arguments:
      // aMethod: The method being encoded.
      // Return Value:
      // Returns the value of the encoded method as
      // a valid SOAP string.
      virtual std::string encodeMethod( SOAPMethod& aMethod );

      // envelopeOpen
      // Description:
      // For this encoder, returns a string that represents the
      // opening of an Envelope element.
      // Arguments:
      // N/A
      // Return Value:
      // See description.
      virtual std::string envelopeOpen();

      // envelopeClose
      // Description:
      //  For this encoder, returns a string that represents the
      // closing of an Envelope element.
      // Arguments:
      // N/A
      // Return Value:
      // See description.
      virtual std::string envelopeClose();

      // headerOpen
      // Description:
      //  For this encoder, returns a string that represents the
      // opening of a Header element.
      // Arguments:
      // N/A
```

```
// Return Value:
// See description.
virtual std::string headerOpen();

// headerContents
// Description:
//   At this point, this is a place holder. I haven't
// implemented anything that allows the use of header
// elements yet. When I need it, I'll get this one done.
// Arguments:
// N/A
// Return Value:
// Returns the contents of the header field.
virtual std::string headerContents();

// headerClose
// Description:
//   For this encoder, returns a string that represents the
// closing of a Header element.
// Arguments:
// N/A
// Return Value:
// See description.
virtual std::string headerClose();

// bodyOpen
// Description:
//   For this encoder, returns a string that represents the
// opening of a Body element.
// Arguments:
// N/A
// Return Value:
// See description.
virtual std::string bodyOpen();

// bodyClose
// Description:
//   For this encoder, returns a string that represents the
// opening of a Body element.
// Arguments:
// N/A
// Return Value:
// See description.
virtual std::string bodyClose();
```

```
// faultOpen
// Description:
//   For this encoder, returns a string that represents the
// opening of a Fault element.
// Arguments:
// N/A
// Return Value:
// See description.
virtual std::string faultOpen();

// faultClose
// Description:
//   For this encoder, returns a string that represents the
// closing of a Fault element.
// Arguments:
// N/A
// Return Value:
// See description.
virtual std::string faultClose();

// faultcodeOpen
// Description:
//   For this encoder, returns a string that represents the
// opening of a Fault:faultcode element.
// Arguments:
// N/A
// Return Value:
// See description.
virtual std::string faultcodeOpen();

// faultcodeClose
// Description:
//   For this encoder, returns a string that represents the
// closing of a Fault:faultcode element.
// Arguments:
// N/A
// Return Value:
// See description.
virtual std::string faultcodeClose();

// faultstringOpen
// Description:
//   For this encoder, returns a string that represents the
// opening of a Fault:faultstring element.
// Arguments:
```

```
// N/A
// Return Value:
// See description.
virtual std::string faultstringOpen();

// faultstringClose
// Description:
//  For this encoder, returns a string that represents the
// closing of a Fault:faultstring element.
// Arguments:
// N/A
// Return Value:
// See description.
virtual std::string faultstringClose();

// faultactorOpen
// Description:
//  For this encoder, returns a string that represents the
// opening of a Fault:faultactor element.
// Arguments:
// N/A
// Return Value:
// See description.
virtual std::string faultactorOpen();

// faultactorClose
// Description:
//  For this encoder, returns a string that represents the
// closing of a Fault:faultactor element.
// Arguments:
// N/A
// Return Value:
// See description.
virtual std::string faultactorClose();

// faultdetailOpen
// Description:
//  For this encoder, returns a string that represents the
// opening of a Fault:detail element.
// Arguments:
// N/A
// Return Value:
// See description.
virtual std::string faultdetailOpen();
```

```
// faultdetailClose
// Description:
//  For this encoder, returns a string that represents the
// closing of a Fault:detail element.
// Arguments:
// N/A
// Return Value:
// See description.
virtual std::string faultdetailClose();

// isEncodingResponse
// Description:
// Used to indicate if the encoder is currently
// closing a SOAP response.
// Arguments:
// N/A
// Return Value:
// true: It is encoding.
// false: Is not encoding.
bool isEncodingResponse();

private:

// m_bIsResponse
// Description: Remembers if this item is encoding
// a SOAP response.
bool m_bIsResponse;

// m_encodedValue
// Description: Keeps the value of the encoded string
// as this object moves itself throughout the encoding process.
std::string m_encodedValue;
};
```

A good number of the functions deal with correctly generating the appropriate begin and end tags for the SOAP-specific elements. These are all declared as virtual in case a client decides to use a different encoding style or for future revisions of the protocol. If a namespace changes, it may just be a matter of creating a SOAPEncoderV12 (version 1.2) that derives from this one and then continuing on.

This class has three methods that will create complete SOAP messages:

- **encodeMethodCall:** Creates a SOAP message for calling a SOAP method.

- **encodeMethodResponse:** Creates a SOAP message for responding to a SOAP call.
- **encodeFault:** Given a SOAPFault instance, generates a valid SOAP Fault response.

These three methods work through cooperation with their caller and the encoded objects. The caller invokes one of the three methods. SOAPEncoder creates the appropriate elements, and then tells the SOAPMethod to encode itself. In the case of a Fault, SOAPEncoder does all the work. Both of the encodeMethodXXX functions call into the protected encodeMethod function.

```
std::string SOAPEncoder::encodeMethod( SOAPMethod& aMethod )
{
  std::string szHeaderContents = headerContents();
  std::string szMethodName = aMethod.methodName();
  std::ostringstream szStream;
  bool bHeaderNeeded = szHeaderContents.length() > 0;
  // Initialize the envelope.
  szStream << envelopeOpen();

  if ( isEncodingResponse() )
  {
    szMethodName += "Response";
  }

  if ( bHeaderNeeded )
  {
    szStream << headerOpen() << szHeaderContents << headerClose();
  }

  szStream << bodyOpen();

  // Set the begin tag for the method element.
  szStream << "<" << szMethodName << ">" << std::endl;

  m_encodedValue = "";

  // Encode the method.
  aMethod.encode( *this );

  szStream << m_encodedValue;

  // Set the end tag for the method element.
```

```
    szStream << "</" << szMethodName << ">" << std::endl;

    // Close the body.
    szStream << bodyClose();

    // Close the envelope.
    szStream << envelopeClose();
    m_encodedValue = szStream.str();
    return m_encodedValue;
}
```

About halfway through the method, the SOAPEncoder passes itself to the SOAPMethod being encoded. Only the method knows what bits need to be encoded. Both clients and servers use this. In the case of a server instance, the SOAPMethod needs to remember the results of the call. Remember, if the call fails, SOAPDispatcher does not try to encode a response.

## *SOAPMethod*

SOAPMethod provides an interface for the things that methods must know how to do. Specifically, it needs to know the following:

- Its name, so the SOAPDispatcher can find it
- How to execute itself given a SOAPElement
- If it fails, how to fill in a SOAPFault
- How to encode itself for execution or response

Because this behavior needs to be defined by derived classes, implementing a derived class means defining this behavior.

```
class SOAPMethod
{
public:
   // Constructor/ Destructor
   SOAPMethod();
   virtual ~SOAPMethod();

   // methodName
   // Description:
   // Used to get the name of the method. This is
   // matched up using the SOAPDispatcher to respond
   // to a call.
```

```
// Arguments:
// N/A
// Return Value:
// Returns the name of the method.
virtual std::string methodName() = 0;

// encode
// Description:
// Transforms the method into something that SOAP
// servers and clients can send. The encoder
// holds the actual data while the client hands
// data to be entered in. This makes a whole
// lot more sense in the samples that should have shipped
// with the library.
// Arguments:
// soapEncoder: Instance of the SOAPEncoder being used
//    to, you guessed it, encode the response.
// Return Value:
// true: Succeeded in encoding the message.
// false: Failed to encode the message.
virtual bool encode( SOAPEncoder& soapEncoder ) = 0;

// execute
// Description:
// Only to be called on the server by the dispatcher,
// this method executes the call and returns
// true if the call succeeded, false if it failed.
// SOAPMethods should keep any return data in a
// member variable. The information will be
// returned via a call to encode.
// Arguments:
// theCall: A SOAPElement (with possible embedded elements)
//    that represents the call.
// Return Value:
// true: Call succeeded.
// false: Call failed.
virtual bool execute( SOAPElement& theCall );

// getFault
// Description:
//   If the call fails, this returns the fault the call generated.
// The actual SOAPFault won't be created unless setFailed() is
// called.
// Arguments:
// N/A
// Return Value:
```

```
    // Pointer to the fault if it exists.
    SOAPFault* getFault();

protected:

    // setFailed
    // Description:
    // Sets the status of the SOAP call to failed and triggers
    // the creation of the SOAPFault.
    // Arguments:
    // N/A
    // Return Value:
    // N/A
    void setFailed();

    // succeeded
    // Description:
    // Tells whether or not the call was successful.
    // Arguments:
    // N/A
    // Return Value:
    // true: Call to execute worked.
    // false: Call to execute failed.
    bool succeeded();

    // m_bSucceeded
    // Description: Stores the success value.
    bool m_bSucceeded;

    // m_pFault
    // Description: Stores a pointer to the fault data (if any).
    std::auto_ptr<SOAPFault> m_pFault;
};
```

Notice that the execute method is not an abstract virtual function. This class may be used on the client, too, where execute will not be needed. The default implementation of this method returns false, just in case a client method decides to implement it. Before looking at the workhorse behind the library, let us take a look at how a SOAP server generates error information.

## SOAPFault

The header file contains all you really need to know. It's error data—important, but not terribly creative.

```
class SOAPFault : public SOAPElement
{
public:
    // Constructor/ Destructor
    SOAPFault();
    virtual ~SOAPFault();


    // getFaultCode
    // Description:
    // Gets the general reason why the call failed.
    // Arguments:
    // N/A
    // Return Value:
    // Returns a string combining the generic fault and
    // any more specific fault data.
    std::string getFaultCode();
    enum FaultCode { Client, Server, MustUnderstand, VersionMismatch };

    // setFaultCode
    // Description:
    // Sets the generic fault code.
    // Arguments:
    // faultCode: One of the values found in the FaultCode enumeration.
    // Return Value:
    // N/A
    void setFaultCode( FaultCode faultCode );

    // setSpecificFault
    // Description:
    // Allows the caller to set the generic and specific
    // reasons for the failure of a call.
    // Arguments:
    // szSpecificFault: The more descriptive reason behind the
    //    failure.
    // faultCode: One of the values found in the FaultCode enumeration.
    // Return Value:
    // N/A
    void setSpecificFault( const std::string& szSpecificFault,
            FaultCode faultCode = Client );

    // faultString
    // Description:
    // Allows the user to set/get the complete fault string.
    // Arguments:
    // N/A
```

```
    // Return Value:
    // See description.
    std::string& faultString();

    // faultActor
    // Description:
    // Allows the user to set/get the fault actor.
    // Arguments:
    // N/A
    // Return Value:
    // See description.
    std::string& faultActor();

    // detail
    // Description:
    // Allows the user to set/get the fault detail.
    // Arguments:
    // N/A
    // Return Value:
    // See description.
    std::string& detail();

private:

    // m_faultCode
    // Description: Generic reason the call failed.
    FaultCode m_faultCode;

    // m_szSpecificFault
    // Description: Specific reason the call failed.
    std::string m_szSpecificFault;

    // m_szFaultString
    // Description: Description of the fault.
    std::string m_szFaultString;

    // m_szFaultActor
    // Description: Intermediary that caught the fault.
    std::string m_szFaultActor;

    // m_szDetail
    // Description: Details behind why the fault occurred.
    std::string m_szDetail;
};
```

## *SOAPParser*

This class probably has the hardest job in the entire SimpleSOAP library.
It takes a SOAP message and transforms it from text to data so the rest of the
library can do something with it. Everything `SOAPEncoder` can do, this class
can understand. The class's public interface only does three things:

- Parse a message.
- Get the namespaces the message declared.
- Return a fault if the class cannot parse the message.

The class also has a number of functions that help it do its job. Functions
exist to extract attributes with begin tags, find namespace declarations, and
extract value data. Like every other class, I put the documentation in the
header file. Here it is to give you a flavor for the class:

```
class SOAPParser
{
public:
  // Constructor/ Destructor
  SOAPParser();
  virtual ~SOAPParser();

  // Maps a namespace identifier to a URN.
  typedef std::map<std::string, std::string> XMLNStoURN;

  // parseMessage
  // Description:
  // Given a SOAP string, parses it into new elements and
  // deposits them into the root SOAPElement passed in via
  // soapMessage.
  // Arguments:
  // szMessage: The message to parse.
  // soapMessage: The root SOAPElement to fill in.
  // Return Value:
  // true: Successful parse.
  // false: Unsuccessful parse.
  virtual bool parseMessage( const std::string& szMessage,
    SOAPElement& soapMessage );

  // getNamespacesInUse
  // Description:
```

```
// Returns the names and URNs of any and all namespaces found
// when parsing the message. If duplicate namespace names are
// used with different URNs, only the last one found will
// appear in the set of return values.
// Arguments:
//   N/A
// Return Value:
// Returns a reference to the internal namespace to URN mapping.
XMLNStoURN& getNamespacesInUse();

// getFault
// Description:
//   If the call fails, this returns the fault the call generated.
// The actaul SOAPFault won't be created unless setFailed() is
// called.
// Arguments:
// N/A
// Return Value:
// Pointer to the fault if it exists.
SOAPFault* getFault();

protected:

// parseMessage
// Description:
// Recursive version of the public interface. The caller
// doesn't need to know that we pass the current position
// within the message string as we parse, but it doesn't
// hurt that the object knows about this.
// Arguments:
// szMessage: Message to parse.
// soapElement: Root element to fill in (might be one of the
// original's subelements).
// nCurrentPos: Current position within szMessage.
// Return Value:
// true: Successful parse.
// false: Unsuccessful parse.
virtual bool parseMessage( const std::string& szMessage,
   SOAPElement& soapElement, long& nCurrentPos );

// setFailed
// Description:
// Sets the status of the SOAP call to failed and triggers
// the creation of the SOAPFault.
// Arguments:
```

```
// N/A
// Return Value:
// N/A
void setFailed();

// extractQuotedString
// Description:
// At a given position within a string, find the string with
// the matching quote types.
// Arguments:
// szString: String to find a "quoted string" within,
// nPos: Position to start at on entrance. Position after
// last
// quote on exit.
// Return Value:
// String minus the quotes used to surround the quoted string.
std::string extractQuotedString( const std::string& szString,
   long& nPos );

// splitNSAndAccessor
// Description:
// Given a "full string" splits the namespace from the rest of
// the string.
// Arguments:
// szFullString: String with namespace and accessor.
// szNamespace: On return, has the namespace name filled in
//    (if present).
// szOther: On return contains the name of the accessor.
// Return Value:
// N/A
void splitNSAndAccessor( std::string szFullString,
   std::string& szNamespace, std::string& szOther );

// extractValue
// Description:
// Extracts the first value it finds in szMessage starting
// at nCurrentPos and puts it into theElement. This stops
// processing when it hits a "<".
// Arguments:
//   theElement: The element to put the value into.
// szMessage: The message to parse.
// nCurrentPos: The message to start extracting the value at.
// Return Value:
// true: Extracted the value successfully.
// false: Failed to extract the value.
```

```
bool extractValue( SOAPElement& theElement,
  const std::string& szMessage, long& nCurrentPos );

// extractAttributes
// Description:
// Given an XML start tag, extracts any attributes and their
// values. Remove any namespace declarations before calling
// this method.
// Arguments:
//   theElement: The element to add the attributes to.
// szBeginTag: The tag to parse.
// Return Value:
// true: Extracted the attributes successfully.
// false: Failed to extract the attributes.
bool extractAttributes( SOAPElement& theElement,
  std::string szBeginTag );

// extractNamespaces
// Description:
// Extracts any and all namespace names. Puts the namespace
// names and their associated URNs into the internal namespace
// to URN map.
// Arguments:
//   szCompleteAccessor: A begin tag. On return, all namespace
//     declarations are removed.
// Return Value:
// true: Extracted the namespaces successfully.
// false: Failed to extract the namespaces.
bool extractNamespaces( std::string& szCompleteAccessor );

// extractBeginTag
// Description:
//   Extracts the "begin tag". If the tag is really an end tag,
// it indicates this via bIsEndTag. This also returns the
//   namespace declared with the element.
// Arguments:
//   szBeginTag: On entrance, contains nothing. On exit, contains
//     the begin tag.
// szNamespace: Contains the namespace of the accessor on exit.
//     If no namespace is used, this is an empty string.
//   szAccessorName: Contains the name of the accessor on exit.
//   szMessage: Contains the message to dig through.
//   nCurrentPos: On entrance, contains the position to start
//     parsing. On exit, contains the spot where the tag
//     closed.
```

```
// bIsEmptyTag: Indicates if the tag is a begin AND an end tag.
//    Ex.: <anEmptyTag value="myData" />
// bIsEndTag: Indicates if the current tag is an end tag.
//    Ex.: </anEndTag>
// Return Value:
// true: Extracted the required information successfully.
// false: Failed to extract the required information.
bool extractBeginTag(
   std::string& szBeginTag,
   std::string& szNamespace,
   std::string& szAccessorName,
   std::string szMessage,
   long &nCurrentPos,
   bool &bIsEmptyTag,
   bool &bIsEndTag);

// Data members

// m_namespaceMap
// Description: Contains the map of namespace name to URN.
XMLNStoURN m_namespaceMap;

// m_pFault
// Description: Stores a pointer to the fault data (if any).
std::auto_ptr<SOAPFault> m_pFault;
};
```

In the class you should have noticed two versions of a method named parseMessage. The one in the public interface allows external classes to request this object's parsing services. The one in the protected interface is a recursive function. A lot of these functions have an argument named nCurrentPos. This argument keeps everybody informed about how far the parse has gone through the message. During the parse, the class instantiates the variable in the public parseMessage method and shares it through the activity.

```
bool SOAPParser::parseMessage( const std::string& szMessage,

   SOAPElement& soapMessage )
{
   long nCurrentPos = 0;
   m_namespaceMap.clear();
   return parseMessage( szMessage, soapMessage, nCurrentPos
         );
}
```

The actual work then happens in its "fraternal" twin.

```
bool SOAPParser::parseMessage( const std::string& szMessage,
  SOAPElement& soapElement, long& nCurrentPos )
{
  bool retval = true;
  std::string szEndTag;

  // Start looking for the start tag.
  std::string szCurrentstring;
  const long KnLength = szMessage.length();

  // Keep marching in the string until we hit the first '<'
  for ( ; ( szMessage[nCurrentPos] != '<' )
     && ( nCurrentPos < KnLength ); ++nCurrentPos )
  {
    // body intentionally left empty.
  }

  // If we got to the end without finding the
  // end tag (or any begin tag), return false.
  if ( nCurrentPos == KnLength )
  {
    setFailed();
    std::ostringstream szStream;
    getFault()->setSpecificFault(
        "ImproperlyFormattedMessage" );
    getFault()->faultString() = "The message either has no
        "begin "
      "tag or is missing the end tag. In either case, "
      "the message was not formatted correctly.";
    return false;
  }

  std::string szBeginTag;
  std::string szNamespace;
  std::string szAccessorName;
  std::string szFullAccessorName;
  bool bIsEmptyTag = false;
  bool bIsEndTag = false;
  for ( ; retval && (nCurrentPos < KnLength); ++nCurrentPos
       )
  {
    // Initialize all variables.
    bIsEmptyTag = false;
```

```
bIsEndTag = false;
szBeginTag = "";
szNamespace = "";
szAccessorName = "";
szFullAccessorName = "";
long nInitialBeginPos = nCurrentPos;

// Get the information contained by the next pair
// of "<>".
retval = extractBeginTag( szBeginTag, szNamespace,
  szAccessorName, szMessage, nCurrentPos, bIsEmptyTag,
  bIsEndTag );

// If we are expecting an end tag, but this isn't
// one, it must be another child item. Start
// parsing at this location and attach a new "tree".
if ( ( szEndTag.length() > 0 ) && (!bIsEndTag ) )
{
  // extract the contents of this item independently
  nCurrentPos = nInitialBeginPos;
  SOAPElement* pElement = new SOAPElement;
  soapElement.addElement( pElement );
  retval = parseMessage( szMessage, *pElement,
        nCurrentPos );

  // We've now parsed all the data within the tree.
  // Go to the top of the loop again. If retval is
  // false, the error data should be filled in
  // and we will drop out of the loop.
  continue;
}

if ( !retval )
{
  // Unwind the stack— we have an error so the rest of
  // the
  // doc doesn't matter.
  setFailed();
  std::ostringstream szStream;
  szStream << "Failed near position " << nCurrentPos <<
    " within the message.";
  getFault()->setSpecificFault(
        "ImproperlyFormattedMessage" );
  getFault()->faultString() = szStream.str();
  break;
```

```
    }

    // If we are at the end of this tag, prepare to close
    // out the current SOAPElement.
    if ( bIsEndTag )
    {
      if ( szEndTag.empty() )
      {
        // We got an end tag when we weren't expecting one.
        setFailed();
        std::ostringstream szStream;
        szStream << "Failed near position " << nCurrentPos
          <<
          " within the message." << "Expected end tag: " <<
          szEndTag << std::ends;
        getFault()->setSpecificFault( "EmptyEndTag" );
        getFault()->faultString() = szStream.str();
        retval = false;
        break;
      }
      if ( szBeginTag != szEndTag )
      {
        // This isn't the end tag we were expecting.
        // Let the user know that the doc isn't formatted
        // correctly.
        setFailed();
        std::ostringstream szStream;
        szStream << "Failed near position " << nCurrentPos
          <<
          " within the message." << "Expected end tag: " <<
          szEndTag;
        getFault()->setSpecificFault( "WrongEndTag" );
        getFault()->faultString() = szStream.str();
        retval = false;
        break;
      }

      retval = true;

      // This was the expected end tag. We are done
      // with parsing for this element.
      break;
    }

    // Pull the namespaces out of the tag. They
```

```
// look like attributes to the rest of the code.
retval = extractNamespaces( szBeginTag );

if ( !retval )
{
  // Gack, something went wrong.
  setFailed();
  std::ostringstream szStream;
  szStream << "Failed near position " << nCurrentPos <<
    " within the message.";
  getFault()->setSpecificFault(
    "NamespaceExtractionFailed",
    SOAPFault::Server );
  getFault()->faultString() = szStream.str();
  retval = false;
  break;
}

// If the given element was specified using a name
// space,
// tack it on to the start of the namespace name.
if ( szNamespace.length() > 0 )
{
  szFullAccessorName = szNamespace + std::string(":");
  soapElement.namespaceName() = szNamespace;
}
szFullAccessorName += szAccessorName;
soapElement.accessorName() = szAccessorName;

// If this is the envelope, check the version.
if ( soapElement.accessorName() == "Envelope" )
{
  bool bFound = false;
  // Check to see if the SOAP namespace was set.
  // If not, we have a VersionMismatch problem.
  for ( XMLNStoURN::iterator it =
    m_namespaceMap.begin();
    it != m_namespaceMap.end(); ++it )
  {
    if ( "http://schemas.xmlsoap.org/soap/envelope/" ==
      it->second)
    {
      bFound = true;
      break;
    }
```

```
      }
      if ( !bFound )
      {
        setFailed();
        getFault()->setFaultCode(SOAPFault::VersionMismatch
            );
        getFault()->faultString() = "Version mismatch "
            "found.";
        retval = false;
        break;
      }
    }

    // set the text for the expected end tag.
    szEndTag = std::string( "/" );
    if ( szNamespace.length() > 0 )
    {
      szEndTag += szNamespace + std::string(":");
    }
    szEndTag += soapElement.accessorName();

    // Pull the attribute information out of the begin tag.
    retval = extractAttributes( soapElement, szBeginTag );
    if ( !retval )
    {
      setFailed();
      std::ostringstream szStream;
      szStream << "Attribute extraction: Failed near
        "position " <<
        nCurrentPos << " within the message." << std::ends;
      getFault()->setSpecificFault(
          "ImproperlyFormattedMessage" );
      getFault()->faultString() = szStream.str();
      break;
    }

    // Take out the value contained between the begin and
    // end tags.
    retval = extractValue( soapElement, szMessage,
        nCurrentPos );
    if ( !retval )
    {
      setFailed();
      std::ostringstream szStream;
      szStream << "Value extraction: Failed near position "
          <<
```

```
      nCurrentPos << " within the message." << std::ends;
    getFault()->setSpecificFault(
        "ImproperlyFormattedMessage" );
    getFault()->faultString() = szStream.str();
    break;
    }
  }
  return retval;
}
```

The remaining functions in the class are fairly compact. `parseMessage` controls the flow of the parse and the rest of the functions handle specific units of functionality. By the time the stack unwinds, you either have a fully parsed message or an error.

This concludes our look at the SimpleSOAP library. Before moving on to the example, we need to take a short look at the networking part of the puzzle.

# SOAPNetwork Library

When sending SOAP messages you need to use other protocols to carry the data. The SOAP specification specifies how SOAP must behave on one protocol: HTTP. A SOAP message does not need to specify the object it needs to act on. It appears that this bit of work is left to the protocol itself. Under HTTP, you can communicate this through the POST and through the SOAPAction. Under SMTP (email), you could do this through the subject line and specify the recipient in the "To:" field.[4] Right now, the SOAPNetwork library has only two classes. SOAPonProtocol specifies an abstract base class that derived classes should implement. SOAPonHTTP derives from SOAPonProtocol and implements the ability to send and receive messages over HTTP. SOAPonProtocol has the following interface:

```
class SOAPonProtocol
{
public:

  // Constructor/Destructor
  SOAPonProtocol();
  virtual ~SOAPonProtocol();
```

---
[4] SOAP on SMTP has not been standardized, so this is just conjecture.

```
// getSendableResponse
// Description: Given a SOAP message that has already been
// translated to some sort of string, this call finishes
// things by adding any text required by the implemented
// protocol.
// szSOAPMessage:
//   The message without any protocol-specific adornments.
// Returns:
//   The message WITH protocol-specific adornments. This method
//   is for use on the server side of a SOAP call.
virtual std::string getSendableResponse(
   const std::string& szSOAPMessage ) = 0;

// send
// Description: Given a SOAPMethod and the related class on
// the server, executes the method and returns the response
// as a string. If any protocol-specifc items will impede the
// parsing of the SOAP part of the message, this item should
// strip that off.
// szClassName:
//   Name of the class that owns the method on the server.
// aMethod:
//   Represents the method being called complete with any arguments.
virtual std::string send( const std::string& szClassName,
   SOAPMethod& aMethod ) = 0;

// getMethodDetails
// Description: When a call comes in, this takes the method,
//   takes out its "guts", and parses the message. This method
//   does not execute the actual message. That is done
//   by another object. The parsing is done here because this
//   object is intimate with the details of the overhead
//   and calling information that comes with the given protocol.
// Arguments:
//   KszMessage: The message in its raw form.
//   szObjectName: On return, this contains the name of the object
//      to execute any methods on.
//   szMethodName: On return, this contains the name of the method
//      the caller wants to execute.
//   theCall: On return, this contains the parsed SOAP message.
// Return value:
//   true: Successfully obtained all needed information.
//   false: Something went wrong during the parse. Look at
//      szObjectName for the fault details as a sendable
//      SOAP string, minus the protocol-specific stuff.
```

```
virtual bool getMethodDetails( const std::string& KszMessage,
   std::string& szObjectName, std::string& szMethodName,
   SOAPElement& theCall ) = 0;
};
```

This base class plays to a grand vision of one server handling messages coming in on multiple protocols. To date, the library has only one implementation of this interface. As a result, the interface itself may be missing some things that it really should have. If this library ever achieves a good level of use it should evolve and change. As of now it is being used on a handful of machines around the world handling some simple tasks. Let's take a look at the one class that does anything in the library: SOAPonHTTP.

## *SOAPonHTTP*

SOAPonHTTP handles all the HTTP-specific functionality. It understands how much of the text received belongs to HTTP and how much belongs to SOAP. It can locate the name of the requested object from the HTTP request header. Finally, it knows how to package a SOAP request or response for the protocol. The class implements the required interface plus a few other methods:

```
class SOAPonHTTP : SOAPonProtocol
{
public:
   // Constructor/Destructor
   SOAPonHTTP();
   virtual ~SOAPonHTTP();

   // getMethodDetails
   // Description: See base class
   // Arguments: See base class
   // Return value: See base class
   virtual bool getMethodDetails( const std::string& KszMessage,
      std::string& szObjectName, std::string& szMethodName,
      SOAPElement& theCall );

   // setHostAndPort
   // Description: Sets the host and port of the destination SOAP
   // server. This method should only be called by SOAP clients
   // (or servers acting as clients).
   // Arguments:
   //   szHost: Name of the machine. Can be numeric or character.
```

```
  // Return value: N/A
  void setHostAndPort( std::string szHost, long nPort = 80 );

  // getSendableResponse
  // Description: See base class
  // Arguments: See base class
  // Return value: See base class
  virtual std::string getSendableResponse(
    const std::string& szSOAPMessage, bool bIsFault = false );

  // send
  // Description: See base class
  // Arguments: See base class
  // Return value: See base class
  virtual std::string send(
    const std::string& szClassName, SOAPMethod& aMethod );

protected:

  // getSendableMessage
  // Description: Called by send to generate a message that
  // is suitable for sending over HTTP.
  // Arguments:
  //   szSOAPMessage: The message being sent.
  // szClassName: Name of the class being called.
  // szMethodName: Name of the method being called.
  // Return value:
  virtual std::string getSendableMessage(
    const std::string& szSOAPMessage,
    const std::string& szClassName,
    const std::string& szMethodName );

private:
  // SocketAddress
  // Description: Contains the address (IP and Port) of the
  //   server. Should only be filled in for SOAP clients.
  SocketAddress m_socketAddress;
};
```

This particular class relies on the TcpServer library to send and receive messages. If you have another library that you want to use, you should be able to do so by making a few minor modifications. I implement the guts using this code:

```
// Constants used by the SOAP HTTP implementation.
const std::string g_KszPost = "POST ";
const std::string g_KszManHeader =
```

```cpp
    "\"http://schemas.xmlsoap.org.soap/envelope/\"";
const std::string g_KszContentType =
    "Content-Type: text/xml; charset=\"utf-8\"";
const std::string g_KszContentLength = "Content-Length: ";
const std::string g_KszSOAPAction = "SOAPAction: ";
const std::string g_KszHTTPversion = "HTTP/1.1";
const std::string g_KszSOAP = "<SOAP";
const std::string g_KszBody = "Body";

std::string SOAPonHTTP::getSendableMessage(
    const std::string& szSOAPMessage,
    const std::string& szClassName,
    const std::string& szMethodName )
{
    std::ostringstream szRetval;
    const long KnLength = szSOAPMessage.length();

    // This simply puts an HTTP header in front of the actual
    // SOAP message.
    szRetval << g_KszPost << "/" << szClassName << " "
        << g_KszHTTPversion << std::endl;
    szRetval << g_KszContentType << std::endl;
    szRetval << g_KszContentLength << szSOAPMessage.length()
        << std::endl;
    szRetval << g_KszSOAPAction << "\"" << szClassName << "#"
        << szMethodName << "\"" << std::endl << std::endl;
    szRetval << szSOAPMessage;
    return szRetval.str();
}

void SOAPonHTTP::setHostAndPort( std::string szHost,
    long nPort /*= 80*/ )
{
        // Initializes the address and port.
    IpAddress ipAddress( szHost );
    m_socketAddress.setIpAddress( ipAddress );
    m_socketAddress.setPort( nPort );
}

bool SOAPonHTTP::getMethodDetails( const std::string& KszMessage,
    std::string& szObjectName, std::string& szMethodName,
    SOAPElement& theCall )
{
    bool retval = true;

    long nPos = KszMessage.find( g_KszPost );
```

```
// Find the first "/" after the first GET.
nPos = KszMessage.find( "/", nPos );

// We know where the object name starts. It ends by the first
// space.
long nEndPos = KszMessage.find( " ", nPos );

++nPos;
szObjectName = KszMessage.substr( nPos, nEndPos - nPos );

std::string szSOAPMessage;

    // Find the start of the SOAP message.
nPos = KszMessage.find( g_KszSOAP );
if ( nPos >= 0 )
{
  szSOAPMessage =
    KszMessage.substr( nPos, KszMessage.length() - nPos
        );
}

// Parse the message now that we have it.
SOAPParser soapParser;
retval = soapParser.parseMessage( szSOAPMessage, theCall
    );
if ( retval )
{
  // If we succeeded, get the name of the
  // method being called. This of course
  // assumes only one method in the body, and
  // that there are no objects outside of the
  // serialization root. This method will
  // need an override if this assumption is invalid.
  SOAPElement* pBody = NULL;
  theCall.getElement( g_KszBody, &pBody );
  if ( NULL != pBody )
  {
    SOAPElement& aMethod = pBody->elementAt( 0 );
    szMethodName = aMethod.accessorName();
  }
  if ( szMethodName.length() <= 0 )
  {
    // Create a SOAP fault
    retval = false;
  }
```

```
    }
    else
    {
      szObjectName =
        SOAPEncoder().encodeFault( *(soapParser.getFault()) );
    }
    return retval;
}


std::string SOAPonHTTP::getSendableResponse(
    const std::string& szSOAPMessage, bool bIsFault
      /*= false*/ )
{
  std::string retval;

      // This HTTP header seems to have a definite
Microsoft
    // feel to it. I will need to see how well this interoperates
    // with a UNIX machine.

    retval = "HTTP/1.1 ";
    if ( bIsFault )
    {
      retval += "500 Internal Server Error";
    }
    else
    {
      retval += "200 OK";
    }
    retval += "\r\nContent-Type: text/xml;"
      "\r\ncharset=\"utf-8\"\r\nContent-Length: ";
    char buffer[33];
    itoa( szSOAPMessage.length(), buffer, 10 );
    retval += buffer;
    retval += "\r\n\r\n";
    retval += szSOAPMessage;
    return retval;
}

std::string SOAPonHTTP::send( const std::string&
szClassName,
    SOAPMethod& aMethod )
{
  SOAPEncoder soapEncoder;
```

```
  // First off, encode the call.
  std::string szCall = soapEncoder.encodeMethodCall( aMethod );

  // Now get the message we want to send.
  std::string szSend = getSendableMessage(
    szCall, szClassName, aMethod.methodName() );
  std::cerr << szSend;
  const long KnBuffSize = 10000;
  char buffer[KnBuffSize];
  memset( buffer, 0, KnBuffSize );
  TcpSocket theSocket;

  // Connect to the server.
  theSocket.connect_to( m_socketAddress );

  // Write out the request.
  theSocket.write( szSend.c_str(), szSend.length() );

  // Read back the response.
  theSocket.read( buffer, KnBuffSize );

  // Copy the contents into the return value.
  szSend = buffer;

  // Close the connection to the server.
  theSocket.close();

  // Return the result of the call.
  return szSend;
}
```

This concludes the SOAP libraries. Let's move on and take a look at how to put all of this together.

# A Simple SOAP Server

To see just how much work this library saved I built a small SOAP client and server. The server supports two methods: add and reverse. add takes two numbers and returns their sum. reverse takes a string and returns that string reversed. This should give you an idea of how to add classes and make them work within the framework. With any luck, it also makes the whole idea of creating your own that much more palatable.

The server contains a few parts. One sets up the ability to actually send and receive requests. Then, we have the SOAPObjectCreator-derived class that creates the SOAPObject. Finally, there are the SOAPMethods. The hardest part involves writing the SOAPMethods. These need the most knowledge of how a SOAP message is constructed. Let's start out with the easy stuff and work our way up.

## Building the Message Processor

Because we are using the TcpServer library, we need to declare a function named networkAppMain. This function opens up a connection on a port on the local machine and listens for new connections.

```
int networkAppMain(int argc, char* argv[])
{
  // Create connection server with well-known port on local host.
  TcpConnectionServer server( SocketAddress( 5043 ) );

  // Perform registration.
  registerObjects();

  TcpSocket socket;
  while (true)
  {
    server.accept( socket ); // Accept incoming connection.
    processSocket( socket );
  }

  return 0;
}
```

I did not use port 80 for the HTTP traffic because I already have a Web server running on this machine. Instead, I listen on a port that I can test on. This port is not used by any other servers I have in use. As you can see, the server simply loops around and around, accepting connections and processing them. It processes all requests in a first-come, first-served order. The server is not designed for high-volume transactions. The fact that most connections wait for a period of time before timing out helps this respond to multiple clients.

So that the server knows what to respond to, it needs to have at least one object in its registry (no, not the Windows Registry). SOAPDispatcher maintains a list of registered objects. Something has to add those objects to the list, and registerObjects performs that task.

```
void registerObjects()
{
  SOAPDispatcher::Instance().registerObject(
    new TSOAPObjectCreator<Ch4SOAP>( std::string("Ch4SOAP") ) );
}
```

Because SOAPDispatcher owns the object, it will make sure that the memory gets cleaned up at program termination. As of now, we still have not seen anything that will actually execute the incoming requests. Here, we look to processSocket. This function does the following:

- Reads the incoming data
- Turns that data into something the SOAPDispatcher can execute
- Tells SOAPDispatcher to process the message
- Returns the response to the caller

```
void processSocket( TcpSocket& socket )
{
  long nBuffSize = socket.receive_buffer_size();
  char* buff = new char[ nBuffSize ];
  std::string szReply;
  std::string szSOAPMessage;
  memset( buff, 0, nBuffSize );

  bool bSendingFault = false;
  try
  {
    socket.read( buff, nBuffSize );
    szSOAPMessage = buff;
  }
  catch( NetworkException& e )
  {
    std::cerr << e.what();
  }
  catch( ... )
  {
    socket.close();
    return;
```

```
}

    // Process the SOAP message- should be the contents of
    // the
    // message from "<SOAP:" to the end of the string.
    SOAPonHTTP soapOnHTTP;
    std::string szObjectName;
    std::string szMethodName;
    SOAPElement theCall;
    if ( soapOnHTTP.getMethodDetails(
        szSOAPMessage, szObjectName, szMethodName, theCall ) )
    {
        szReply = SOAPDispatcher::Instance().processMessage(
            szObjectName, szMethodName, theCall, bSendingFault );
    }
    else
    {
        // Create a SOAP fault. Client error- the message could
        // not be understood.
        std::cerr << "Couldn't parse the message" << std::endl;
        bSendingFault = true;
        szReply = szObjectName;
    }
    szReply = soapOnHTTP.getSendableResponse( szReply, bSendingFault );
    socket.write( szReply.c_str(), szReply.length() + 1 );
    socket.close();

    delete[] buff;
}
```

That's all there is to processing a message using the library. And yes, it would be fairly easy to reduce all of this down to requiring the programmer to implement the `registerObjects` function and embedding the rest in the SOAPNetwork library. I prefer the approach shown here over using a library because this gives me a little more access to what is coming in and going out. Using this capability, users of the library can view the incoming data, log it, or do whatever they need to do. This should help any debugging effort and I feel this benefit outweighs the inconvenience of copying this function into a project. Besides, the library and the sample code do nothing with `Header` entries other than parse them and put them into `SOAPElements`. You may need to process these in your own `processSocket`.

## Responding to SOAP Requests

Because the example builds the required SOAPObjectCreator using the template, we just need to write the SOAPObject and the server is done. The methods that the derived SOAPObject can execute should only be accessible through the parent object's getMethodList call. To really hide this, you can play some tricks. Ch4SOAP uses one of my favorites: Write a forward declaration for a struct and keep a pointer to it as a data member. Then, define that struct inside the class's implementation file.

```
class Ch4SOAP : public SOAPObject
{
public:
  Ch4SOAP();
  virtual ~Ch4SOAP();

private:
  struct MyData;
  std::auto_ptr<MyData> m_pData;
};
```

Because MyData will evolve as it is being built, this trick helps minimize the number of modules the compiler needs to touch each time we add a new method. On a small project, the impact of this change is negligible. On a large project, this could save a lot of time. I demonstrate it here knowing that if anyone chooses to use this library, he or she will likely mimic a lot of the examples. MyData contains the two SOAPMethods we need to implement.

```
struct Ch4SOAP::MyData
{
  class addMethod : public SOAPMethod
  {
  public:
    addMethod() : returnValue( 0 ) {}
    virtual std::string methodName() { return "add"; }
    virtual bool encode( SOAPEncoder& soapEncoder );
    virtual bool execute( SOAPElement& theCall );

  private:
    long returnValue;
  } m_add;

  class reverseMethod : public SOAPMethod
```

```
  {
  public:
    virtual std::string methodName(){ return "reverse"; }
    virtual bool encode( SOAPEncoder& soapEncoder );
    virtual bool execute( SOAPElement& theCall );

  private:
    std::string returnValue;
  } m_reverse;
};
```

It contains two member variables: m_add and m_reverse. The Ch4SOAP constructor adds these methods to the main list of methods the object supports.

```
Ch4SOAP::Ch4SOAP() :
  m_pData( new MyData )
{
  insertMethod( &(m_pData->m_add) );
  insertMethod( &(m_pData->m_reverse) );
}
```

Both of the methods are fairly simple. Let's take a look at addMethod's implementation. To execute the call, it needs to check a number of things before moving forward. First, it needs to know if it needs to understand anything. Second, it has to check to make sure that the right number of arguments came through. Finally, it has to execute the call. To check and see if mustUnderstand was set, I wrote the following helper function:

```
static bool mustIUnderstand(SOAPElement& theCall)
{
  SOAPElement* pHeader = NULL;
  theCall.getElement( "Header", &pHeader );
  bool retval = false;
  if ( pHeader != NULL )
  {
    // check if anybody has mustUnderstand set to true.
    long nNumElements = pHeader->numElements();
    long nNumAttributes = 0;
    SOAPAttribute soapAttribute;
    for ( long i = 0; i < nNumElements; ++i )
    {
      SOAPElement& aHeaderElement = pHeader->
              elementAt( i );
```

```
      if ( aHeaderElement.getAttribute( "mustUnderstand",
        soapAttribute ) )
      {
        retval = soapAttribute.value() == std::string("1");
      }
    }
  }

  return retval;
}
```

The rest of the checking gets done in the class's execute method.

```
bool Ch4SOAP::MyData::addMethod::execute( SOAPElement& theCall )
{
  bool retval = true;

  // Added for faults only.
  std::ostringstream szStream;

  // Check out the header elements. If any have a "mustUnderstand",
  // we won't understand and need to fail.
  if ( mustIUnderstand( theCall ) )
  {
    retval = false;
    setFailed();
    getFault()->setFaultCode( SOAPFault::MustUnderstand );
    szStream << "This object does not understand any "
      "mustUnderstand header entries." << std::ends;
    getFault()->faultString() = szStream.str();
  }
  else
  {
    // Grab the body and get the first two elements.
    SOAPElement* pBody = NULL;
    theCall.getElement( "Body", &pBody );
    if ( NULL != pBody )
    {
      if ( pBody->numElements() == 1 )
      {
        SOAPElement& theMethod = pBody->elementAt( 0 );
        if ( theMethod.accessorName() == methodName() )
        {
          if ( theMethod.numElements() == 2 )
```

```
            {
                long a = atoi( theMethod.elementAt( 0 ).
                    value().c_str() );
                long b = atoi( theMethod.elementAt( 1 ).
                    value().c_str() );
                returnValue = a + b;
            }
            else
            {
                retval = false;
                setFailed();
                getFault()->setSpecificFault(
                    "InvalidArgumentCount" );
                // Since this fault happened in the body, set
                // the detail Fault element too.
                getFault()->faultString() =
                    "Invalid number of arguments.";
                szStream << "The fault occurred because the "
                    << "add method expected 2 arguments but "
                    << "received "
                    << theMethod.numElements()
                    << " arguments.";
                getFault()->detail() = szStream.str();
            }
        }
        else
        {
            retval = false;
            // If you are using the SOAPDispatcher, this code
            // should not be reachable.
            setFailed();
            getFault()->faultString() = "Invalid method name.";
            getFault()->setSpecificFault( "MethodName" );
            szStream << "The fault occurred because the add "
                << "method expected to be called using the "
                << "name \"add\", not \" "
                << theMethod.accessorName() << ".";
            getFault()->detail() = szStream.str();
        }
        }
    }
    }
    return retval;
}
```

To encode the method, `SOAPDispatcher` will come along and tell `SOAPEncoder` to generate a valid SOAP string. It will do its thing and ask the method to encode its return value.

```
bool Ch4SOAP::MyData::addMethod::encode( SOAPEncoder& soapEncoder )
{
  bool retval = true;
  soapEncoder.encodeArg( returnValue );
  return retval;
}
```

Using an external client and adding some code to write out the exchange, we have the exchange shown in Figure 4–4. The client in this situation was a Visual Basic (VB) application that uses the Microsoft SOAP Toolkit v2. Here is the critical VB function:

```
Private Sub Command1_Click()
  Dim Serializer As SoapSerializer
  Dim Reader As New SoapReader
  Dim ResultElm As IXMLDOMElement
  Dim FaultElm As IXMLDOMElement
```

*Figure 4–4*   Request and response for the Add call using SOAP over HTTP.

```
Dim Connector As SoapConnector

Set Connector = New HttpConnector
Connector.Property("EndPointURL") = "http://local"&-
    "host:5043/Ch4SOAP"
Connector.Connect

Connector.Property("SoapAction") = "add"
Connector.BeginMessage

Set Serializer = New SoapSerializer
Serializer.Init Connector.InputStream

Serializer.startEnvelope
Serializer.startBody
Serializer.startElement "add", , , "m"
Serializer.startElement "a"
Serializer.writeString Text1.Text
Serializer.endElement
Serializer.startElement "b"
Serializer.writeString Text2.Text
Serializer.endElement
Serializer.endElement
Serializer.endBody
Serializer.endEnvelope

Connector.EndMessage

Set Reader = New SoapReader
Reader.Load Connector.OutputStream

If Not Reader.Fault Is Nothing Then
  MsgBox Reader.faultstring.Text, vbExclamation
Else
  MsgBox Text1.Text & " + " & _
    Text2.Text & " = " & CLng(Reader.RPCResult.Text)
End If

Set Connector = Nothing
Set Reader = Nothing
Set Serializer = Nothing
```

This function is part of the application shown in Figure 4–5. Now that the server is working, let's write a client with the library.

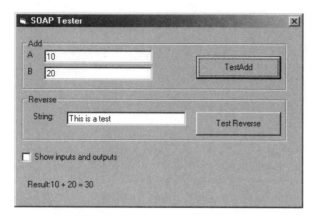

***Figure 4–5***   Visual Basic client calling SimpleSOAP server. This is the client interface.

# A Simple SOAP Client

Using the SimpleSOAP library, writing a SOAP client is even easier than writing the server. The example here needs network capabilities and the TcpServer library provides them once again. The `networkAppMain` function simply sets the target host and port based off of command-line parameters. Other than this, the main function remains ignorant of the fact that this is a networked application.

```
int networkAppMain( int argc, char* argv[] )
{
  TestSOAPClient testSOAP;

  if ( argc < 3 )
  {
    std::cout << "Standard usage is " << argv[0]
      << " [IP Address] [port]" << std::endl;
    return 1;
  }

  // Set the end point
  testSOAP.m_szEndPointIP = argv[1];
  testSOAP.m_nPort = atoi( argv[2] );
  long a = 10;
  long b = 20;
```

```
try
{
  // This may throw an exception (can't connect, etc.)
  std::cout << a << " + " << b << " = "
    << testSOAP.add( a, b ) << std::endl;
}
catch ( std::exception& e )
{
  std::cerr << e.what() << std::endl;
}

std::cout << "Normal termination of " << argv[0] <<
    std::endl;
return 0;
}
```

The `TestSOAPClient` class does all the SOAP-specific work. Its external interface hides this for all except the port and host information.

```
class TestSOAPClient
{
public:
  TestSOAPClient();
  virtual ~TestSOAPClient();

  int add( int a, int b );
  void setEndPoint( const std::string& szEndPoint, long nPort );
private:
  struct SOAPMethodTable;
  std::auto_ptr<SOAPMethodTable> m_pMethodTable;
};
```

Again, you can see that I am hiding the method data from users of the class. Because this class will have member data changing a lot during development, it just seemed like a good idea. On a small project, this construct will not yield much in terms of improving build times. This still has the benefit of hiding bits of the implementation from those reading the header file. The SOAP bits even manage to stay out of the class. This knowledge gets delegated to the `SOAPMethodTable` struct. Just look:

```
TestSOAPClient::TestSOAPClient() :
  m_pMethodTable( new SOAPMethodTable )
{
}
```

```
TestSOAPClient::~TestSOAPClient()
{

}

int TestSOAPClient::add( int a, int b )
{
  m_pMethodTable->m_addSOAP.m_szEndpoint =
    m_pMethodTable->m_szEndPointIP;
  m_pMethodTable->m_addSOAP.m_nPort = m_pMethodTable->
      m_nPort;
  return m_pMethodTable->m_addSOAP.add( a, b );
}

void TestSOAPClient::setEndPoint( const std::string&
    szEndPoint,
  long nPort )
{
  m_pMethodTable->m_szEndPointIP = szEndPoint;
  m_pMethodTable->m_nPort = nPort;
}
```

That's it. The part that handles making the call and interpreting the response is just as clean:

```
struct TestSOAPClient::SOAPMethodTable
{
  class addSOAP : public SOAPMethod
  {
  public:
    addSOAP(): a(0), b(0), m_nPort(0){}

    virtual ~addSOAP(){}

    virtual std::string methodName()
    { return std::string( "add" ); }

    virtual bool encode( SOAPEncoder& soapEncoder )
    {
      soapEncoder.encodeArg( a );
      soapEncoder.encodeArg( b );
      return true;
    }

    long add( int na, int nb )
    {
```

```
      long retval = 0;
      a = na;
      b = nb;
      SOAPonHTTP soapOnHTTP;
      soapOnHTTP.setHostAndPort( m_szEndpoint, m_nPort );
      std::string szReturn =
        soapOnHTTP.send( "Ch4SOAP", *this );
      SOAPParser soapParser;
      SOAPElement soapElement;
      if ( soapParser.parseMessage( szReturn, soapElement )
          )
      {
        SOAPElement* pBody = NULL;
        soapElement.getElement( "Body", &pBody );
        if ( NULL != pBody )
        {
          // Get the value of the element inside
          // the response
          if ( ( pBody->numElements() == 1 ) &&
            ( pBody->elementAt( 0 ).numElements() == 1 )
            )
          {
            retval = atoi( pBody->elementAt( 0 ).
              elementAt( 0 ).value().c_str() );
          }
        }
      }
      return retval;
    }

    std::string m_szEndpoint;
    long m_nPort;
  private:
    int a;
    int b;
  } m_addSOAP;

  std::string m_szEndPointIP;
  long m_nPort;
};
```

I still think that is an awful lot of code to write just to execute a procedure on another computer. However, when you compare this to the code required to manually instantiate a COM or CORBA object on a remote machine, this is par for the course.

# Summary

This chapter presents a library that can act as a SOAP server or client. If you know exactly how a given SOAP server receives and sends messages, this library will allow you to create a client that can operate over a Local Area Network (LAN) or the Internet. As a SOAP server, this library can allow you to do some pretty quick turnarounds on calls. Why did I create yet another SOAP implementation when so many already exist? SOAP is not only a simple protocol to use, but it is simple to implement. By actually writing all the required components, I can put some weight behind these claims. The implementation for this chapter was not intended to be a toy example. Instead, I wrote it to be robust and fault tolerant. Is it? Let's just say that I fully expect to be fixing bugs for a year or more as the library gets used more often.

# Fun Things to Try

This chapter presents a number of opportunities for you to experiment with the code and try to write your own SOAP clients and servers. Here are a few things you might want to try out:

1.  The server also contains a method to reverse an arbitrary string. Extend the client to call this method and display the reversed string on the console. You can take input from the command line or via a prompt.

2.  None of the example code sends binary data. Write a client and server that can send an arbitrary file as a part of the SOAP message.

3.  Using an existing SOAP server, write a client to send and receive a few messages from it.

4.  Write your own server using the library. Use another SOAP library and write a client to connect to the server. This may sound boring, but you will enjoy the thrill when the two applications actually start talking to each other.

# Part 2

# RELATED TECHNOLOGIES

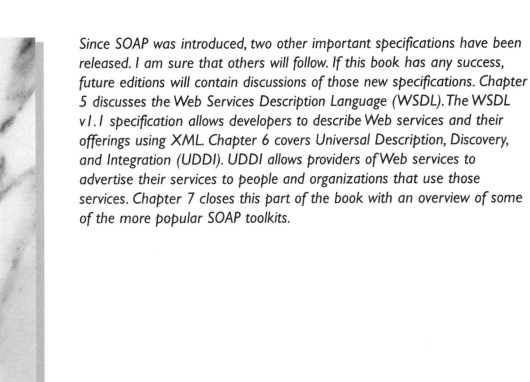

*Since SOAP was introduced, two other important specifications have been released. I am sure that others will follow. If this book has any success, future editions will contain discussions of those new specifications. Chapter 5 discusses the Web Services Description Language (WSDL). The WSDL v1.1 specification allows developers to describe Web services and their offerings using XML. Chapter 6 covers Universal Description, Discovery, and Integration (UDDI). UDDI allows providers of Web services to advertise their services to people and organizations that use those services. Chapter 7 closes this part of the book with an overview of some of the more popular SOAP toolkits.*

# Chapter 5

# WEB SERVICES DESCRIPTION LANGUAGE

Imagine that for whatever reason, you have chosen to allow Web-based access to a set of services. Maybe you have an e-commerce application or a simple application programming interface (API) to a network-enabled device. Depending on the request you may return a SOAP response, an XML document, or an image. How do you tell the user this information? You can use paper documentation and then let the user program against that information. You can provide language-specific libraries that create the requests the "right way." What do you do if you want to allow for discovery of services as well as provide for the possibility that connections may change? What do you do if you provide for SOAP connections over more than just HTTP? You have a few choices: either write your own discovery mechanism or use the Web Services Description Language (WSDL) and a Universal Description, Discovery, and Integration (UDDI) registry.[1] This chapter concentrates on WSDL, an XML format for describing network-based services.

Some people in the SOAP community see WSDL as ornamentation for something that could be done with XML Schema Documents (XSD) alone. In a way, that faction is correct. You could specify the type data as well as incorporate some attributes or other elements into the schema that describes the Web service endpoints. But how would you build tools to use these

---

[1] We cover UDDI in the next chapter.

specialized documents? Would you try to alter the XSD specification? Would you find some way of making a SOAP-specific extension to XSD to avoid altering XSD itself? When SOAP came out, we did not see a lot of acceptance of the "just XSD" approach. Instead, IBM, Microsoft, and other companies tackled the endpoint definition problem by creating various SOAP definition document types. After just a few months of independent existence, these ideas were consolidated into WSDL. Why? The creators of the SOAP tools, Open Source advocates as well as corporate entities, wanted a way to specify the following things:

- The exchange method (response/request, solicit/response, one-way, multicast, etc.)
- The input and output message types (document or procedure oriented)
- The location of the service (i.e., the endpoint)
- Message schema
- Fault information

The WSDL 1.1 specification is mute on the subject of how to discover the location of a WSDL document. The specification only details what the documents mean and how to compose them. UDDI provides the discovery mechanism, and WSDL tells you how to use what you found.[2] If you find yourself wondering why WSDL might be a good thing, you have not had to answer questions such as these:

- How do I transmit an XML document as my sole response?
- How do I send a picture as my response?
- How do I send a gigabyte of data without base64 encoding it?

You see, the SOAP specification never says that you can return something other than SOAP as a response. It never says you cannot do this either. For whatever reasons, many people have assumed that if SOAP goes out, SOAP must come back. WSDL clears up this misconception and provides a mechanism for you to tell your callers what to expect as a return value. It uses three existing specifications to do all this: SOAP 1.1, HTTP GET/POST, and MIME.

---

[2] You can convey this information using something other than WSDL. Chapter 6 covers when to deviate from the norm.

# WSDL Overview

The WSDL document uses a number of common terms in very specific ways. These specific meanings do not always jive with the currently accepted usage of the terms. This section defines those terms and shows a WSDL example.

Every WSDL document defines a service as a collection of *ports*. In this context, think of ports as URLs, not TCP/IP entities. A port defines the location of the *service*. A service may exist at multiple locations but can only respond to a well-defined set of *messages*. The message describes the data being communicated. Each message consists of some sort of data defined using a type definition known to both the sender and receiver. *Types* should be defined using XSD unless some other method makes more sense. The combination of port and messages represent the collection of *operations* and defines the *port type*. Associating a protocol with a data format defines a reusable *binding*. You define a port by associating a network address with a binding. A collection of ports defines a service. WSDL documents use these elements to define a network service:

- **Types:** Container for datatype definitions. XSD can be used to describe a type.
- **Message:** Defines the data being communicated. Includes data inputs and outputs.
- **Operation:** Abstract definition of an action a service can perform.
- **Port:** Single endpoint defined by a binding and a network address.
- **Port type:** Describes the set of operations one or more ports support.
- **Binding:** Concrete protocol and data format specification for a given port type.
- **Service:** A collection of related ports.

Before we cover these items in detail, we should cover the namespace prefixes used in the WSDL specification. I have found that I tend to use the same ones. The prefixes can be found in Table 5-1.[3] I will also continue to use the informal syntax found in that document. In particular:

---

[3] Section 1.2 of the WSDL 1.1 document..

| Table 5–1    Prefixes used by the WSDL 1.1 specification | | |
|------|------|------|
| *Prefix* | *Namespace URI* | *Definition* |
| wsdl | http://schemas.xmlsoap.org/wsdl/ | WSDL namespace for WSDL framework. |
| http | http://schemas.xmlsoap.org/wsdl/http/ | WSDL namespace for HTTP GET & POST binding. |
| mime | http://schemas.xmlsoap.org/wsdl/mime/ | WSDL namespace for MIME binding. |
| xsd | http://www.w3.org/2001/XMLSchema | Schema namespace defined by XSD, updated to reflect current usage. |
| tns | (various) | The "this namespace" (tns) prefix is used as a convention to refer to the current document. |
| (other) | (various) | All other namespace prefixes are samples only. In particular, URIs starting with `http://example.com` represent some application-dependent or context-dependent URI. |

- The syntax will appear as an XML instance. The values indicate datatypes instead of actual values.
- I will append three different characters to represent the cardinality of an element or attribute: ? represents 0 or 1, * represents 0 or more, and + represents 1 or more.
- If an element name ends in an ellipsis (…), that indicates the removal of irrelevant attributes or elements.
- `<— extensibility element —>` serves as a placeholder for elements from some other, unknown namespace (like ## in XSD).
- If an example starts with `<? xml`, it contains enough information to conform to the WSDL specification. Anything else is just a fragment and requires more information before it will conform.

# Defining a Web Service

Any Web services document contains a set of definitions. When looking at a WSDL document, you need to remember that these are only XML documents. They contain elements that derive a special meaning from their associated namespace and schema. WSDL defines the following elements in its XSD:

- **definitions:** All XML documents need one root level document, and the WSDL specification chooses this one.
- **documentation:** This element can contain arbitrary text and elements. You can inject a `documentation` element any time you think the human reader might benefit from extra information.
- **message:** Abstract definition of the data sent or received by the service. These consist of logical parts. Each part has an association within a type system.
- **portType:** Defines the set of operations available on a given port.
- **operation:** Names the operation and lists the expected inputs and outputs. This element may also contain a `fault` subelement that describes any error data the `operation` may return.
- **input:** Describes the elements a given operation takes as input parameters. It also links the `input` back to a specific message.
- **output:** Describes the elements a given operation returns as output parameters. It also links the `output` back to a specific message.
- **fault:** Specifies the layout of any fault data that may be returned.
- **binding:** Specifies the protocol and data formats for the operations and messages defined by a given `portType`.
- **service:** Used to group related ports.
- **port:** Specifies the address for a given binding. This typically takes the form of a URN.

The layout of a typical WSDL document looks like this:

```
<wsdl:definitions name="nmtoken"? targetNamespace="uri"?>

  <import namespace="uri" location="uri" />*

  <wsdl:documentation... />?

  <wsdl:types>?
    <wsdl:documentation... />?
    <xsd:schema.../>*
    <– extensibility element –>
  </wsdl:types>

  <wsdl:message name="nmtoken">*
    <wsdl:documentation... />?
    <part name="nmtoken" element="qname"? type="qname"? />*
  </wsdl:message>

  <wsdl:portType name="nmtoken">*
    <wsdl:documentation... />?
    <wsdl:operation name="nmtoken">*
      <wsdl:documentation... />?
      <wsdl:input name="nmtoken"? message="qname">?
        <wsdl:documentation... />?
      </wsdl:input>
      <wsdl:output name="nmtoken"? message="qname">?
        <wsdl:documentation... />?
      </wsdl:output>
      <wsdl:fault name="nmtoken"? message="qname">*
        <wsdl:documentation... />?
      </wsdl:fault>
    </wsdl:operation>
  </wsdl:portType>

  <wsdl:binding name="nmtoken" type="qname">*
    <wsdl:documentation... />?
    <– extensibility element –>*
    <wsdl:operation name="nmtoken">*
      <wsdl:documentation... />?
      <– extensibility element –>*
      <wsdl:input name="nmtoken"?>?
        <wsdl:documentation... />?
        <– extensibility element –>*
      </wsdl:input>
```

```
        <wsdl:output name="nmtoken"?>?
          <wsdl:documentation... />?
          <-- extensibility element -->*
        </wsdl:output>
        <wsdl:fault name="nmtoken"?>*
          <wsdl:documentation... />?
          <-- extensibility element -->*
        </wsdl:fault>
      </wsdl:operation>
    </wsdl:binding>

    <wsdl:service name="nmtoken">*
      <wsdl:documentation... />?
      <wsdl:port name="nmtoken" binding="qname">*
        <wsdl:documentation... />?
        <-- extensibility element -->*
      </wsdl:port>
      <-- extensibility element -->*
    </wsdl:service>

    <-- extensibility element -->*

</wsdl:definitions>
```

In the preceding text, you should have noticed the import element. This element allows you to associate a namespace with a document location. You can use it to build service definitions as well as to reuse any and all of the definitions in the document. The WSDL document uses a few XML examples to show the benefits of the import element. The first version of this request does not use it, allowing a reader to go through the document without a need to reference anything else.

```
<?xml version="1.0"?>
<definitions name="StockQuote"
  targetNamespace="http://example.com/stockquote.wsdl"
  xmlns:tns="http://example.com/stockquote.wsdl"
  xmlns:xsd1="http://example.com/stockquote.xsd"
  xmlns:soap="http://schemas.xmlsoap.org/wsdl/soap/"
  xmlns="http://schemas.xmlsoap.org/wsdl/">

  <types>
    <schema targetNamespace="http://example.com/stockquote.xsd"
      xmlns="http://www.w3.org/2001/XMLSchema">
      <element name="TradePriceRequest">
        <complexType>
```

```
        <all>
          <element name="tickerSymbol" type="string" />
        </all>
      </complexType>
    </element>
    <element name="TradePrice">
      <complexType>
        <all>
          <element name="price" type="float" />
        </all>
      </complexType>
    </element>
  </schema>
</types>

<message name="GetLastTradePriceInput">
  <part name="body" element="xsd1:TradePrice" />
</message>

<message name="GetLastTradePriceOutput">
  <part name="body" element="xsd1:TradePriceResult" />
</message>

<portType name="StockQuotePortType">
  <operation name="GetLastTradePrice">
    <input message="tns:GetLastTradePriceInput" />
    <output message="tns:GetLastTradePriceOutput" />
  </operation>
</portType>

<binding name="StockQuoteSoapBinding"
type="tns:StockQuotePortType">
    <soap:binding style="document"
    transport="http://schemas.xmlsoap.org/soap/http" />
  <operation name="GetLastTradePrice">
    <soap:operation soapAction=
      "http://example.com/GetLastTradePrice" />
    <input>
      <soap:body use="literal"
        namespace="http://example.com/stockquote.xsd"
        encodingStyle=
          "http://schemas.xmlsoap.org/soap/encoding/" />
    </input>
    <output>
      <soap:body use="literal"
        namespace="http://example.com/stockquote.xsd"
```

```
            encodingStyle=
               "http://schemas.xmlsoap.org/soap/encoding/" />
      </output>
    </operation>
  </binding>

  <service name="StockQuoteService">
    <documentation>My first service</documentation>
    <port name="StockQuotePort" binding="tns:StockQuoteBinding">
      <soap:address location="http://example.com/stockquote"
          />
    </port>
  </service>

</definitions>
```

A document like this one can become more complicated as the number of services grows. The import element gives you the ability to split this up into separate documents. The definitions can reuse the files to define various services, types, and other pieces found in a WSDL document. The WSDL 1.1 specification shows how to do that by splitting up the StockQuoteService definition. The type definitions are nothing more than an embedded XML schema. Making it a separate document is fairly straightforward. By separating the schema you can also use this same document to define the schema used in a listing of closing stock prices or some other such item. I have taken the liberty of altering the examples in the 1.1 specification to more closely match the element names in the larger example.

File: *http://example.com/stockquote/stockquote.xsd*

```
<?xml version="1.0"?>
<schema targetNamespace="http://example.com/stockquote.xsd"
  xmlns="http://www.w3.org/2001/XMLSchema">
  <element name="TradePriceRequest">
    <complexType>
      <all>
        <element name="tickerSymbol" type="string" />
      </all>
    </complexType>
  </element>
  <element name="TradePrice">
    <complexType>
      <all>
        <element name="price" type="float" />
```

```
      </all>
    </complexType>
  </element>
</schema>
```

So far, so good. The next file defines the operations available on a specific `portType`.

File: *http://example.com/stockquote/stockquote.wsdl*

```
<?xml version="1.0"?>
<definitions name="StockQuote"
  targetNamespace="http://example.com/stockquote/definitions"
  xmlns:tns="http://example.com/stockquote/definitions"
  xmlns:xsd1="http://example.com/stockquote/schemas"
  xmlns:soap="http://schemas.xmlsoap.org/wsdl/soap/"
  xmlns="http://schemas.xmlsoap.org/wsdl/">

  <import namespace="http://example.com/stockquote/schemas"
    location="http://example.com/stockquote/stockquote.xsd" />

  <message name="GetLastTradePriceInput">
    <part name="body" element="xsd1:TradePrice" />
  </message>

  <message name="GetLastTradePriceOutput">
    <part name="body" element="xsd1:TradePriceResult" />
  </message>

  <portType name="StockQuotePortType">
    <operation name="GetLastTradePrice">
      <input message="tns:GetLastTradePriceInput" />
      <output message="tns:GetLastTradePriceOutput" />
    </operation>
  </portType>

</definitions>
```

Finally, put the pieces together to define the bindings for the particular `portType`. Using this, you could use separate files to define bindings for SOAP, HTTP, MIME, or anything else that makes sense.

File: *http://example.com/stockquote/stockquoteservice.wsdl*

```
<?xml version="1.0"?>
<definitions name="StockQuote"
  targetNamespace="http://example.com/stockquote/service"
```

```
xmlns:tns="http://example.com/stockquote/service"
xmlns:soap="http://schemas.xmlsoap.org/wsdl/soap/"
xmlns="http://schemas.xmlsoap.org/wsdl/">

<import namespace="http://example.com/stockquote/definitions"
   location="http://example.com/stockquote/stockquote.wsdl" />

<binding name="StockQuoteSoapBinding" type="tns:StockQuotePortType">
   <soap:binding style="document"
      transport="http://schemas.xmlsoap.org/soap/http" />
   <operation name="GetLastTradePrice">
      <soap:operation soapAction=
         "http://example.com/GetLastTradePrice" />
   </operation>
</binding>

<service name="StockQuoteService">
   <documentation>My first service</documentation>
   <port name="StockQuotePort" binding="tns:StockQuoteBinding">
      <soap:address location="http://example.com/stockquote"
         />
   </port>
</service>

</definitions>
```

## Language Extensibility and Binding

WSDL uses the term *binding* to refer to the action of associating the protocol and data format information with a `message`, `portType`, or `operation`. Some elements in the binding are used to represent a specific technology. The specification refers to these as *extensibility elements*. You would normally use these to specify binding information specific to a given protocol or message format. For example, HTTP extensibility elements would specify a specific Web page within a Web site and SMTP elements would declare an email address. Any namespaces used to identify data about the extensibility element have to use a namespace not tied to the WSDL namespace. Appendix A3 from the WSDL document, reproduced in Table 5–2, indicates where these elements might appear inside of a WSDL definition. To indicate whether or not the element is required, you can use the boolean `wsdl:required` attribute whose default value is false ("0"). We see examples of extensibility elements later in the chapter when we cover the SOAP, HTTP, and MIME bindings.

**Table 5–2    WSDL 1.1 Appendix A3.**

| Location of Extensibility Element | Meaning | Possible Use |
|---|---|---|
| Definitions | The extensibility element applies to the entire WSDL document. | Introduce extra information or definitions to the WSDL document. |
| Definitions/types | The extensibility element is a type system. | Specify the types used in a format other than XSD. |
| Definitions/service | The extensibility element applies to the service. | Introduce extra information or definitions to the service. |
| Definitions/service/port | The extensibility element applies to the port. | Specify an address for a port. |
| Definitions/binding | The extensibility element applies to the binding as a whole. | Provide protocol-specific information that applies to all of the operations in the portType being bound. |
| Definitions/binding/operation | The extensibility element applies to the operation as a whole. | Provide protocol-specific information that applies to both the input and the output. |
| Definitions/binding/operation/input | The extensibility element applies to the input message of the operation. | Provide protocol-specific information that applies to the input. |
| Definitions/binding/operation/output | The extensibility element applies to the output message of the operation. | Provide protocol-specific information that applies to the output. |
| Definitions/binding/operation/fault | The extensibility element applies to the fault message of the operation. | Provide protocol-specific information that applies to the fault. |

## Encoding Type Information

WSDL uses XSD as its preferred type system. This allows for maximum flexibility and platform neutrality—mostly due to the widespread adoption of XML. You can use XSD to specify the type information even if you do not use

XML to transfer the data over the wire. This allows you to specify bindings to protocols that are binary in nature. When doing this, you should follow these rules:

- Only use elements to describe the types. Do not use any attributes. Why? There are a variety of reasons. Mainly, it simplifies the creation of SOAP messages and standardizes the meaning of a type. For example, if attributes are used, should the deserialized attribute be an instance variable or a class variable? Also, a person may write the deployed WSDL file. This would allow the running Web service to use a less capable (and smaller) XML parser that ignores attributes and only processes elements.

- If a piece of data is specific to the binding, leave it out of the type information. For example, put the HTTP address in the binding information, not the type data.

- Use the `soap:Array` type to represent array types, even if the resulting form uses something other than the encoding specified by the SOAP v1.1 document in Section 5.

## Messages

All `messages` contain one or more `parts`. The `message` definition associates each `part` with a type using a message-typing attribute. Because of this, you can extend the set of attributes as needed. WSDL defines the attributes `element` and `type` for use with XSD. Use `element` to refer to an XSD `element` using a `QName`. Use `type` to refer to an XSD `simpleType` or `complexType` using its `QName`. For example, your schema may define the following:

```
<schema>
  <element name="aliasForItem" type="tns:Item" />
  <complexType name="Item">
    <element name="price" type="float" />
    <element name="productName" type="string" />
  </complexType>
</schema>
```

Using the preceding schema, you could then express the same `message` definition in two separate but equivalent ways:

```
<message name="itemInformation">
  <part name="theElement" element="aliasForItem" />
</message>
```

or

```
<message name="itemInformation">
  <part name="theElement" type="Item" />
</message>
```

You can define other attributes as long as they do not use the WSDL namespace.

All messages are abstract in nature. The degree of abstractness depends on how well the binding maps to the message definition. If a binding maps to a binary-only protocol such as DCE RPC, consider the message a human-readable abstraction of the underlying data. If the binding maps to something like SOAP, the abstraction will map fairly closely to the actual wire format. There is no such thing as a concrete message.

## Port Types

It bears repeating that the term *port* in WSDL does not mean the same thing as *port* in the world of socket-based network programming. With respect to sockets, a port uniquely identifies an open connection on a particular network address. Typically, the port is represented by a positive integer. In the WSDL world, a `portType` instance refers to a specific collection of `operations`. The `portType` may be bound to a specific TCP/IP port, but that simply represents a clash of the nomenclature. For example, HTTP defaults to port 80, but you can also specifically set the TCP/IP port in the named port (e.g., http://www.scottseely.com:8080/myWebService.asmx).

Each `portType` defines a collection of `operations`. Each `operation` may contain up to three elements: `wsdl:input`, `wsdl:output`, and `wsdl:fault`. Using these, you can declare the type of transmission primitive supported by the `operation` and the endpoint.

A few of the primitives make use of the `parameterOrder` attribute. `operations` do not specify whether or not they should be used with RPC-like bindings. When you desire this type of behavior, this attribute allows you to specify the parameter order. The attribute contains a list of message part names separated by a single space. The following rules apply for the named parts:

- The order reflects the order of parameters in the RPC signature.
- The list does not include the return value part.
- In/out parameters appear in the input and output messages.
- In parameters only appear in the input message.
- Out parameters only appear in the output message.

This information included in the attribute only serves as a hint. One can safely ignore this if the RPC signature does not matter. However, if the message is bound to something like DCE RPC, then the order does matter. The `parameterOrder` attribute is always optional and can be omitted, even with an RPC-like binding.

## Transmission Primitive: One-Way

One-way transmission occurs when the `operation` declares an `input` element and no `output` element. A one-way `operation` looks like this:

```
<wsdl:definitions...>
  <wsdl:portType name="nmtoken">
    <wsdl:operation name="nmtoken">
      <wsdl:input name="nmtoken"? message="qname" />
    </wsdl:operation>
  </wsdl:portType>
</wsdl:definitions>
```

If implemented, a one-way transmission would have one of the following function/method definitions:[4]

- VB: `Public Sub OneWay()`
- C# or Java: `public void OneWay()`
- C/C++: `void OneWay()`

In one-way `operations`, you cannot specify fault information. Why? The caller does not expect to hear anything and as a result, does not (and should not) listen for a response.

[4] Don't read anything into my language choices. I picked these languages because I use them in the book. Hey, you have to have some way to decide which languages you skip!

## Transmission Primitive: Request-Response

In request-response, the caller is told to expect an answer from any calls. The binding determines how the request and response actually operate. The messages may cross the wire as a request/response pair over one connection or may go across as two requests over two connections. Because request-response allows for a response, it also allows for the possibility of returning fault information. A request-response definition does not have to declare fault information. This primitive has the following generic format:

```
<wsdl:definitions...>
  <wsdl:portType name="nmtoken">
    <wsdl:operation name="nmtoken" parameterOrder="nmtokens">
      <wsdl:input name="nmtoken"? message="qname" />
      <wsdl:output name="nmtoken"? message="qname" />
      <wsdl:fault name="nmtoken" message="qname" />*
    </wsdl:operation>
  </wsdl:portType>
</wsdl:definitions>
```

If implemented, a request-response transmission would have one of the following function/method definitions:

- VB: `Public Function RequestResponse() as Int`
- C# or Java: `public int RequestResponse()`
- C/C++: `int RequestResponse()`

## Transmission Primitive: Solicit-Response

This primitive looks similar to request-response:

```
<wsdl:definitions...>
  <wsdl:portType name="nmtoken">
    <wsdl:operation name="nmtoken" parameterOrder="nmtokens">
      <wsdl:output name="nmtoken"? message="qname" />
      <wsdl:input name="nmtoken"? message="qname" />
      <wsdl:fault name="nmtoken" message="qname" />*
    </wsdl:operation>
  </wsdl:portType>
</wsdl:definitions>
```

The only difference is that `output` and `input` are swapped. Abstractly, these two differ from each other the same way pull technology differs from push.[5] In pull, the computer providing information typically packages the data on the fly. In push, the provider delivers prepackaged information whenever solicited. The provider does not know who will ask for information, but it is always ready for the request. Logically, this still acts like request-response. The actual difference would probably lie in the function implementation. For the function, one possible usage is pass by reference where you send a value with known data and expect to get the same logical instance back, although modified, on return. If implemented, a solicit-response transmission would have one of the following function/method definitions:

- VB: `Public Sub SolicitResponse( ByRef aStruct as someStruct )`
- C# or Java: `public void SolicitResponse( someStruct value )`
- C++: `void SolicitResponse( someStruct& value )`
- C: `void SolicitResponse( someStruct* value )`

## Transmission Primitive: Notification Operation

A one-way `operation` may consist of a request such as "Notify me whenever Acme stock goes above $30/share or below $15/share."[6] Then, the requester goes silent while waiting to hear any news. This primitive represents "the news." It looks like this:

```
<wsdl:definitions...>
  <wsdl:portType name="nmtoken">
    <wsdl:operation name="nmtoken">
      <wsdl:output name="nmtoken"? message="qname" />
    </wsdl:operation>
  </wsdl:portType>
</wsdl:definitions>
```

---

[5] They are the same ideas with different names. It seems that "push" developed a nasty reputation in the 1990s. The name may have changed but the idea still remains.

[6] The registration would be done using request-response. That way, your application at least knows if the endpoint understood the request for notifications.

If implemented, a notification transmission would have one of the following function/method definitions:

- VB: `Public Sub Notification(ByVal value as Int )`
- C# or Java: `public void Notification( int value )`
- C/C++: `void Notification( int value )`

For any of the preceding primitives, the name attribute of any `input`, `output`, or `fault` must be unique within the enclosing `portType`. To avoid the need to name all of these elements, WSDL provides some defaults depending on the name of the `operation`. On one-way and notification primitives, the name defaults to the name of the `operation`. In request-response, the name defaults to *operation*`Request` for the input element and *operation*`Response` for the output. For solicit-response, the input and output are *operation*`Solicit` and *operation*`Response`, respectively.

## Binding

Using a `binding`, you can define the message format and protocol details for the `operations` and `messages` defined by a given `portType`. This element must specify exactly one protocol and cannot specify address information. The `portType` may have one or more `bindings`. They have the following grammar:

```
<wsdl:definitions...>
  <wsdl:binding name="nmtoken" type="qname"> *
    <-- extensibility element (1) --> *
    <wsdl:operation name="nmtoken">
      <-- extensibility element (2) --> *
      <wsdl:input name="nmtoken"? /> ?
        <-- extensibility element (3) --> *
      </wsdl:input>
      <wsdl:output name="nmtoken"? /> ?
        <-- extensibility element (4) --> *
      </wsdl:output>
      <wsdl:fault name="nmtoken"? /> *
        <-- extensibility element (5) --> *
      </wsdl:fault>
    </wsdl:operation>
  </wsdl:portType>
</wsdl:definitions>
```

The name attribute for the binding provides a unique name for all bindings defined with the entire WSDL document. The type attribute references the portType made concrete by the binding. Optional extensibility elements can be used to specify the concrete grammar for the input, output, and fault messages. You can also add extra information for the operation or the entire binding.

## Ports and Services

A port defines the address for a given binding. You may recall that in the discussion on portType, I claimed that the WSDL port differs from a TCP/IP port. This is still true: Addresses are all in the eye of the related protocol. An address of 1 may have the following meanings:

- Device on RS-485 wire that has an ID of 1
- Port 1 on the local machine
- And so on

A service groups related ports. The definition of the two elements takes the following form:

```
<wsdl:definitions...>
  <wsdl:service name="nmtoken"> *
    <wsdl:port name="nmtoken" binding="qname"> *
      <-- extensibility element (1) -> *
    </wsdl:port>
  </wsdl:service>
</wsdl:definitions>
```

In this situation, the extensibility element provides address information for the port. A port can specify only one address and cannot specify anything other than address information. For both the service and the port, the name attribute must be unique to the WSDL document. ports within a service have the following relationship:

- The ports do not communicate with one another. For example, the output of one port is not the input of another.
- A service may contain several ports whose bindings map back one portType or that map to different addresses.

Because the `ports` provide equivalent behavior, they represent alternatives. Using this you can provide the same service over HTTP, email, SOAP, or some other protocol. You can also provide the same service at different locations, allowing the user of the service to select a faster or closer machine.

- You can determine the `portTypes` offered by a `service` by examining its `ports`. Using this information a user can determine if a given machine supports all the `operations` needed to complete a given task.

# SOAP Binding

WSDL defines how to send and receive requests using SOAP by defining a set of extensibility elements. These elements provide the following information:

- The `binding` uses the SOAP v1.1 protocol.
- It specifies an address for a SOAP endpoint.
- It specifies the URI for the `SOAPAction` HTTP header if the transmission occurs over HTTP.
- It lists definitions for the SOAP `Header` elements that may appear in the SOAP `Envelope`.
- It provides a method to specify the SOAP roots using XSD.

The set of SOAP bindings continues to evolve because of the growing number of implementations of SOAP over protocols other than HTTP. As a result, other SOAP bindings can be derived using the grammar defined in Section 3 of the WSDL document as a basis. For example, these bindings may need alternate addressing schemes and may not require the `SOAPAction` at all.

The grammar for the SOAP `binding` extensibility elements looks like this:

```
<definitions...>
  <binding...>
    <soap:binding style="rpc|document" transport="uri" />
    <operation...>
      <soap:operation soapAction="uri"? style="rpc|document"? />?
```

```
    <input>
      <soap:body parts="nmtokens"? use="literal|encoded"
        encodingStyle="uri-list"? namespace="uri"? />
      <soap:header element="qname" fault="qname"? />*
    </input>
    <output>
      <soap:body parts="nmtokens"? use="literal|encoded"
        encodingStyle="uri-list"? namespace="uri"? />
      <soap:header element="qname" fault="qname"? />*
    </output>
    <fault>
      <soap:fault name="nmtoken" use="literal|encoded"
        encodingStyle="uri-list"? namespace="uri"? />
    </fault>
  </operation>
</binding>

<port>
  <soap:address location="uri" />
</port>
</definitions>
```

Using this grammar, you could create the following WSDL document. It specifies a service that gets the last trading price for a stock and binds that service to SOAP.

```
<?xml version="1.0"?>
<definitions name="StockQuote"
  targetNamespace="http://example.com/stockquote.wsdl"
    xmlns:tns="http://example.com/stockquote.wsdl"
    xmlns:xsd1="http://example.com/stockquote.xsd"
    xmlns:soap="http://schemas.xmlsoap.org/wsdl/soap/"
    xmlns="http://schemas.xmlsoap.org/wsdl/"
    xmlns:xsd="http://www.w3.org/2001/XMLSchema">

  <message name="GetLastTradePriceRequest">
    <part name="tickerSymbol" element="xsd:string"/>
    <part name="time" element="xsd:timeInstant"/>
  </message>

  <message name="GetLastTradePriceResponse">
    <part name="result" type="xsd:float"/>
  </message>

  <portType name="StockQuotePortType">
    <operation name="GetLastTradePrice">
```

```
        <input message="tns:GetLastTradePriceRequest"/>
        <output message="tns:GetLastTradePriceResponse"/>
     </operation>
  </portType>

  <binding name="StockQuoteSoapBinding" type="tns:StockQuotePortType">
     <soap:binding style="rpc"
        transport="http://schemas.xmlsoap.org/soap/http"/>
     <operation name="GetLastTradePrice">
        <soap:operation
          soapAction="http://example.com/GetLastTradePrice"/>
        <input>
           <soap:body use="encoded"
             namespace="http://example.com/stockquote"
             encodingStyle=
                "http://schemas.xmlsoap.org/soap/encoding/"/>
        </input>
        <output>
           <soap:body use="encoded"
             namespace="http://example.com/stockquote"
             encodingStyle=
                "http://schemas.xmlsoap.org/soap/encoding/"/>
        </output>
     </operation>>
  </binding>

  <service name="StockQuoteService">
     <documentation>My first service</documentation>
     <port name="StockQuotePort"
         binding="tns:StockQuoteBinding">
        <soap:address location=
           "http://example.com/stockquote"/>
     </port>
  </service>
</definitions>
```

Let's take a look at the meaning of the elements related to the SOAP binding.

## soap:binding

This element signifies that the entire binding is bound to SOAP. This includes the SOAP `Envelope`, `Header`, `Body`, and `Fault`. To bind a `binding` to the SOAP format you must use the `soap:binding` element. `soap:binding` contains two optional attributes. `transport` indicates which

SOAP transport mechanism the `binding` corresponds to. Use the URI value `http://schemas.xmlsoap.org/soap/http` to indicate the HTTP binding in the SOAP specification. You can use other URIs to indicate other transport mechanisms such as SMTP or straight TCP.

## *soap:operation*

This element provides information on the whole `operation`. It contains a `soapAction` attribute that specifies the expected HTTP `SOAPAction` header. Do not change this value when making a request. You only need to supply this attribute when using HTTP with SOAP.

The other attribute this element has is `style`. It indicates the type of `operation`: RPC-oriented or document-oriented. Use the value "`rpc`" to indicate that the message contains parameters and returns values. The value "`document`" indicates that the message contains documents. Using this information the programmer can select an appropriate programming model and set of tools. For example, a C++ programmer could typically get away with using the library presented in Chapter 4 to handle RPC-oriented `operations`. They would need something more complete for a document-oriented `operation`. If it uses a SOAP binding but does not supply the `style` attribute, the style is "`document`".

## *soap:body*

The `soap:body` element specifies how the parts of a message appear within the SOAP `Body` element. The parts may be defined by concrete schema definitions or abstract type definitions. For abstract definitions, the SOAP engine serializes the message elements according to some set of rules defined by an encoding style. An encoding style such as the one defined by the SOAP v1.1 specification allows for some degrees of variation in the message format for some of the abstract types. For example, the type system may define an element in the message as `xsd:integer`. If the reader is responsible for understanding and translating all derived types into `xsd:integer` (e.g., `xsd:short` or `xsd:long`) then we consider the message to be "reader makes right." For a server to avoid this, a message might have a concrete definition. In this case, no matter how an application uses or processes the information it may demand the information in a specific format. If the creator of the message must conform exactly to the provided schema, we call this "writer makes right."

This element can be used to define RPC-oriented and document-oriented messages. If RPC-oriented, then each part within the message is a parameter or return value. For document-oriented messages each part appears in the body as a document. RPC-oriented messaging satisfies the desire to use a Web service as an RPC mechanism. Document-oriented messaging allows for applications like Electronic Data Interchange (EDI) to be performed using SOAP and XML.

The optional `parts` attribute tells the reader of the WSDL document which parts appear within the message's SOAP `Body`.[7] If a document omits this attribute, all parts defined by the `message` must appear in the SOAP `Body`.

`soap:body` must always include the use attribute. Valid values are `literal` and `encoded`. When set to `encoded`, each part within the message references an abstract type using the `type` attribute. The abstract types produce a concrete message when the encoding specified by the `encodingStyle` is applied. The `name`, `type`, and `namespace` attributes specified by the `part` definition all contribute as inputs to the encoding. The `namespace` attribute only applies if not explicitly defined by the abstract `types`. "Reader makes right" applies to these messages if the encoding style allows for variations in its format. The encoding specified by SOAP does allow for some variations.

If you want the "writer makes right" rules to happen, set `use` to `literal`. This means that each `part` references a concrete schema. In this case, the `encodingStyle` attribute may be used to hint at which encoding was used to derive the encoding. In any case, the reader of the message will only accept the variation specified by the `part` definition.

The `encodingStyle` attribute contains a list of URIs, each separated by one space. This works like the `encodingStyle` attribute in SOAP—encodings are listed from most restrictive to least restrictive.

## *soap:fault*

The `soap:fault` element specifies the part used by the SOAP `Fault` element. The `name`, `use`, `encodingStyle`, and `namespace` elements function the same way as in `soap:body`. The element can only have one part.

---

[7] If SOAP and multipart MIME are used together, some parts of a message may appear elsewhere.

## soap:header

The `soap:header` element provides the ability to define headers that appear in the SOAP `Header` element. You do not have to list every header that might appear because intermediaries and other specifications in the WSDL document might cause other unknown headers to appear in the actual payload. You specify the header type via the `element` attribute. The schema for this attribute cannot include definitions for the SOAP `Header` `actor` and `mustUnderstand` attributes.

The fault attribute is optional. Like the `soap.body` fault attribute, this defines exactly one `type` that describes the error. The SOAP specification states that `Header` element errors must be returned in a `Header`. This mechanism allows the WSDL document to specify what errors to expect.

## soap:address

The `soap:address` binding associates a URI with a port. When binding a port to SOAP, one address must be specified. Anything else is wrong.

# HTTP GET and POST Binding

The WSDL specification includes a binding for the HTTP GET and POST verbs to describe how a Web browser and a Web site interact. Using this, applications other than Web browsers can access the Web site. The binding does the following:

- Indicates if the `binding` uses HTTP GET or POST.
- Specifies an address for the `port`.
- Gives a relative address for each `operation`. The address is relative to the `port` address.

This `binding` provides one way to answer the question "How do I return X using SOAP?" This question comes up every time someone wants to transmit binary data or an XML document and they have bandwidth concerns. The answer to this question is simple: Do not use SOAP. Instead, bind the

Web service to HTTP and skip the SOAP part all together. The grammar for the HTTP GET and POST extensibility elements looks like this:

```
<definitions...>
  <binding...>
    <http:binding verb="nmtoken" />
    <operation...>
      <http:operation location="uri" />
      <input...>
        <- mime elements ->
      </input>
      <output...>
        <- mime elements ->
      </output>
    </operation>
  </binding>

  <port...>
    <http:address location="uri" />
  </port>
</definitions>
```

Using this grammar, you can write the following WSDL document:

```
<definitions...>
  <message name="m1">
    <part name="part1" type="xsd:string"/>
    <part name="part2" type="xsd:int"/>
    <part name="part3" type="xsd:string"/>
  </message>

  <message name="m2">
    <part name="image" type="xsd:binary"/>
  </message>

  <portType name="pt1">
    <operation name="o1">
      <input message="tns:m1"/>
      <output message="tns:m2"/>
    </operation>
  </portType>

  <service name="service1">
    <port name="port1" binding="tns:b1">
      <http:address location="http://example.com/"/>
    </port>
```

```
    <port name="port2" binding="tns:b1">
      <http:address location="http://example.com/"/>
    </port>
    <port name="port3" binding="tns:b1">
      <http:address location="http://example.com/"/>
    </port>
</service>

<binding name="b1" type="pt1">
    <http:binding verb="GET"/>
    <operation name="o1">
      <http:operation location="o1/A(part1)B(part2)/(part3)"/>
      <input>
        <http:urlReplacement/>
      </input>
      <output>
        <mime:content type="image/gif"/>
        <mime:content type="image/jpeg"/>
      </output>
    </operation>
</binding>

<binding name="b2" type="pt1">
    <http:binding verb="GET"/>
    <operation name="o1">
      <http:operation location="o1"/>
      <input>
        <http:urlEncoded/>
      </input>
      <output>
        <mime:content type="image/gif"/>
        <mime:content type="image/jpeg"/>
      </output>
    </operation>
</binding>

<binding name="b3" type="pt1">
    <http:binding verb="POST"/>
    <operation name="o1">
      <http:operation location="o1"/>
      <input>
        <mime:content type="application/x-www-form-urlencoded"/>
      </input>
      <output>
        <mime:content type="image/gif"/>
        <mime:content type="image/jpeg"/>
```

```
      </output>
    </operation>
  </binding>
</definitions>
```

In all instances, the input consists of some data in the request string and then returns either a gif or jpeg file. Valid requests include the following:

```
port1: GET, URL="http://example.com/o1/A1B2/3"
port2: GET, URL="http://example.com/o1?p1=1&p2=2&p3=3"
port3: POST, URL="http://example.com/o1", PAYLOAD="p1=1&p2=2&p3=3"
```

All these requests use the same inputs, but each has a different format. The rest of this section discusses what all the elements really mean.

## *http:address*

The `http:address` element contains one, mandatory attribute: `location`. This serves as the base URI for the port. The `location` attribute on this element serves as the base for any relative URIs specified by the `location` attribute in the `http:operation` element.

## *http:binding*

The `http:binding` element has one attribute: `verb`. Most often you will set this to GET or POST. If another verb makes sense and the Web host understands it, use it.

## *http:operation*

The `http:operation` element uses its `location` attribute to define a relative URI for the `operation`. This attribute works in conjunction with the `http:address` element to define the full URI for the HTTP request. The URI value must always be relative to the URI specified by the `location` attribute of the `http:address` element.

## *http:urlEncoded*

The presence of the `http:urlEncoded` element indicates that the sender should encode the message parts within the HTTP request URI using the

URI encoding rules (name1=value&name2=value…). The parameter names correspond to the names of the message parts. This can be used with GET to specify the URL encoding or with POST to specify a FORM-POST. When using GET, append "?" as needed.

### http:urlReplacement

Use the http:urlReplacement element to indicate that the parts of the message have been encoded into the HTTP request URI using a replacement algorithm. The algorithm works like this:

- Look at the relative URI specified within http:operation for a set of search patterns. This occurs before combining the value of the location attribute in http:address.
- One search pattern exists for each message part. The search pattern appears as the name of the message part surrounded by parentheses. For example, the pattern might be operation/A(part1)b(part2)c(part3).
- For each match, substitute the value of the corresponding message part at the location of the match. Continuing with the example, suppose the values of part1, part2, and part3 are 22, Computer, and Speaker, respectively. The encoded string would be operation/A22bComputercSpeaker.
- Match up all parts before performing the replacements. Assume that the first value in the example was actually (part2). If substitutions occurred along with the replacement scan, we could wind up with extra parts or some other confusion.

Finally, message parts may not have repeating values. You cannot ask the message sender to send the same parameter two or more times.

## MIME Binding

WSDL also defines a way to bind abstract types to concrete messages using some MIME format. The specification defines bindings for these MIME types:

- multipart/related
- text/xml
- application/x-www-form-urlencoded (used to submit a form in HTML)
- Others by specifying the MIME type string

WSDL does not define an XML grammar for each and every MIME type because of the sheer number of MIME types and the rate at which the list grows. If a MIME type string can define the content, then you can use the mime element. Otherwise, make sure that the sender and receiver understand any additional grammars that you or others may define.

The MIME binding defines the following extension elements:

```
<mime:content part="nmtoken"? type="string"?/>

<mime:multipartRelated>
  <mime:part> *
    <- mime element ->
  </mime:part>
</mime:multipartRelated>

<mime:mimeXml part="nmtoken"?/>
```

They show up within the WSDL document in the input and output elements. If more than one element appears, these represent alternatives.

```
<definitions...>
  <binding...>
    <operation...>
      <input...>
        <- mime elements ->
      </input>
      <output...>
        <- mime elements ->
      </output>
    </operation>
  </binding>
</definitions>
```

This simple grammar provides the ability to write the following WSDL document using a MIME binding.

```
<definitions...>
```

```
<types>
  <schema...>
    <element name="GetCompanyInfo">
      <complexType>
        <all>
          <element name="tickerSymbol " type="string"/>
        </all>
      </complexType>
    </element>
    <element name="GetCompanyInfoResult">
      <complexType>
        <all>
          <element name="result" type="float"/>
        </all>
      </complexType>
    </element>
    <complexType name="ArrayOfBinary" base="soap:Array">
      <all>
        <element name="value" type="xsd:binary"/>
      </all>
    </complexType>
  </schema>
</types>

<message name="m1">
  <part name="body" element="tns:GetCompanyInfo"/>
</message>

<message name="m2">
  <part name="body" element="tns:GetCompanyInfoResult"/>
  <part name="docs" type="xsd:string"/>
  <part name="logo" type="tns:ArrayOfBinary"/>
</message>

<portType name="pt1">
  <operation name="GetCompanyInfo">
    <input message="m1"/>
    <output message="m2"/>
  </operation>
</portType>

<binding name="b1" type="tns:pt1">
  <operation name="GetCompanyInfo">
    <soap:operation soapAction="http://example.com/GetCompanyInfo"/>
    <input>
```

```
            <soap:body use="literal"/>
        </input>
        <output>
          <mime:multipartRelated>
            <mime:part>
              <soap:body parts="body" use="literal"/>
            </mime:part>
            <mime:part>
              <mime:content part="docs" type="text/html"/>
            </mime:part>
            <mime:part>
              <mime:content part="logo" type="image/gif"/>
              <mime:content part="logo" type="image/jpeg"/>
            </mime:part>
          </mime:multipartRelated>
        </output>
      </operation>
    </binding>

    <service name="CompanyInfoService">
      <port name="CompanyInfoPort"binding="tns:b1">
        <soap:address location="http://example.com/companyinfo"/>
      </port>
    </service>
</definitions>
```

## *mime:content*

The mime:content element functions as a catch-all for any MIME content you may want to use. Use this element if you do not need to tell the consumer of the message anything other than the MIME type string. This element has two attributes: part and type. If the message only contains one part, then the part attribute is optional. Otherwise, use it to indicate the part of the message being bound.

The type attribute holds the MIME type string. This attribute has two portions separated by a /. Either portion might be a wildcard, *. If the document does not specify a type, any MIME type can fit the requirements. The following examples illustrate various meanings:

- To return arbitrary XML documents:
  ```
  <mime:content type="text/xml" />
  ```
- To return arbitrary text types:
  ```
  <mime:content type="text/*" />
  ```
- To return arbitrary any MIME type:
  ```
  <mime:content type="*/*" />
  ```
  or
  ```
  <mime:content />
  ```

## mime:multipartRelated

The `mime:multipartRelated` element allows the aggregation of an arbitrary set of MIME-formatted parts into one message. This is accomplished through the MIME type `multipart/related`. This element describes the concrete message format.

The `mime:part` element, contained by `mime:multipartRelated`, describes each part of the multipart message. A MIME element appearing within `mime:part` describes the MIME type for that part. If multiple MIME elements appear, they represent alternatives.

## soap:body

You can use the MIME binding with SOAP requests. Moreover, you can use the `soap:body` element as a MIME element. Doing so indicates that the MIME content type is `text/xml` and that the content has an enclosing SOAP `Envelope`.

## mime:mimeXml

Sometimes, you may know the XML schema for a given element. Use the `mime:mimeXml` element whenever this is true. The element contains one attribute: `part`. This attribute refers to the `message part` that defines the schema of the root XML element. You can omit this attribute only if the message contains one `part`.

# Summary

WSDL provides many capabilities not originally presented in the SOAP specification. Using it, you can define services on HTTP servers, email, and SOAP servers. As we will see in the case study in Part 3, WSDL allows us to tackle some of the harder problems presented by SOAP. Specifically, it answers questions such as these:

- How do I send an image without encoding it?
- How do I return an object that does not easily decompose into XML?
- How do I return XML as a response?

Instead of looking at the world of RPCs, which SOAP does well, WSDL tackles the larger issue of providing services over the Web. It also provides a way to define what these services look like—an XML header file. It also allows you to advertise how to access a service and what to expect in return over multiple delivery channels. This is very handy, especially when coupled with a registry service like UDDI, covered in the next chapter.

# Chapter 6

# UNIVERSAL DESCRIPTION, DISCOVERY, AND INTEGRATION

A lot of people believe that the ability to discover and use Web services will make the integration of disparate connected systems easier. To do this, a standard has to exist and the location of the information has to be well known. To this end, Universal Description, Discovery, and Integration (UDDI) was created. This chapter explains some of the basic terminology and technology behind UDDI. Full coverage of UDDI and its specification is beyond the scope of this book.

UDDI specifies what the API for a Web-based registry looks like. Anyone can implement one of these and any client can access it. An *operator site* implements a UDDI registry. Using one of these registries you can find general information about a business as well as the Web services it provides.

The UDDI specification comes up with basic ideas of how to run these sites. To pay for the operation of these sites as well as encourage their use, site operators are encouraged to provide the basic lookup services for free. More advanced services, such as advertising Web services via the registry, pay for the operation of the site. Companies will likely do this to take advantage of simply being registered. As UDDI takes off, more people will use the registries to search for potential trading partners using the classification and categorization codes used by various businesses.

All UDDI-compatible registries implement the interface described by the UDDI Programmer's API Specification.[1] These registries provide the following information:

- *Who?* You can find basic information about a business such as its Dun & Bradstreet number, name, and contact information.

- *What?* You can get classification information to help find the right type of business. For example, you would not want to be digging for Web services for agricultural companies when you wanted to ship a package (unless you are shipping botanical products). Expect to find codes such as Standard Industry Codes (SIC), North American Industry Code Standard (NAICS), United Nations/Standard Products and Services Classification (UN/SPC), and others to be used by these registries. You can also get descriptions of the types of electronic services that are available.

- *Where?* The registry provides information about the URI used to access a service.

- *How?* The registry describes how a given interface functions.

Why would you need all of this information? Regardless of how elegant an application is, someone will still need to decide which APIs to call and will need to take care of any issues in using those services. A good number of these services will need things such as authorization codes and payment information. People implementing these services will still need to eat!

# UDDI Basics

Before we go into how to use UDDI, I want to take a few pages and explain why you would want to use UDDI for your own projects. UDDI looks at how to solve a specific class of problems: discovering and using Web services on a wide area network (WAN) like the Internet. This can also work on an intranet to advertise and update the location of Web services. We cover two items in this section: a usage scenario and the definition of a tModel.

---

[1] Ariba, Inc., International Business Machines Corporation, and Microsoft Corporation own the copyright on the specification.

# A UDDI Usage Scenario

Before going into detail about how UDDI actually works, let's take a high-level look at how someone might use it. In this scenario, a developer needs to provide order tracking for a commerce application. As an added responsibility, he or she must find out what companies deliver nationally and internationally. To tackle this task, the developer opens up a UDDI search engine and queries several registries for package delivery companies with national and international capabilities. The developer then saves the results of the search.

Still somewhat interactive, the developer drills down on the results. A few of the companies have a national presence, but do not service the area the warehouse is located in. Those get eliminated from the list of possibilities. The list now known, he or she asks order fulfillment to contact the remaining companies and set up account information. While the people in order fulfillment set up these relationships, our intrepid programmer looks at the various interfaces offered and writes some code to get tracking information from each of them. The code is tested against the various test servers set up by each of the companies. The developer tests to make sure that he or she understands what the service provider offers. If you provide a service, you will need to provide test equipment for the customer's learning period.[2] These test machines need not be as capable as the machines used by the live service. Once everything works, the service moves into production and customers can now track their packages via the interface. To the customers, it appears that everything runs on the company's computers, even though things such as tracking come from machines that may be very far away.

# tModels

UDDI defines a tModel[3] as the definition of a specification. This is metadata—"data about data." Using tModels, programmers and their programs can check services to see if the service is compatible with a given specification. A tModel defines what interface the underlying service implements. If you program to an interface, you should be able to use a new service without

[2] Credit card verification services came into being quite a while ago. I have heard stories of companies being charged tens of thousands of dollars because a developer was making sure that he or she was able to verify credit card numbers correctly. After a few businesses complained of these large bills, "dummy" verification services started to appear so that people could test and debug their applications.

[3] From what I understand, this is supposed to be short for TypeModel and was the "least hated" name. People familiar with the history of Ford Motor Company have been known to ask questions like "And what would the aModel be?" The Model T and Model A were the first two popular cars produced by Ford.

modifying your original program. Standards organizations, trade groups, or individual organizations may define these interfaces. What does this mean for companies developing and purchasing UDDI-enabled products?

Those who develop these products now have the ability to target specific markets and create services that either implement or use the pre-defined tModels. For others, it means that they do not always need to have a group on their staff writing programs that access specific tModels. Instead, they can purchase software that performs the tasks already. Some existing standards, such as Electronic Data Interchange, or EDI, will be standardized fairly quickly. Others will appear as needed.

# Where Does UDDI Fit in?

By now, you should have an idea of where to use UDDI and a general understanding of how it communicates interface information. The next question is with all the other stuff out there, where does UDDI fit in?

The World Wide Web has done a lot for the Internet. Soon after it was introduced, we got XML—a standardized SGML grammar. In short order, numerous XML initiatives showed up. Because of all this activity, we have a standardized set of technologies for use in Web-based services. Table 6–1 shows the Interop Stack as it stands today. UDDI represents the next layer in this stack that enables Web services. Future standards will provide things such as transaction management, object pooling, and other high-level services.

The UDDI specification describes the Web services and provides an interface for a framework that can describe any kind of Web service. WSDL describes the Web service location information and UDDI provides the programmatic interface for discovering that WSDL document.

| Table 6–1    Interop Stack. |
|---|
| **Interop Stack**    Universal Service Interop Protocols (not defined yet) |
| Universal Description, Discovery, and Integration (UDDI) |
| Simple Object Access Protocol (SOAP) |
| Extensible Markup Language (XML) |
| Common Internet Protocols (HTTP, TCP/IP, SMTP) |

# UDDI Information Types

The information model used by UDDI is defined using XML Schema. Like WSDL and SOAP, UDDI uses XML because of the availability of XML on many different platforms. At the time of the initial UDDI draft, the schema specification had passed most of the hurdles and was about to become a W3C recommendation.

The UDDI schema defines four types of information needed to access Web services:

- Business information
- Service information
- Binding information
- Service specification information

Appendix A of the UDDI specification contains a Unified Modeling Language (UML) object diagram. This diagram, reproduced as Figure 6–1, shows the relationship of the various entities in the UDDI information model. Although not explicitly stated in the diagram, no single instance of a core structure type ever has more than one parent. On the other hand, an individual element may be referenced by multiple other elements.

## *businessEntity*

The `businessEntity` element describes the business information. It contains basic information about a business such as its name, Dun and Bradstreet numbers, stock symbol, categorization information, and contact names. A UDDI registry uses this element to provide a sort of business yellow pages. The registry uses the basic information provided by the `businessEntity` to provide searching on business type as well as to locate a business based on unique identifiers.

## *businessService*

The `businessEntity` element contains links to more specific information about the services provided by that business. The `businessService` element contains information regarding a group of related Web services.

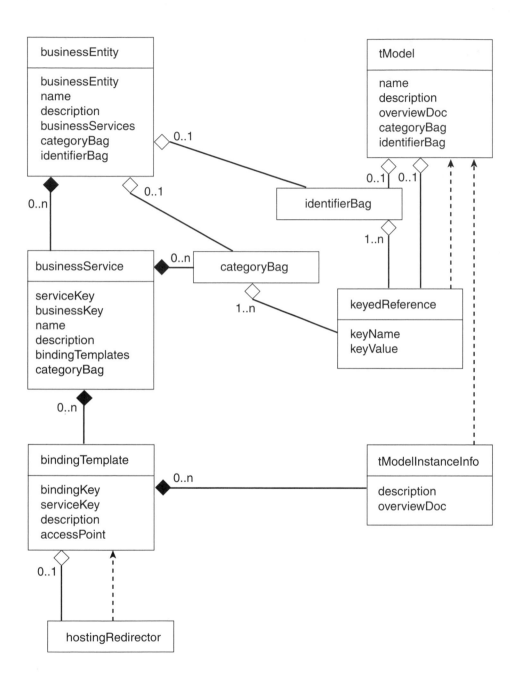

***Figure 6–1*** UDDI information model.

These services are related by either business process or as a category of services. These groupings all depend on how the site operator or implementer of the services chooses to do this. The groups may contain subgroups that further define the services.

This element also contains other information such as additional features that a user must hook up with before invoking the desired service. For example, the user of the service may have to register with a message router, or load balancer, or simply log in.

## bindingTemplate

Each `businessService` contains one or more `bindingTemplate` elements. The `bindingTemplate` contains information about what the service looks like (the `tModel` element) and where to access the service itself (`hostingRedirector`). The `bindingKey` and `serviceKey` attributes provide enough information to identify an interface implemented by a Web service.

## tModel

The `tModel` element describes the data and how to access it. A `tModel` can describe just about anything, from a natural language translation service to a simple calculator. Normally, a `tModel` is used to determine compatibility as well as for keyed namespace references. These elements are composed of a key, a name, possibly a description, and a URL that points somewhere. That URL should point to a document that contains more information about the concept represented by the `tModel`.

Commonly, you will find references to one `tModel` from many individual `businessEntity` data sets. The element may describe a commonly used data structure or set of services. It may also reference a common set of standards. In EDI, whole industries have agreed on a common reference model to transmit data between partners. A `tModel` may reference one of those common standards. For example, it would not be unusual to see life insurance companies represent insurance quotes and policyholder information using the exact same layouts. As a result, many different companies may reference one `tModel`.

# The Programmer's API

The UDDI specification defines a programmatic API to the registry data. This API is composed of two logical pieces: the Inquiry API and the Publisher's API. All operator sites must implement the entire API. The Inquiry portion allows programs to connect to and browse the UDDI registry. It also comes in handy when a Web service is invoked and then fails for some reason. The Publisher's portion of the API helps manage information related to the businessEntity or tModel elements. The entire API is built on SOAP. All of the calls in the API use the request-response model.

## The UDDI Invocation Model

The bindingTemplate element models each individually advertised Web service. Typically, a program will call these services based on cached bindingTemplate information. Typical usage of the UDDI registry's Inquiry API works like this:

1. Program accesses a UDDI registry to find information about a known service.
2. Program caches information from first use for subsequent uses.
3. Program invokes services based on cached information.
4. If the invocation succeeds, you are done.
5. If invocation fails, ask for data about the service.
6. If the data is the same as the cache, the call fails.
7. If the data is different from the cache, retry the call.
8. If the call succeeds, refresh the cache.
9. If the call fails, fail the call.

Using the preceding method allows users of the registry to achieve higher throughput because they do not need to get the UDDI-specific information before executing the call. By refreshing on failure only, the caller can assume the best and plan for the worst. This type of thing can happen when a service changes hosting, when the primary server fails and a backup comes online, or when the business upgrades a server.

## Security

The UDDI document does not specify how to secure access to the UDDI registry. You can assume that you will need authenticated access to use the Publisher's API. Each operator site must select and implement an authentication protocol that will still allow the Publisher's API to work. The operator site is also responsible for figuring out how to sign up new users. The Inquiry API should be left open for anyone to access.

## Versioning

The writers of the UDDI specification made sure that the API could handle versioning. After all, some of the calls will need to handle extra functionality, the content of the core elements may change, and the number of core elements may grow. To handle this turn of events, any calls using the API must use a version element named `generic`. All operator sites must support the current `generic` value and at least one prior version if applicable. Unlike SOAP, the authors of the UDDI specification chose to use regular old numbers for versioning. The current version is 1.0. For a call such as `find_business`, the initial element within the SOAP `Body` looks like this:

```
<find_business generic="1.0" xmlns="urn:uddi-org:api">
   ...
</find_business>
```

## Query Patterns

When digging into a UDDI registry, you will probably follow one of three query patterns. The one used depends on what you want to accomplish. These patterns are identified in the UDDI specification as the **browse**, **drill-down**, and **invocation** patterns.

### Browse Pattern

For users to discover what services they want to use, they need to find those services first. The UDDI yellow pages data has a hierarchical structure. If a user wanted to see all the services available on a UDDI operator site, they might use a tool[4] to look at all the publicly available information. To do so, they would use the browse pattern. Users may search for all businesses that begin with "Acm." Once they find an interesting businessEntity, they select a member of the result set and look for a candidate service by drilling down on the information (a combination of the drill-down and browse patterns). This pattern uses the find_xxx API calls.

## Drill-Down Pattern

Once you have a key for one of the four main UDDI datatypes, you can use that key to access all the details of a given data instance.[5] Once you have the item, you can find all of its related elements. This pattern uses the get_xxx API calls.

## Invocation Pattern

When using UDDI to find and connect to services, you still need to write applications to use those services. UDDI does not solve development issues. UDDI does solve some deployment issues. Namely, it allows services to move from machine to machine as necessary without needing to rewrite or otherwise manually intervene to keep the application running. The basic invocation pattern, already outlined by this chapter in the section "The UDDI Invocation Model," permits this to happen. The basic pattern looks like this:

1. Call the function using the cached bindingTemplate information.
2. If the call cannot be executed, update the bindingTemplate information.
3. Try again.

Using this pattern, you and your partners have the freedom to move machines, merge companies, and recover from disasters without telling everyone using the service about the changes. Simply update the information at the operator site and all should be well.

---

[4] This tool could take the form of a standalone client application or a Web-based application.

[5] These keys have meaning across replicated operator sites. If two sites do not share a common replication source, their data and keys will not be in sync—they have no reason to synchronize with each other.

# Summary

UDDI is something you will use with SOAP if you are exposing services to the world. Details on the API, operator sites, and other information can be found at http://www.uddi.org. I included this chapter solely to tell you what UDDI is and what it can do for you. It would be a shame if you implemented a great Web service and did not know that you could advertise it somehow. By the time of the publication of this book, other books should exist or be on their way highlighting UDDI in full detail. The documents at the UDDI Web site do contain enough information to implement an operator site or browser if you are so inclined.

# Chapter 7

# AVAILABLE
# SOAP
# IMPLEMENTATIONS

This chapter discusses a few of the more popular commercially available and freely available SOAP servers. Because it is so easy to write a SOAP client and server, many implementations exist. The authors of these implementations get to piggyback on the enthusiasm and implementations that standardized XML brought about. This left them only needing to implement that little bit of SOAP-specific code to get things working. When picking an implementation to discuss, I used the following criteria:

1. From postings on the DevelopMentor SOAP discussion list, did someone announce it (i.e., I need to know it exists)?
2. Do people use it?
3. Is there a better one?

SOAP implementations come in two flavors: ones that are language specific and ones that are ORB specific. Of course, they must all receive SOAP messages and send them back. That is what the public interface of any SOAP application does. The private side of the interface, the one that does any work, is a little different. The SOAP messages need to be translated into some sort of actionable code somewhere. If the service is simple enough, it can be coded as an XML style sheet (XSLT). Most Web services are not that trivial.

For those, some sort of code needs to exist on the other side. We look at those implementations in this chapter.

You will note that the number of open-source implementations is a bit larger than the number of commercial ones. This only reflects the fact that open-source projects do not have nondisclosure agreements. If commercial is important to you, do not worry. I am fairly certain that other commercial versions will materialize over time.

What can you expect in these short reviews? I give summaries of the basic marketing information available from the various vendors and project home pages. The case study in the book uses the two dominant SOAP solutions: Apache (which runs on most operating systems) and the SOAP Toolkit on Windows.[1] Later in the book, you will get a better feel for these two because I actually had to learn them well.

Let's take a look at the various offerings.

# Apache

**Type:** Open-source
**Language(s) supported:** Java
**Available platforms:** Most Posix-compliant platforms (Many UNIX, Windows, and others)
**Home page:** *http://www.apache.org/SOAP*

Apache began its life in 1995 as a UNIX-based HTTP server. Since then, it has become the leading Web server on many operating systems and has branched out to take on more projects. The Apache Software Foundation (ASF) was created to take ownership of all of the projects, including the following:

- **Apache HTTP Server:** A Web server that aims to support the current HTTP standards. It runs on modern desktop and server operating systems.
- **Apache XML Project:** This project has received a great deal of support from many individuals and companies. Among the list of projects is SOAP, contributed by IBM.
- **Jakarta:** The home for various server-side Java projects. Contains things such as Tomcat and a Web Distributed Authoring and Versioning (WebDAV) implementation.

---

[1] I don't have any real numbers to back up this claim. Instead, this represents a gut feel from traffic I have seen in various discussion lists and newsgroups.

- **Java Apache:** Other Java-related projects. The ASF intends to merge this with Jakarta.
- **mod_perl:** An implementation of Perl for the Apache HTTP server. Using this, you can write Apache modules (essentially, add-on components) in Perl.
- **PHP:** Apache's answer to Microsoft's Active Server Pages (ASP).
- **Apache Tcl:** The project that serves as a catchall for Tcl-Apache integration efforts. Tcl is a cross-platform scripting language that is very popular on UNIX. Ports exist for many other operating systems.

Setup is a breeze compared with most other UNIX applications. On most Linux distributions, Apache will be set up for you automatically. If you intend to write most of your SOAP objects from scratch in Java and you have to use UNIX, I would recommend using Apache for the full implementation. Apache sports one of the biggest and best support organizations out there. It is the most popular Web server, with 59.69% of all Web sites running the software.[2] When looking at this number, keep in mind that the majority of Web pages are still served up by commercial applications. It fully supports WSDL and almost all of SOAP v1.1.

# IdooXoap

**Type:** Open-source
**Language(s) supported:** C++ and Java
**Available platforms:** Java 1.3, Apache
**Home page:** *http://www.idoox.com*

Version 1.0 of the IdooXoap toolkit was released on December 15, 2000. Zvon (*www.zvon.org*) created this distribution and then gave it away under a BSD-style (Berkeley Software Distribution) open-source license. The C++ version of this toolkit is far more capable than the one presented in this text. It supports WSDL as well as almost 100% of the SOAP specification. The documentation on IdooXoap appears to be fairly thin, sticking mostly to documentation on SOAP and XML schema instead. Still, this appears to be a very good choice for someone looking to do SOAP using only C++.

---

[2] Numbers courtesy of Netcraft at *http://www.netcraft.com/survey/*. This reading was taken in November 2000.

# Iona

**Type:** Commercial
**Language(s) supported:** C++ and Java
**Available platforms:** Various UNIX platforms, OS/390, and Windows through their iPortal and Orbix 2000 products
**Home page:** *http://www.iona.com*

Iona is one of the companies that got involved with SOAP shortly after the release of the v1.0 specification. They are a leading vendor of CORBA and COM-to-CORBA bridge technology. Iona has two products that will support SOAP: iPortal and Orbix 2000.

## *iPortal*

iPortal functions as a portal and integration product for various popular messaging standards. It may receive a SOAP message formatted according to one of a number of emerging standards including RosettaNet, BizTalk, HL7, ACORD, finXML, and fpml. It takes that message and passes it to the appropriate back-end component. Based on the initial request, the message comes out with a compatibly formatted return message. The SOAP part of the basic communication is shown in the graphic in Figure 7–1, supplied by Iona.

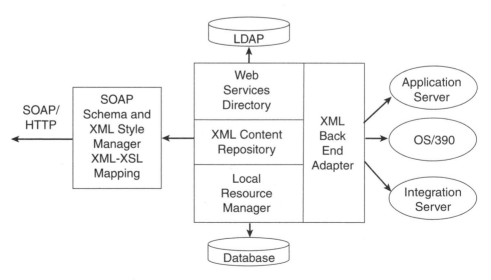

***Figure 7–1***    Iona iPortal SOAP adapter.

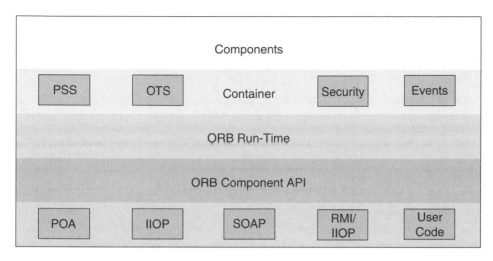

***Figure 7–2***   Iona Orbix ORB layering model.

iPortal works by parsing the SOAP message and then translating it into something consumable by the program providing the service. Essentially, the product works as a universal translator for XML.

## *Orbix 2000*

This product allows you to expose existing CORBA services as Web services through a SOAP interface. Using it, you can take services already exposed via IIOP and add a SOAP interface to the object as well. This back-end product allows you to write your objects in Java, C++, or any other CORBA-aware language and then call them from any SOAP-compliant application without having to use matching object models. This provides for a SOAP server without reliance on a pre-existing Web server. This fits into the overall Orbix product according to the Iona-supplied diagram pictured in Figure 7–2.

# Microsoft

Microsoft currently provides two items for SOAP. One, the SOAP Toolkit, is free, and it provides tools for developing SOAP-based Web services using COM and Internet Information Server. The other, Visual Studio Net, allows people to develop Web services under the latest evolutionary step in COM: the Common Language Runtime (CLR).

## SOAP Toolkit v2

**Type:** Commercial but free
**Language(s) supported:** COM compliant languages
**Available platforms:** Windows
**Home page:** *http://msdn.microsoft.com/soap*

This first version of this product started life as a sample application for the Microsoft Developer's Network (MSDN). SOAP was supposed to be a simple thing to implement and so the MSDN team attacked it that way. A funny thing happened on the way to this one becoming a series of articles for Microsoft: People got excited and started using it for production systems. So, the product grew from an MSDN sample to a full-grown, free, supported Microsoft product. A new team took over the concept (SOAP for COM) and built something more capable[3] and supportable than the first version of the toolkit. This product has no reliance on the Microsoft .Net technologies. Why? It supplies SOAP to people who need it on Windows now. Many customers just do not feel comfortable running things like beta technologies (e.g., Net) on their machines. The toolkit provides comfort for those people.

The toolkit has a fairly functional SOAP implementation. It integrates with Internet Information Server (the Internet's Number 2 Web server at 20.09% of all Web sites[4]) and has good performance. If you have a number of COM objects that you need to expose as Web services, you should definitely give the SOAP Toolkit a look.

## Visual Studio.Net

**Type:** Commercial
**Language(s) supported:** CLR-compliant languages
**Available platforms:** Windows
**Home page:** *http://www.microsoft.com*

As of this writing, this product is in its beta period. Unless you can afford to live on the cutting edge of Microsoft technology, you may want to stay away from this one until Microsoft ships the product. That said, if you can get your

---

[3] Of course, this is a matter of perspective. I think that my perspective is somewhat tainted, because at the time of this writing, I work for the person who implemented the v1 Internet Services Application Programming Interface (ISAPI) listener (that's Matt Powell in case you are curious).

[4] Numbers courtesy of Netcraft at *http://www.netcraft.com/survey/*. Numbers were based on November 2000 readings.

hands on the prerelease versions of the product and can afford minor rewrites as it evolves toward its finished state, this one offers a lot of benefits to the Windows-savvy SOAP developer. You get benefits because the product does not use SOAP as a separate add-on or product. It is simply something that you can access from any of the .NET languages. My experience has been that even the early internal beta releases have been very stable.

# pocketSOAP

**Type:** Open-source
**Language(s) supported:** COM-compliant languages
**Available platforms:** All 32-bit Windows (including CE)
**Home page:** *http://www.pocketsoap.com*

This is a SOAP client COM component for the Windows family and was originally targeted at PocketPC. Since then, Simon Fell has also created a version that works on Windows 9x/Me/NT4/2000/XP. The package includes an HTTP transport for making HTTP-based SOAP requests. He separated the transport from the main SOAP core. As a result, users can add other transports as needed.

# RogueWave

## *XML-DB Link and*
## *XML Services Framework*

**Type:** Commercial
**Language(s) supported:** CORBA-compliant languages as well as
                         Structured Query Language (SQL)
**Available platforms:** Various UNIX platforms and Windows
**Home page:** *http://www.roguewave.com*

The XML Services Framework provides mechanisms to expose CORBA services as Web services. The framework takes the incoming messages, and translates them into CORBA. For the response, the CORBA message is

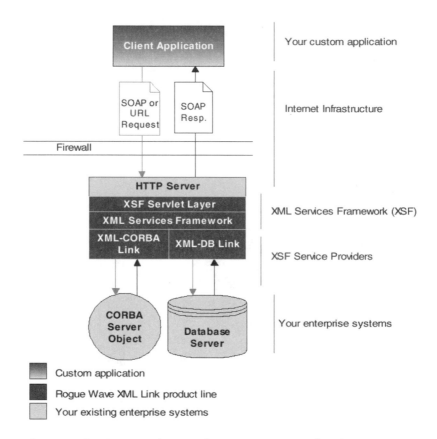

**Figure 7–3**    Conceptual usage of RogueWave XML Link with SOAP.

translated back to SOAP and sent to the client. XML-DB Link sits on top of the XML Services Framework and allows you to expose stored procedures and SQL queries via the framework. This product aims to enhance server-side security by only exposing the objects and queries you specify. You can then place your entire infrastructure behind a firewall and use the framework as the bridge between the public and private sides of your enterprise. A conceptual drawing, provided by RogueWave, is shown in Figure 7–3.

This particular option is very tempting if you have already bought into one of RogueWave's other offerings: DBTools.h++. Many shops like to use DBTools.h++ because it works well on many different platforms. I suspect that the integration between these products is pretty good, making this a natural choice for any SOAP work you may need to do.

# SOAP::Lite

**Type:** Open-source
**Language(s) supported:** Perl
**Available platforms:** Various UNIX platforms and Windows
**Home page:** *http://www.soaplite.com*

If you know Perl and need to use SOAP, this is the library you want to use. The author, Paul Kulchenko, has been very active in the SOAP newsgroups and quick to patch any bugs with the library. This works well with the Microsoft and Apache implementations of SOAP, which means it will talk to pretty much everything.

With SOAP::Lite, you get a lot. It fully supports UDDI and WSDL. The author has followed the v1.1 specification very well, and he has populated his site with plenty of documentation and examples.

# White Mesa

**Type:** Open-source
**Language(s) supported:** C++
**Available platforms:** Windows
**Home page:** *http://www.whitemesa.com*

This allows you to build an RPC-based SOAP server and client using C++ on the client and a WinNT service as the server. The SOAP service accepts requests using the HTTP binding as long as those requests are formatted according to the rules in SOAP v1.1. The server interprets the request, creates the correct COM object, invokes the requested message, and returns information back to the client. The server uses WSDL to find out about the requested SOAP service. The WSDL files provide information about what to do with a particular message, as well as parameter data typing.

This implementation works very well if you are a Windows developer who needs a small, fast implementation of SOAP. As an added benefit, you do not need Internet Information Server for this one to work. It does a fairly good job handling most simple datatypes. Complex types such as structures do not work with this implementation.

# Zope

**Type:** Open-source
**Language(s) supported:** Python
**Available platforms:** Various UNIX platforms and Windows
**Home page:** *http://www.zope.org*

Zope is a Python-based Web server. At the time of this writing, the Zope team is in the process of adding support for SOAP to accompany its XML-RPC support. You can do some things with this product that you cannot with many others. You can edit your Web pages over the Web using some of the product's administrative tools. The product is driven to be collaborative. It supports WebDAV for editing. WebDAV is a set of extensions to HTTP that allows users to edit and manage files on Web servers.

Python is a fairly easy language to learn. It is an object-oriented scripting language that has developed a well-deserved reputation for being powerful and flexible.

# Summary

Several products exist that will allow you to develop SOAP clients and servers in the language and platform of your choice. A fair number of these choices provide a full-featured Web server in the mix. This may or may not be a good thing, depending on the device you want to use to host the SOAP application. As the device gets smaller, you will probably need to gravitate toward a more and more specialized XML parser and SOAP implementation. You may even have to go so far as to create a grammar for Lex and Yet Another Computer Compiler (YACC) so that when the production is found, it calls the right function.

Hopefully, this chapter has helped save you the pain of reinventing the wheel. I have tried to include the SOAP libraries and engines that I know about. If you know of any more good ones that are not included, please send them to me, *scott@scottseely.com*, so that I can mention them on My web site (www.scottseely.com) and in any subsequent editions of this text. I would really appreciate a summary of the capabilities of any you mention.

# Part 3

# CASE STUDY:
# A WEB-BASED
# AUCTION SYSTEM

*SOAP appears to be a very beneficial technology, but can you really use it to build cross-platform applications? Yes, you can.  This case study shows the construction of an application that uses Java, Visual Basic, and C#.  It runs on UNIX, Windows, and .NET. The various pieces use SOAP to communicate with each other, providing easy interoperability. The case study uses three of the most popular SOAP toolkits: Apache SOAP, Microsoft SOAP Toolkit v2, and .NET's SOAP implementation.*

# Chapter 8

# AUCTION SYSTEM AND REQUIREMENTS

So far, this book has covered a lot of information. To show you how to use all this technology, the chapters in this section present a case study using SOAP as the primary communication mechanism between computers and components. We take a look at a fairly common situation: A company has a platform with a lot of critical data that is needed by another, incompatible platform. Frequently, this occurs within organizations and between trading partners. For our case study, we will enter the land of make-believe.

## Background

A fictional company, Sammamish Liquidation Associates (SLA), is about to enter the online auction world. SLA has a customer information database as well as some customer management applications that it runs on a UNIX machine. They have had this information and code for years and do not want to take any chances in breaking things. The biggest risk the company took was migrating all customer-related applications and data to Linux.

Recently, the company decided to offer a new option to its customers that have excess inventory to get rid of: auctions. SLA decided that this should all be done online. As a result, the Web development team got the task of setting up a Web site. As luck would have it, the Web team grew out of the company's Visual Basic talent. The group knows Microsoft tools inside and out and has little or no UNIX experience. The company did give one directive: All customer information must continue to use the UNIX system. The tools and data on that system are too valuable to risk a conversion. Besides risking losing tested code, the business also risks a loss of manpower. In typical "us versus them" mentality, employees on either side of the fence would rather quit than use the "other" platform. Fortunately, both sides agreed that using standards is a good idea. The internal platforms are all Internet capable and will use SOAP and WSDL to communicate.

The various leads on these teams presented this information to management. Management liked the ideas and then suggested that they might be interested in hosting the auction information as a Web service in the future. As a result, they would like any and all parts of the auction interface available through SOAP. They also thought that they might host several distinct auctions for bigger clients. The idea was to be able to set up an auction anywhere that ties into the auction Web service for business logic. After the meeting, someone in management wrote up the requirements. What follows is the document that person came up with.

# Executive Summary

A number of our customers have traditionally relied on us to help find buyers for their excess inventory. They also rely on us to arrange delivery for any items we manage to help them sell. We believe that we can help move that inventory more effectively by adding another channel to our sales path: online auctions. A number of our customers like this idea. They have the potential to get a higher price than they would if the excess was sold through more traditional channels (bulk to surplus stores, discounts to retailers, etc.).

We currently have an existing customer management system that can also handle processing payments through major credit card companies. This system will be enhanced to handle adding new bidders that are not corporations. We do not have anything that really could handle the inventory management and tracking requirements for an auction system and will need to design that from scratch.

This system will be composed of four subsystems:

- **Bidder enrollment and management:** Adds new bidders to the system and allows them to place bids on items for auction.
- **Item enrollment and management:** Adds items for auction to the database and defines how they will be auctioned off.
- **The bidding system:** Pulls items from the item database and puts them on the Internet. Manages bids, starts and stops bidding, and notifies people when they have made a successful bid or have gone out of the bidding.
- **Reporting:** Provides users with information about orders based on seller, bidder, shipped items, and other items.

The rest of this document defines the requirements for these sub-systems.

# Bidder Enrollment and Management

We will manage the bidders by adding them to the existing customer management system. For this system, we will need to add an interface accessible from the Windows machine. This interface does not need to be accessible to the Internet or other outside networks. The following information needs to be collected when a bidder enrolls:

- Title (Mr., Ms., Mrs., Dr., etc.)
- First name
- Last name
- Two lines for address information
- City
- State/Province
- Zip/Postal Code
- Daytime phone number
- Evening phone number
- Email address
- Shipping information (name, city, state/province, zip/postal code)

The shipping information may change from order to order, but it is important to know the default shipping address. The user must be able to update this information at a later time using a username and password. The username and password do not need to be tied into the bidder subsystem. It may be part of logging in to bid on an item.

# Item Enrollment and Management

When an item goes up for auction, a number of things need to be known about it:

- Owner of item (who will deliver after auction)
- Description of the item
- Picture of the item (if available)
- Number of items in lot
- Category (selected from predefined list)
- Reserve price (if any)
- Yankee auction or Dutch auction[1]
- Auction start date
- Auction end date
- Approximate item weight (for shipping cost approximation)
- Approximate item dimensions (height, width, length)

These requirements introduce a couple of new terms. The *reserve price* is the minimum bid required to win the item. If the owner of the item sets the reserve at $10[2] and the winning bid goes to $8, the owner is not obligated to sell the item. The winning bid never gets collected and the item never gets sent. On the other hand, if the winning bid is $10 or greater, the owner must sell the item and the winning bidder must pay.

Auctions will often have many identical individual items available. Few people will buy 20 identical cordless phones, but 20 people may each buy one cordless phone. A *Yankee auction* format states that when the auction closes

---

[1] This is not meant to be derogatory toward any cultural group. Yankee and Dutch are terms widely used to describe two popular methods of auctioning multiple identical items.

[2] For the sake of the examples, assume all currencies are U.S. dollars.

and a particular lot includes two or more of the same item, each winning bidder pays the minimum bid required to win the item. For example, let's say that three cordless phones are available. The three winning bids are $20, $18, and $16. When the auction closes, all three winning bidders will pay $16, the smallest winning bid. A *Dutch auction* works more to the seller's favor. In a Dutch auction, those three winning bidders would pay what they bid: $20, $18, and $16.

This system must have a Web-based interface and should prevent people from posting bogus items. We should also be able to block people from adding items. If a particular individual develops a reputation for not delivering goods then he or she should be barred from using the system.

This system needs to define auction start and end times. More exactly, the system must allow us to define the start and end times of an auction "day." An auction day does not need to run for 24 full hours. It may run 8 a.m. to 5 p.m. If an auction begins on May 1 and ends on May 6, the auction will start at 8 a.m. on May 1 and end at 5 p.m. on May 6.

# The Bidding System

The bidding system allows potential buyers to look at items currently available for auction. Customers should be able to browse based on category. The following views should be available to the user:

- Opening page that shows categories of items.
- Categorized page that shows item name, brief description, current minimum winning bid, and auction close time. Items that are going to be for auction in the near future (within two days) should be featured on the bottom of the page.
- When actually looking at an item, the user should be able to see all active bids and some brief information about who owns the bid (e.g., $15 Boise, Idaho). This will help the user decide how much to bid.
- When placing a bid, the bidder must log in and supply payment information. If not a current user, the bidder can use this as an opportunity to create a new account.

All of these items must be prototyped in the specification phase. When the bidder actually "wins" an item, the system needs to charge their credit card.

If the card is successfully charged, the system should send an email message telling the winner that he or she won. As soon as the item is shipped, the user should get another email indicating when it shipped and providing any available tracking information.

# Reporting

A few basic reports are needed to know what the auction system is doing for us. This section defines a few basic reports. Others may become apparent as the product develops.

## Active Items

This report details the items currently being auctioned. The report needs to detail the following items:

- Seller name
- Item name
- Number of items
- Auction format (can just be Y for Yankee or D for Dutch)
- Reserve price
- Highest winning bid
- Lowest winning bid
- Auction end date for item

A user of this report should be able to specify either a specific seller name or retrieve all active items.

## Upcoming Items

This report shows all items that have not been sold yet. This report comes in handy when verifying items for auction with a seller. We may have a periodic need to verify stock at our warehouse or at the seller's warehouse. It will also let us know when we may need to solicit extra items or request that sellers postpone some sales for a lull in the auction calendar. The report should contain the following items:

- Seller name
- Item name
- Number of items
- Auction format (can just be Y for Yankee or D for Dutch)
- Reserve price
- Auction start date for item
- Auction end date for item

This report has three variable parameters: seller name, start date, and end date. If no name is specified, all sellers should be returned. If no start date is used, assume January 1, 2000 (or some other sane start time). If no end date is used, use today plus 10 years (if today is April 5, 2001, then the end date is April 5, 2011).

## Items to Ship

Once an auction is over and the winners have been notified, the seller needs a report detailing which items need to be shipped as well as where to ship them. This report could be done to list all sold items, but will normally be used on a seller-by-seller basis. You should be able to generate all of the individual reports with one button push. This report has a slightly different layout than others. This one does not contain simple detail lines. Instead, it should look something like this:

```
North Lake Widgets                            Page 1
_____

Item: Screwdriver Set (Part No. 12-988-212)
    No. of Pieces              Address
        2                      Scott Seely
                               817 E. Imperial Dr.
                               Hartland, WI 53029

        1                      Norma Lindberg
                               733 Wheelock Ave.
                               Hartford, WI 53027

Item: Undercar Scooter (Part No. 17-222-819)
    No. of Pieces              Address
        5                      David Bradshaw
                               3513 208th Pl. NE
                               Redmond, WA 98052
```

Assume 25 lines per page. Do not worry about page-wrapping items. When you hit line 25, simply wrap around to the next page and keep going. If you want to be fancy, assume that no address contains more than four lines.

# Summary

This chapter tries to mimic the types of requirement documents I am used to seeing. You will notice that a number of the requirements are fairly vague and others are detailed. This reflects the reality of the business: People who want these systems often only know that they want the system to do. Our job as programmers is to create something that meets those wants. Obviously, the vague items will require the most work—because the developer will surely get it wrong. Chapter 9 contains the developer response to the requirements document: the design document.

The system described here works well as a sample system for a SOAP application. For a real auction system, you would want search capabilities, a page to highlight specials, and, more likely than not, a better user interface that what will be created here.[3] You would also want to actually process the credit card information. Think about how you would describe those features for someone to implement. In the meantime, let's move on to the design and fill in the holes in the requirements.

[3] This is not a book on HTML, so I can get away with that.

# Chapter 9

## AUCTION SYSTEM DESIGN

Before getting into how the whole system will look, I need to go over some practical constraints that I have imposed on the example. This book has a number of hidden constraints created by the target audience. For example, the majority of people reading this book develop software for the Windows platform. As a result, any Linux example must use tools available on Windows. One of the strengths of using any open-source code is that you can almost always find a Windows version of the same product.

I designed this case study as a proof of concept for an auction system. Finished products contain a lot of design points that have nothing to do with SOAP. When discussing what I did, I would have to go into discussions about user interface design, database optimizations, and other off-topic items. I will have to do some of this with the proof of concept, but the level of detail is not as deep as it would be for a full system. Hopefully, the project will convince you that SOAP can make it easy for you to build cross-platform, Internet-ready applications.

As we go through the various features, I make lists of things you may want to add to make the sample more capable. What can you expect in this chapter and those that follow? In this chapter, you will see high-level designs and use cases for the major subsystems:

- Bidder enrollment and management
- Item enrollment and management
- The bidding system

I will not be designing all the reports. Given the descriptions in the previous chapter, you should be able to generate a set of SOAP methods that can return records for formatting into reports. They are all fairly simple methods and should give you an opportunity to do some experimentation with SOAP.

By now, you must be wondering what tools I picked. For databases, I picked mySQL and the Microsoft Data Engine (MSDE). mySQL runs well on Windows and Linux. As an added benefit, it has a stable, easy-to-use Java Database Connectivity (JDBC) driver. MSDE is a free database engine for small databases. For all intents and purposes, you can think of MSDE as a scaled-down version of Microsoft SQL Server. It allows databases to grow up to two gigabytes and uses the same syntax as its big brother. As an added benefit, you can use Microsoft Access[1] to create, design, and view MSDE databases.

For development tools, I picked some fairly simple ones. I did not want to scare people away and from what I have seen, most people are not intimidated by Java or Visual Basic. I highly recommend Sun's Forte for Java. Forte is based on my favorite Java Integrated Development Enviroment (IDE): NetBeans. I tried a number of IDEs when Java first came out and NetBeans was the only one that clicked with me. Before it came out, I did a lot of my Java programming with text editors and a command line. Then, NetBeans released their product and I became an IDE user again.

As for VB 6.0, it is not free but almost everyone seems to have it. I do not use any of its advanced features, so you should be able to get away with the cheapest, lowest power version out there. Another reason behind this choice was that more people use VB than any other individual language on Windows. This choice makes the book accessible to more Windows programmers. If you must use C++, most of the code should be an easy translation if you #import the COM objects and use Active Template Library (ATL).

Any tools that I can distribute have been included on the book's CD-ROM. All of the tools have links that I maintain at *http://www.scottseely.com/soapbooktools.htm*.

I hope I have adjusted your expectations and explained my reasoning. With that out of the way, let's go back to our little bit of fiction take a look at how the system is designed.

---

[1] I've used both Access 2000 and Access 2002 to do this. I have not tried with earlier versions of Access.

# Bidder Enrollment and Management

SLA has invested a lot of time and money developing software that manages customer data. These systems integrate with our shipping and order management systems. We need to do some minor modifications to these applications to get winning bids from the auction system. We can implement that phase of the project once we complete the bidding system. We need to allow the bidding system to interact with the customer management applications so that it can create, look up, edit, and delete customer data. We intend to expose the following customer data:

- Full name
- Email address
- Shipping and billing address
- Home, work, and fax phone numbers

We store this information in a mySQL database. We use JDBC and Java to access the data. Because the Apache SOAP implementation supports Java, we should only need to make a few enhancements to expose this information via a Web service. Apache's SOAP contains a class called `BeanEncoder`. As long as we follow the Java Bean design pattern for the objects we want to serialize over SOAP, we should be fine. The Web service will only write to the `Customer`, `Address`, and `PhoneNumber` tables. Figure 9–1 shows the relationship between these tables.

We also have to tie customer data to specific types of customers: sellers and bidders. The bidding system keeps track of which Customer records are in which table. For the time being we want to make sure that a seller cannot be a bidder and a bidder cannot be a seller.

Given the way that the data is arranged, we do not get any benefits (yet) from sharing the common mySQL database. An existing customer cannot simply state that "I am Acme, Inc." and have the computer associate that customer with that company. The mySQL database does not include authentication rules. It does allow for records that only differ by ID, so this restriction will not cripple us. To enable authentication, the MSDE database uses an e-mail address as the primary key and a password as the "secret" that allows the user to manipulate the account. Figure 9–2 shows the relationship between the mySQL and MSDE databases.

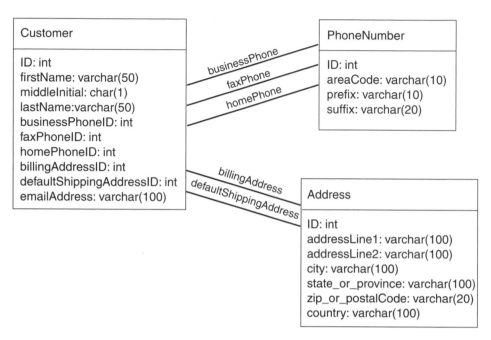

***Figure 9–1***   Customer database table relationships.

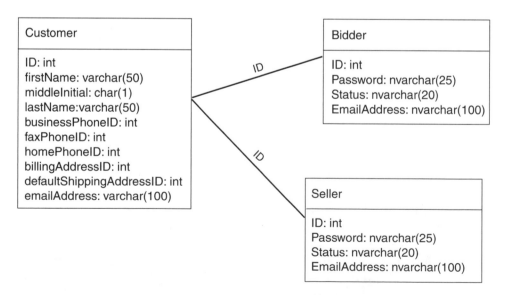

***Figure 9–2***   mySQL to MSDE database table relationships.

## *Customer Use Cases*

The objects must allow the following use cases:

## Create a New Customer

People who have never been a customer before will want to bid on the auction items. Given that we want this situation (i.e., new customers), we need some way of tracking them should they successfully bid on an item. When a user places a bid, he or she needs to enter his or her email address and a password. If the email address does not exist in the system, the user will be routed to a sign-up screen. The user cannot select a password at this time. Why? We want to limit the number of phony bids. The system will generate a new password and email it to the user as soon as he or she submits and saves the customer data. The user can then use that password to place a bid.

## Edit Customer Information

Our customers may have changes to their email address or other personal data. They need to be able to change the following items:

- Billing address
- Shipping address
- Home phone
- Fax phone
- Work phone

## Get Customer

We need to be able to look up customers based on email address as well as customer ID. This lookup should return the full set of customer information: name, email, addresses, and phone numbers.

## Delete Customer

A customer may give us bogus information: shipping address, billing address, or credit card data. We don't want to keep these users in our system, so this provides a method of removing them. Likewise, people may request that we remove their information from our database. We need to be able to delete those customers from our system.

## Change Password

When a customer is created, we generate a password for that customer. Odds are pretty good that new customers will not want to keep the password. Why? Normal people have problems remembering passwords such as `mfQveTmsaZ`. So, we need to provide a facility for them to change the password to something more memorable. We recognize that this may leave the account open to things such as a dictionary attack[2]. Because of this, the system must email a notice of the change to the account owner in case someone guesses and then changes the password. If a fraudulent change occurs, we have to recognize that a number of bad bids may be submitted. Our legal advisors will have to come up with something that explains what our responsibilities are in the event that the worst happens.

# Item Enrollment and Management

As a liquidation firm, we do have a fair amount of code invested in managing items as well. A lot of this system also deals with the location of items within our own warehouse. We want our customers to be able to auction items without moving them to our facilities. This should reduce shipping costs because goods will not have to move twice. Currently, goods ship once to our warehouse and then to the buyer. With this auction system, we will actively seek out items for auction as well as maintain the Web presence.

When maintaining the items, we need two tools:

- **Category editor:** Allows our site operators to add, remove, and modify item categories.
- **Item editor:** Allows our clients to add, remove, and modify their surplus items.

---

[2] A *dictionary attack* attacks authentication mechanisms. One way of performing the attack is by getting a valid username and then using words found in a dictionary (think Webster's) as guesses for the password. Such attacks are fairly easy to automate and are very common.

Because these features will run on Windows, we will continue to store data in an SQL Server database.[3]

# Category Management

Category management helps organize the contents of the auction site. Like the classified ads in the newspaper, it helps buyers find what they are looking for. For example, a buyer looking for stereo speakers would look in a category such as *Electronics* and then drill down into *Audio* and finally, *Speakers*. At this point in time, we believe that SLA should manage this functionality for clients. When clients want to add an auction item, they should email us with a request to add a new category if none of the existing categories cover the product. Although cumbersome and time consuming, this process should help reduce the number of redundant and unnecessary categories.

Like a lot of components in this system, the category management piece needs to have the business logic exposed via a SOAP interface. This way, potential licensees (as well as us) can develop and change the user interface as often as needed.

# Category Management Use Cases

For the prototype, we will do this by only giving the administrators access to the category management system. If clients cannot find an appropriate category or want a category changed, they can submit the request via email or by calling the technical assistance help line. The following use cases must be satisfied by the management interface.

## Add New Category

Users must be able to add a new category. They must be able to add categories to the toplevel (no parents) or beneath any other category as well. The SOAP interface will impose no limits on how deeply the user can nest the categories. The site administrators may impose category depth limits. At some point, the categories might become too fine grained.

---

[3] This code uses the super-scaled-down version of SQL Server—MSDE. Why? Because I can redistribute it for free so that you have something to experiment with.

## Edit Category

Not every category will have a typo-free name or description. Alternatively, the name or description may need to change because it is not accurate enough. Someone may have entered *Computer* when the only computer type available is a notebook. Because of this, the category may need to be changed to *Notebook Computer*. These changes need to happen without changing the category's ID—a seller may have already associated products with the category we want to more accurately label.

## Delete Category

A category or family of categories may have fallen out of use. This may happen under a number of situations:

- A client who provides a certain type of stock goes out of business or stops working with us.
- Over the course of a few months, we stop getting items in that category.
- We decide to not auction a certain type of item for liability reasons (e.g., firearms, jewelry, automobiles).

When a category is deleted, it should remove any child categories as well. When performing this cascading delete, the code should make sure that no items reference that category or any of its children. In the case where a category or its child is referenced, the delete must stop. A partial delete might happen in the case where only one child is referenced. Some of its siblings may be removed before the child is found. If the proof of concept is accepted, we will have to discuss wrapping the delete in a transaction or if we should allow things to continue in this manner.

## Item Management

We want to allow our sellers to add items to the auction site on their own. This way, sellers can add items as they get them instead of contacting our salespeople or operations people to do it for them. Likewise, they can update the information or delete the items as needed.

## *Item Management Use Cases*

### Add Item

The interface needs to allow sellers to add items so that they can post what they want to sell. At a minimum, sellers need to fill in the following columns in the Item table:

- Name
- Description
- Category
- Auction start/end date
- Auction type
- Quantity

Auctions cannot start before the current date and the end date must be at least one day past the start date. The quantity field can contain any value between 0 and 1,000,000.

### Edit Item

After adding an item, the seller may want to fill in extra information or reduce the number of items available during a specific auction period. In ongoing auctions, sellers can sometimes maximize their offers by auctioning off smaller numbers of items more frequently. People become more competitive when chasing one of three items in five separate auctions instead of 15 items offered in one auction. No one can make changes once an auction begins. We do not want to allow sellers to change the rules once the auction begins.

### Delete Item

Sellers may want to pull an item before it goes up for auction. Like in the Edit Item use case, you cannot delete an item once the auction has begun. At that point in time, the seller has committed to selling the item. If the auction has not begun, the seller can delete whatever item he or she wants to delete.

# The Bidding System

To place bids, the bidder needs to be able to discover a few pieces of information:

- The item categories
- Items available in those categories
- Details of individual items
- Active bids on individual items

Like the other subsystems, the business logic must be exposed via SOAP. If nothing else, this prepares the company for future plans to expose the auction service via a UDDI registry.

Of all the parts of our system, we expect that this piece will get the most use. Why? If we market the service correctly and generate enough traffic, people will use this system to see what we have for sale. With any luck, they will sign up for an account and place some bids as well. Hopefully, we will make a good impression on prospective clients as well.

## Bidding System Use Cases

### Entrance to Web Site

When users come to the Web site, they should see a welcome message as well as links to do the following items:[4]

- View items for auction
- Create a new bidder account
- Request a new seller account
- Add auction items

The rest of the use cases define what the user should see and what the site should do when the user goes to the `View Items for Auction` part of the Web site.

[4] This section defines the part of the site that adds auction items. All the other pieces are defined in this chapter except for requesting a new seller account. The seller account functionality looks a lot like the functionality for creating a customer account.

## User Selects View Items for Auction

A screen should come up that allows the user to select an item category. When the user selects a particular category, the page should also display the items available for auction in that category. Because categories may contain sub-categories, we could either display all items in that category and its sub-categories or only the items linked to that specific category. At this point in time, we will only display the items linked to the category and not items in subcategories. If the beta users do not like this particular choice, we will modify it to display items in subcategories as well.

## Site Displays Items in Category

If a category has no items available for sale, the site must display a message to the user stating that it found no items for sale. If the category does have associated items, the page should show an item summary including this information:

- Item name
- Number available for this auction
- Item reserve price
- Auction type
- If the auction has not begun yet, a message to notify the user
- If the auction is over, a message to notify the user

The item name must link to a page that displays all of the details about the item including any active bids.

## User Selects Item

When users select an item, they should see a page giving all the details about an item:

- Name
- Description
- Auction type
- Reserve price
- Quantity available

- Auction begin date
- Auction end date
- Approximate height
- Approximate length
- Approximate width
- Approximate weight

Beneath this information, the user should see a table containing all of the active bids. We want to help bidders understand what it will take to make a winning bid. This table should display the following information:

- The offer in U.S. dollars
- The number of items the bidder requested
- The comment made by the bidder

To allow bidders to place bids, the page must contain a link or button allowing a user to place a bid. Users may also want to return to the previous page to keep looking at the items. This link must bring them back to the same category view that they came from.

## Logging In

When bidders want to place a bid, we need to verify their identity. Before they bid they need to log in using their email address and password. If the password/email combination matches, we will ask them to place a bid. Otherwise, they should stay on the login page. That page should display a message stating that they entered an invalid password/email combination.

## Placing a Bid

Once we know who the bidder is, we will allow him or her to place a bid. To help the bidder remember what they are bidding on and help them make a good offer, the bid screen should display the following information about the item:

- Name
- Description
- Quantity available
- Reserve price

We also need to get some information from the bidders. In particular, they have to provide the following information:

- Bid quantity
- The actual offer
- Credit card details (card type, number, and expiration date)
- Comment

The bidder must supply the quantity, offer, and credit card details. The credit card expiration date must be for some time after the current month. When accepting the quantity, verify that the value lies between one and the quantity available. Finally, make sure that the bidder's offer exceeds the reserve price. If any of these conditions are not met, inform the user.

## Placing the Bid

When placing a bid, we have quite a few items to check out. We want to make sure that all the items in the lot are spoken for before people start getting notices that they have just lost their bid. When a bidder puts in an offer, the system performs a number of checks. If the quantity without bids is less than or equal to the number requested, save the bid. In cases in which the amount requested exceeds the amount of product without a bid, get a list of the existing bids in ascending offer order. If enough items exist for which the offer price for each item is less than the price for the bid we are trying to save, we will remove items from the lower valued bids until we have enough products to satisfy the current offer. Otherwise, we will tell the bidder that we cannot satisfy his or her bid. If any lower valued bid is reduced to zero items, delete the bid from the database. The system should send an email message to any bidders whose offers are reduced or deleted.

# Summary

I wrote the previous requirements primarily through use cases. Although UML and other software engineering disciplines often require a number of pictures and greater detail when creating a design and set of use cases, your typical proof of concept starts out as something like the previous document. These requirements give the impression that someone has an idea and documents what it looks like. Once the proof of concept is complete, the group can go back and figure out what the rest of the system should look like. The only time I have ever received more detail in an initial requirements document was when the creators of the document had built such a system in the past. I actually like the vague documents. It gives me an opportunity to dig into the problem and understand what I am trying to do. It also forces me to understand the rules behind the system I am trying to design. Business people like this situation because a software engineer can typically learn the problem domain faster than the project sponsors can learn how to program.

With these admittedly vague requirements, we should still be able to build the proof of concept for the auction system. It will not be a fully functional, business-ready system. We will see that SOAP is a viable technology for cross-process, cross-machine communication. The remaining chapters show the development of the system and highlight the SOAP-related features. The end of each chapter contains suggestions for things you can do to add on to the system and maybe bring it closer to being a finished product. This gives you something to play with and experiment on. I often learn best when adding a small feature instead of building a project from the ground up. I hope this approach works for you, too.

# Chapter 10

# BIDDER ENROLLMENT

T his chapter looks at how I implemented the bidder enrollment subsystem. While going through this, I try to highlight any difficulties I ran into. One of the biggest benefits of a case study is that it highlights how to do something and shows where potential pitfalls lie. I show you where I did well and where I made any mistakes. This chapter focuses on one of the more interesting interoperability problems SOAP solves well. It focuses on allowing different languages, computers, and platforms talk to each other. For practicality, I developed everything on Windows 2000, got the Java parts running on Linux, and then cheered.[1]

This chapter covers the Java and Visual Basic environments. The Java piece only acts as a server component. It exposes the ability to add, modify, and delete customer data over SOAP. The VB environment consumes that service and exposes a few of its own.

---

[1] Some of you may have read some of my material at *http://msdn.microsoft.com/webservices*. Just so you know, Microsoft employees use alternative operating systems, too. Hey, how can you talk about interoperability if you never try something different?

243

# The Java Environment

I started out calling this part of the project the "UNIX" environment. After actually implementing everything, I realized that all the issues I ran into had little to do with UNIX and lots to do with Java. This is true for one reason: UNIX does not care about the CLASSPATH environment variable or how you access the database, but Java does. In this section, we look at the following items:

- Setup
- Coding
- Deployment
- Testing

# Setting Up the Java Environment

The Java environment, whether it is running on Linux or Windows, requires the following components:

1.  mySQL
2.  mySQL JDBC driver
3.  Apache SOAP v2.0
4.  Apache Tomcat
5.  JDK 1.3
6.  Xerces XML Java Library
7.  Java editor[2]

To set things up, just follow the instructions provided with the various packages. You can usually find these instructions in a README file. As long as you follow the instructions to the letter, everything will work out just fine. Still, you are bound to miss a couple of things. When I set up everything, I usually had no problems setting my CLASSPATH correctly. However, I did

---

[2] I used Java Forte CE (Community Edition) to edit the Java code. This editor was originally called NetBeans before Sun Microsystems, the creator of Java, purchased them.

make mistakes when setting up Tomcat. For starters, I always seem to forget to create an environment variable named `TOMCAT_HOME` and point it at Tomcat's home directory. The other item is setting the SOAP application path so that Tomcat can handle SOAP requests. It requires you to enter the following information in the `server.xml` file:

```
<Context path="/soap" docBase="C:\soap-2_2\webapps\soap"
  debug="1" reloadable="true">
</Context>
```

If you have even a little typo in this statement, you will see your SOAP calls mysteriously fail. I spent an evening tracking down why my SOAP messages would not get through before discovering this was the problem.

For those of you not used to common Java setup issues, here is another one: You need to make sure that your `CLASSPATH` environment variable is also set up correctly. You will need the following items in your `CLASSPATH`:

- Full path to `xerces.jar`
- Full path to `soap.jar`
- Base path to the mySQL JDBC driver
- Path to where the Java code for the sample application will go

My `CLASSPATH` contains the following directories (all separated by semi-colons):

- `C:\xerces-1_2_3\xerces.jar`
- `C:\soap-2_2\lib\soap.jar`
- `C:\mysql\jdbc2\mm.mysql.jdbc-2.0pre5\`
- `C:\SOAP\CaseStudy\auctionUNIXInterface\`

Once all this is in place, you should be ready to use SOAP with Java.[3]

## Coding the Java Data Access Layer

This piece of the system exposes the customer database to SOAP-capable clients. The system contains objects with the same names, properties, and relationships as the tables they link to (Figure 9–1). The classes all use the get/set JavaBean pattern. As we see in the next section, this makes deployment of the objects a lot easier. The primary Java objects are:

---

[3] You can download this from the XML Apache home page: *http://xml.apache.org*.

Database Connection Using JDBC

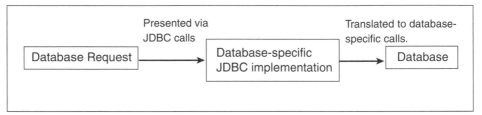

Database Connection Using JDBC-to-ODBC Bridge

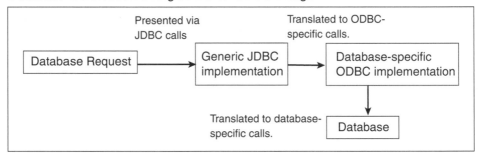

**Figure 10-1**   Database intermediaries.

- `Address`
- `Customer`
- `PhoneNumber`
- `CustomerSOAP`

The first three objects, `Address`, `Customer`, and `PhoneNumber`, all handle database interaction. All of these objects can load, save, and delete a record. The `Customer` object is responsible for deleting any related `PhoneNumber` and `Address` records. Besides these classes, we have one class, `util`, which knows how to get a database connection as well as the last ID added to the database.

Java talks to databases using JDBC. Java is distributed with a JDBC-to-Open Database Connectivity (ODBC) bridge. Database vendors can also create JDBC-specific implementations. What does JDBC do? To understand that, you have to understand how you would talk to a database if something like ODBC or JDBC did not exist. Most databases ship with a library that allows clients to directly access the database. Often, this library provides the fastest way to talk to a database but forces the customer to spend a lot of time simply discovering how to talk to a specific database. ODBC solved this problem by defining a standard interface that vendors had to implement to claim

ODBC compliance. Customers then spend their time learning how to talk to ODBC and pick the database on factors other than "I know this one's library already." Java did the same thing for databases when it introduced JDBC. A direct JDBC connection will often be faster than a JDBC-to-ODBC connection. The reason is fairly simple: The number of interfaces the connection needs to go through goes up by 50% when using the ODBC bridge from Java (illustrated in Figure 10–1).[4] When our objects talk to the database, they use a direct JDBC connection. A class named `util` owns the code that opens the database.

```
/**GetDefaultConnection
  Desc.: Returns a SQL connection to the
    caller. It only initializes the JDBC driver
    once during the application.
*/
public Connection GetDefaultConnection() throws Exception
{
  Connection retval;
  // Only load the MySQL driver into the driver manager
  // once.
  if ( !m_driverLoaded )
  {
    Object obj;

    // Instantiate the class by its name. It registers itself
    // with the driver manager.
    obj = Class.forName("org.gjt.mm.mysql.Driver").newInstance();
    if ( obj != null )
    {
      m_driverLoaded = true;
    }
  }

  // When this leaves proof of concept stage, load this
  // from a configuration
  // file.
  retval = DriverManager.getConnection(
    "jdbc:mysql://localhost/CustomerDB/?user=dbuser" );
  return retval;
}
```

---

[4] Please don't just count boxes and say "Your math stinks." I did not count the originating request as an interface the request needs to go through. I also did not include things like "What if the JDBC connection uses Remote Method Invocation (RMI) or SOAP?" What happens in those situations? The number of interfaces goes up and the overall impact of ODBC goes down.

I know this has little to do with the world of SOAP, but surprisingly little of using Java as a server has to do with SOAP. That is a big bonus for those of you who want to deploy existing code to the Web. As we see later in the chapter, this also applies to existing COM objects. I will take advantage of this and spend a little more time going over a piece of code I had a bit of difficulty figuring out.

When generating unique IDs, you can do a few different things. You can use Globally Unique Identifier (GUID) as the row ID. Although this approach gives us the ability to produce a large number of unique keys, it impedes a developer's ability to debug. If you have ever tried to visually match one of these 128-bit hex numbers, you know what I am talking about. Another approach I have used is to create a table with the sole purpose of holding a unique number to use as the ID. The table will hold one column or row per table that requires an ID. When adding a row, a program will lock the table, read the ID, increment it, and write the incremented number back to the database. This can make inserting records a little slow. Fortunately, this last solution has been implemented so many times that database vendors have added this feature, often called auto-increment, to databases, including mySQL. To use the feature, create an integer field as the primary key and mark it as `auto_increment`. For example, the `phoneNumber` table gets created with the following SQL statement:

```
CREATE TABLE phoneNumber
        (ID int(4) AUTO_INCREMENT PRIMARY KEY NOT NULL,
                areaCode varchar(10) NOT NULL,
                prefix varchar(10) NOT NULL,
                suffix varchar(20) NOT NULL);
```

When using an `auto_increment` field, do not specify the value of the field when doing an insert. On most databases, doing this will cause the insert to fail. This brings up another issue: getting the value of the newly inserted row. After all, you will want to link to it at some point in time. With mySQL, you can do it with the following lines of code:

```
/** GetLastInsertedID
  Desc.: Returns the ID of the last ID created on the Statement
    using an auto_increment field.
  Input:
    stmt: Statement object used to execute an insert (if it wasn't, you
      will get a zero back).
    tableName: Name of the table the insert was performed on.
  Returns:
```

```
      Number of the last recorded insert using the statement
      on the named table.
*/
public int GetLastInsertedID( Statement stmt, String
  tableName )
  throws Exception
{
  int retval = -1;
  ResultSet resultSet = stmt.executeQuery(
    "SELECT LAST_INSERT_ID() AS lid FROM " + tableName );

  // Move to first (and last) record in the resultset.
  resultSet.next();
  retval = resultSet.getInt( "lid" );
  resultSet.close();

  return retval;
}
```

How does this get used? Given that all of the code for the objects looks
more or less the same, I decided to take the shortest of the object save methods as an example. It shows how the two previous methods get used and how
easy it is to use JDBC within a Java program.

```
public boolean save() throws Exception
{
  boolean retval = true;
  boolean isInsert = false;
  util ut = new util();

  Connection conn = ut.GetDefaultConnection();
  if ( null != conn )
  {
    Statement stmt = conn.createStatement();
    String sql;
    if ( m_ID < 1 )
    {
      // Phone number hasn't been saved yet. Do an insert.
      sql = "INSERT INTO phoneNumber (areaCode, prefix, "+
        " suffix )" +
        " VALUES ('" + m_areaCode + "','" + m_prefix +
        "','" +
        m_suffix + "')";
      isInsert = true;
    }
```

```
    else
    {
      // Phone number has been saved. Do an update.
      sql = "UPDATE phoneNumber SET areaCode='" + m_areaCode +
        "', prefix='" + m_prefix +
        "', suffix='" + m_suffix + "' WHERE ID=" + m_ID;
    }
    stmt.executeUpdate( sql );
    if ( isInsert )
    {
      m_ID = ut.GetLastInsertedID( stmt, "phoneNumber" );
    }
    retval = true;
    stmt.close();
    conn.close();
  }
  return retval;
}
```

That looks like enough of the behind-the-scenes code. By now, you should have a good feel for the data access layer. The objects themselves are presented through a special interface: `CustomerSOAP`.

## *Writing a SOAP Interface*

No specifications exist for maintaining object references across SOAP boundaries. That does not mean that some specification will never be layered on top of SOAP. It just means that you should shoot for a stateless interface when exposing your objects to the Web. While working on the Java interface, I occasionally ran into problems when trying to connect to Tomcat. Here are just a few of the things I ran into:

- On startup, Tomcat may take a little time to respond. Retries seem to fix that.

- When changing the interface, often you need to redeploy the application. Restarting the server never hurts either.
  Whenever I did change an interface, I always had to stop and start Tomcat to make sure that the changes were accepted and available.

- With the SOAP 2.2 release, it is easier to write a deployment file than to use the Tomcat HTML interface. The HTML interface does allow you to deploy and remove interfaces. This tool loses its utility when the item being deployed becomes mildly complex. I noticed that once I had something mildly substantial deployed, I would forget or misspell the critical details. After doing that twice, I wrote a deployment file.

To handle the first issue, I recommend writing a simple "Hello World" type interface. You do not necessarily have to make this a part of your final deployment interface, but you will want it available for test time. CustomerSOAP calls this test function testConnection.

```
public String testConnection()
{
  String retval = new String();
  retval = "Connection is active";
  return retval;
}
```

The Java part of the system can store, retrieve, and delete basic customer data. The system needs to be able to look up a customer by ID or by email address. A caller can only delete a customer if it knows the correct ID. Because the system is stateless, I decided that saving a customer meant saving everything—address, phone numbers, the whole lot. The CustomerSOAP::saveCustomer method is one of the more interesting methods from a "just how much does the environment do for you" perspective. Why? With minimal effort, Apache SOAP will automatically serialize and deserialize your objects. CustomerSOAP::saveCustomer takes a Customer object as a parameter.

```
public int saveCustomer( Customer theCustomer ) throws Exception
{
  int retval = 0;

  if ( theCustomer.getID() == 0 )
  {
    Customer temp = lookupByEmailAddress(
      theCustomer.getEmailAddress() );

    // If this customer already exists, simply set the ID
    // to that of the existing one and save the changes.
    if ( temp.getID() > 0 )
    {
```

```
        theCustomer.setID( temp.getID() );
      }
   }
   if ( theCustomer.save() )
   {
      retval = theCustomer.getID();
   }
   return retval;
}
```

Maybe you expect this to just work over the network because you have
seen a lot of other really good Java code or you are familiar with RMI. After
implementing the SOAP engine found in Chapter 4, I thought it was very
cool that the Java environment made it so easy for the objects to go from one
form to the other and back again. This all happens thanks to a class named
BeanSerializer, from the org.apache.soap.encoding.soapenc
package. As long as you provide a bunch of get/set method pairs, you can send
basic objects and objects composed of objects with almost no effort. You do
need to map each object you intend to send to an entity that knows how to
serialize and deserialize that named object. This is the deployment file I used
for the Web service in the case study.

```
<isd:service xmlns:isd="http://xml.apache.org/xml-soap/deployment"
   id="urn:scottseely.com:CustomerSOAP">
   <isd:provider type="java"
      scope="Application"
      methods="lookupByID lookupByEmailAddress saveCustomer
         deleteCustomerByID testConnection">
      <isd:java class="com.scottseely.auction.CustomerSOAP"
         static="false"/>
   </isd:provider>
   <isd:mappings>
      <isd:map encodingStyle="http://schemas.xmlsoap.org/soap/encoding/"
         xmlns:x="urn:scottseely.com:CustomerSOAP" qname="x:customer"
         javaType="com.scottseely.auction.Customer"
         java2XMLClassName=
            "org.apache.soap.encoding.soapenc.BeanSerializer"
         xml2JavaClassName=
            "org.apache.soap.encoding.soapenc.BeanSerializer"/>
      <isd:map encodingStyle="http://schemas.xmlsoap.org/soap/encoding/"
         xmlns:x="urn:scottseely.com:CustomerSOAP" qname="x:address"
         javaType="com.scottseely.auction.Address"
         java2XMLClassName=
            "org.apache.soap.encoding.soapenc.BeanSerializer"
```

```
        xml2JavaClassName=
          "org.apache.soap.encoding.soapenc.BeanSerializer"/>
      <isd:map encodingStyle="http://schemas.xmlsoap.org/soap/encoding/"
        xmlns:x="urn:scottseely.com:CustomerSOAP" qname="x:phoneNumber"
        javaType="com.scottseely.auction.PhoneNumber"
        java2XMLClassName=
          "org.apache.soap.encoding.soapenc.BeanSerializer"
        xml2JavaClassName=
          "org.apache.soap.encoding.soapenc.BeanSerializer"/>
    </isd.mappings>
  </isd:service>
```

When deploying a Web service, you must identify the service with an iden-tifier that is unique on the Tomcat server. This appears as the ID attribute in the isd:service element. The next element, isd:provider, indicates the methods exported by the particular language (in our case, Java).[5] The final items in the XML document convey the following pieces of information:

- XML namespace for the object. This typically matches the URI provided in the isd:service id attribute.
- The name of the element when present in the SOAP Body.
- The name of the Java class to create or read from when receiving or sending the class.
- The name of the class that can convert the class from Java to XML.
- The name of the class that can convert the class from XML to Java.

To get an idea of the power here, let's take a look at the return value from a call to CustomerSOAP::lookupByID. The only code I wrote looks like this:

```
public Customer lookupByID( int theID ) throws Exception
{
  Customer retval = new Customer();
  retval.load( theID );
  return retval;
}
```

---

[5] This element indicates the intention of the Apache SOAP package: to support more languages than just Java.

This generates the following call and return value:

*Call*

```
<SOAP-ENV:Envelope
  xmlns:SOAP-ENV="http://schemas.xmlsoap.org/soap/envelope/"
  xmlns:xsi="http://www.w3.org/1999/XMLSchema-instance"
  xmlns:xsd="http://www.w3.org/1999/XMLSchema"
  xmlns:csoap="urn:scottseely.com:CustomerSOAP">
  <SOAP-ENV:Body>
    <ns1:lookupByID
      xmlns:ns1="urn:scottseely.com:CustomerSOAP"
      SOAP-ENV:encodingStyle=
        "http://schemas.xmlsoap.org/soap/encoding/">
      <theID xsi:type="xsd:int">1</theID>
    </ns1:lookupByID>
  </SOAP-ENV:Body>
</SOAP-ENV:Envelope>
```

*Return Message*

```
<SOAP-ENV:Envelope
  xmlns:SOAP-ENV="http://schemas.xmlsoap.org/soap/envelope/"
  xmlns:xsi="http://www.w3.org/1999/XMLSchema-instance"
  xmlns:xsd="http://www.w3.org/1999/XMLSchema">
  <SOAP-ENV:Body>
    <ns1:lookupByIDResponse
      xmlns:ns1="urn:scottseely.com:CustomerSOAP"
      SOAP-ENV:encodingStyle=
        "http://schemas.xmlsoap.org/soap/encoding/">
      <return xsi:type="ns1:customer">
        <middleInitial
            xsi:type="xsd:string">C</middleInitial>
        <billingAddress xsi:type="ns1:address">
          <ID xsi:type="xsd:int">3</ID>
          <zipCode xsi:type="xsd:string">98000</zipCode>
          <addressLine2
            xsi:type="xsd:string">Suite 104</addressLine2>
          <addressLine1
            xsi:type="xsd:string">123 Main</addressLine1>
          <state xsi:type="xsd:string">WA</state>
          <city xsi:type="xsd:string">Anytown</city>
          <country xsi:type="xsd:string">USA</country>
        </billingAddress>
        <emailAddress
```

```
          xsi:type="xsd:string">scott@scottseely.com</emailAddress>
        <defaultShippingAddress xsi:type="ns1:address">
          <ID xsi:type="xsd:int">4</ID>
          <zipCode xsi:type="xsd:string">12345</zipCode>
          <addressLine2
            xsi:type="xsd:string">Office 102</addressLine2>
          <addressLine1
            xsi:type="xsd:string">321 Broadway</addressLine1>
          <state xsi:type="xsd:string">KN</state>
          <city xsi:type="xsd:string">Metropolis</city>
          <country xsi:type="xsd:string">England</country>
        </defaultShippingAddress>
        <homePhone xsi:type="ns1:phoneNumber">
          <ID xsi:type="xsd:int">6</ID>
          <areaCode xsi:type="xsd:string">414</areaCode>
          <prefix xsi:type="xsd:string">144</prefix>
          <suffix xsi:type="xsd:string">4141</suffix>
        </homePhone>
        <faxPhone xsi:type="ns1:phoneNumber">
          <ID xsi:type="xsd:int">5</ID>
          <areaCode xsi:type="xsd:string">231</areaCode>
          <prefix xsi:type="xsd:string">123</prefix>
          <suffix xsi:type="xsd:string">3321</suffix>
        </faxPhone>
        <businessPhone xsi:type="ns1:phoneNumber">
          <ID xsi:type="xsd:int">4</ID>
          <areaCode xsi:type="xsd:string">800</areaCode>
          <prefix xsi:type="xsd:string">008</prefix>
          <suffix xsi:type="xsd:string">8080</suffix>
        </businessPhone>
        <ID xsi:type="xsd:int">1</ID>
        <firstName xsi:type="xsd:string">Scott</firstName>
        <lastName xsi:type="xsd:string">Seely</lastName>
      </return>
    </ns1:lookupByIDResponse>
  </SOAP-ENV:Body>
</SOAP-ENV:Envelope>
```

Like I said, the fact that this works so easily is very cool. The Java code exposes a few more methods via SOAP.

- `boolean deleteCustomerByID( int theID )`: Given a customer ID, this method deletes that customer. If successful, the function returns `true`.

- `Customer lookupByEmailAddress( String emailAddress )`: Every email address accessible over the Internet is unique. This method allows lookups to happen using the email address instead of record ID.

- `int saveCustomer( Customer theCustomer )`: Takes a `Customer` record and saves it to the database. This method has a backup plan for saving unidentified customers that already exist in the database. If the `Customer` object comes in with the ID set to zero (unknown/not set), then this method does a quick check to make sure no one else is using that email address. If someone is, that record gets updated. Otherwise, an insert happens. Of course, if the record ID is set to a positive value, an update is assumed. The return value indicates the record ID of the just saved `Customer`.

- `String testConnection()`: Already discussed, but in case you skipped that part, this method simply returns "Connection is active."

# Securing Access to the Web Service

I agonized a bit about where to put this discussion. It is not necessarily a lengthy topic, but I figured that it should show up somewhere that would make security-minded folks get worried. I just got done explaining that the Java-based Web service allows an individual to delete a user simply by supplying a positive integer greater than zero. If alarm bells did not go off for you, do not worry. Some people simply think about security more than others. Before you get too worried, I want to state that I believe that the Java side of this could be deployed to a live site if done correctly.[6] The Java implementation exists to give the Windows folks, at our fictitious company, the ability to manage customer records on the Java side using SOAP. How would we make sure that the bad guys could not access our SOAP methods?

---

[6] Just so you do not get the wrong impression, I did deploy this live on a small network. I just did not secure it.

The first thing we would do is make sure that the UNIX machines sit behind a firewall of some sort that does not allow incoming connections from the public Internet. Next, we can install a router between the UNIX machines and the Windows machines. This router should only accept connections over port 8080 (the port that Tomcat uses) originating from the Windows machines. Finally, we need to make sure that the Windows code works correctly. Most likely, a set of tests verifying that what should happen does happen would suffice. I do not want to advocate paranoia of "the other team" for those of you that choose SOAP as an interoperability solution for internal products. You do need to remember that you can be a bit more lax with internal folks than external ones.

If you decided to deploy a service such as this one to the public Internet, you would want to change the methods a bit. At this level, you would want some way to authenticate the caller. Many ways exist to accomplish this task. You can use Secure Sockets Layer (SSL) certificates to verify the identity of callers (and they can do the same to verify your identity). Every SOAP call could require a username and password in addition to other required parameters (i.e., the ones that make sense in the context of the function). For another option, you could also use digest authentication in HTTP (RFC 2617). Through the use of hashed nonces, no passwords are sent, and only the users knowing the password used for the hash can access your documents. Finally, you could have the user log in first and then issue them a key good for a given time duration. That key would then accompany every SOAP call.[7]

You also need to do some things with respect to incoming parameters. If anything will allow a person to perform buffer overflows, check the size of the incoming arguments. As a result, I highly recommend using variable types (e.g., classes, built-in types, etc.) that do not depend on fixed-size buffers. You also want to perform sanity checks on string length. If someone is trying to break your system, they may also try memory overruns (string never ends). Crackers understand how to use and exploit buffer overflow attacks. After social engineering,[8] it is the next easiest way to break your system. What does a buffer overflow look like? Here's some C code that demonstrates the problem:

---

[7] When my team implemented the Server Side Favorites example for MSDN, this was the route we chose.

[8] *Social engineering* is the art of getting other people to divulge usernames and passwords, and getting others to run malicious programs, all by using deceit to gain access to their computers or accounts. The ILOVU virus is one example of a social engineering attack.

```
void overflowExample( char buffer[] )
{
  // For various reasons, we assume a buffer of length 3 characters makes
  // sense. (Total length is 3 characters + null terminator
  // = 4 characters.)

  char manipBuff[4];

  // Buffer overflow opportunity happens on next line, corrupting stack.
  strcpy( manipBuff, buffer );
  // not too sure what happens next
  ...More code to execute
  }
```

What should you do? One option is shown here, but many options exist.

```
void fixedOverflowExample( char buffer[] )
{
  char manipBuff[4];

  if ( strlen ( buffer ) < 4 )
  {
    // Tragedy averted.
    strcpy( manipBuff, buffer );
  }
  ...More code to execute
}
```

Assuming incoming parameters and the source of the inquiry check out, you also want to restrict access to your machine. In the happy land of development, we often develop code without any restrictions on what we can do to our own machines. Eventually, the product will go up against a security review of some kind. By that time you need to figure out how to keep the bad guys out. When exposing a service over the Web, you may want to consider placing a router on that connection that blocks all ports not explicitly required by your Web service. If the service accepts secure and open connections, that means opening up two ports on the router, probably 80 (HTTP) and 443 Secure Socket Layer (SSL). You can further restrict trespassers by only accepting connections from a small set of machines.

In all these cases, you should definitely involve any security people you have on hand. If you do not have any, try to make sure that your budget includes money for a security consultant who can audit your code and your deployed solution prior to publishing the availability of the Web service.

Things being what they are, the project budget may not allow for the addition of a security consultant. In this worst case, get a book and find out best practices for securing Web sites. The same general concepts apply to securing the machines the Web services run on.

Before continuing to look at how the Windows applications talk to the Java ones, I want to leave you with this thought: When you design your Web service, state who will use the service in the project requirements. Once that is known, assign someone on the team to figure out how secure the service needs to be. Many of you will only need to secure the machine, not the access to the service. If it functions as a revenue stream, you will need to make sure that only organizations and people who have paid for access get access. Because this book does not aim to explain how to make money with Web services, I return to the case study.

# The VB Environment

The VB side of things is not much different from the Java side. We have a data access layer that talks to MSDE. Another set of objects talks to the UNIX piece via SOAP. The top layer talks to the rest of the world by exposing a SOAP interface.

## Data Access Layer

The section of the application described by this chapter focuses on managing bidders, so, this section examines that part of the data access layer. The `AuctionPersist` component contains all the COM objects responsible for saving, loading, and deleting data from the MSDE database. The `Bidder` component handles bidder-related data. This layer uses ActiveX Data Objects (ADO) to talk to the database. Like the Java objects, the VB objects have the ability to save, load, and delete data. To give you a feel for what this code looks like, here is the `Bidder.Save` method:

```
Public Sub Save()
   Dim sql As String
   Dim aShared As New SharedObj

   ' Check if this bidder already exists in the database.
   If (aShared.GetCount("Bidder", "EmailAddress='" & _
```

```
      aShared.SafeSQLString(EmailAddress) & "'") > 0) Then
      ' Perform an update
      sql = "UPDATE Bidder SET ID=" & ID & ", Password='" & _
         aShared.SafeSQLString(Password) & _
         "', Status='" & aShared.SafeSQLString(Status) & _
         "' WHERE EmailAddress='" & _
         aShared.SafeSQLString(EmailAddress) & "'"
   Else
      ' Perform an insert
      sql = "INSERT INTO Bidder (ID, Password, Status, EmailAddress) " & _
         "VALUES (" & ID & ", '" & aShared.SafeSQLString(Password) & _
         "', '" & aShared.SafeSQLString(Status) & "', '" & _
         aShared.SafeSQLString(EmailAddress) & "')"
   End If

   aShared.ExecuteSQL sql, aShared.GetConnection

   Set aShared = Nothing
End Sub
```

Within the function, you may have noticed an object type called `SharedObj`. `SharedObj` acts as a container for several related SQL functions. Why would I use a class when I could have just as easily used a module? If I have a bunch of utility functions that share a common purpose, I put them in a class. If the utility functions do not have that much in common, I go with a module. What else is in the `SharedObj` class?

Its name implies what it is used for—it contains a bunch of shared code. The `GetCount` method gets the number of records that match some given criteria in the named table.

```
Public Function GetCount(ByVal tableName As String, _
   Optional ByVal whereClause As String = "") As Long
   Dim rs As ADODB.Recordset
   Dim sql As String

   GetCount = -1
   sql = "SELECT Count(*) as theCount FROM " & tableName
   If (Len(whereClause) > 0) Then
      sql = sql & " WHERE " & whereClause
   End If

   Set rs = ExecuteSQL(sql)
```

```
   If (Not rs.EOF) Then
      GetCount = rs("theCount")
   End If

   Set rs = Nothing
End Function
```

ExecuteSQL opens up the database connection if none is provided and returns the record set resulting from the call. All the SQL calls follow the same pattern: Construct an SQL statement, execute it, and examine the result. The code to execute the SQL statement always involves the following lines:

```
Public Function ExecuteSQL(ByRef sql As String, _
   Optional ByRef aConn As Connection = Nothing) As ADODB.Recordset

   Dim releaseConnection As Boolean

   releaseConnection = False
   If (aConn Is Nothing) Then
      Set aConn = GetConnection
      releaseConnection = True
   End If

   Set ExecuteSQL = New ADODB.Recordset
   Debug.Print sql
   ExecuteSQL.Open sql, aConn, adOpenDynamic, adLockOptimistic

   If (releaseConnection) Then
      Set aConn = Nothing
   End If
End Function
```

The function allows you to pass in an active connection if you need it for other activities. You would retain the active connection if you needed to do something such as get the last inserted ID.[9] GetConnection is the last function I want to look at in this class.

```
Public Function GetConnection() As ADODB.Connection
   Set GetConnection = New ADODB.Connection
   GetConnection.Open "File Name=" & GetAuctionUDLPath
End Function
```

---

[9] See the discussion on auto_increment in the Java section of this chapter.

The function `GetAuctionUDLPath` simply opens a UDL file stored in the same directory as the `AuctionPersist` Dynamic Link Library (DLL). Many of you may not have heard of UDL files—I know I did not hear of them until I started working for Microsoft.[10] When deploying applications, you typically want some way to update the database configuration when deploying it to different servers. To make it easy to store information regarding where your database is located, Microsoft uses UDL files, also known as Microsoft Data Link files. I prefer using these to using registry settings to store database log-in and location information. Using the registry, you wind up doing one of two things: educating users on how to edit the registry or writing some custom code to do this for them. UDL files get around this by providing a user interface for editing the file itself. As needed, just double click on the file from within Windows Explorer and change as needed. An education issue still exists, but this at least keeps the user out of the registry. The next example shows the contents of a UDL file on my machine. The last two lines in this sample are actually one line—the content would not fit on one book line:

```
[oledb]
; Everything after this line is an OLE DB initstring
Provider=SQLOLEDB.1;Password=thePW;Persist Security
Info=True;
   User ID=sa;Initial Catalog=Auction;Data Source=.
```

Figures 10–2 and 10–3 show the user interface for this file. Figure 10–2 shows the screen that allows you to pick the Ole DB provider. Ole DB is Microsoft's database connection technology. The fields on the Connection tab change depending on the Ole DB provider. In this case, the Ole DB provider is SQL Server. MSDE is just a size-constrained version of SQL Server allowing for databases up to two gigabytes. That is about all the interesting information on the data access layer. Let's move on to the part that talks to the Java SOAP provider.

## The VB-to-Java Connection

Between the time that I wrote the proposal for this book and the time I actually wrote this chapter, Microsoft released their SOAP Toolkit v2. Version 2 added a number of enhancements over Version 1. Version 1 started out life as an MSDN example. The MSDN Architecture team thought it would be a good way to show people how to support SOAP in their own applications. By

[10] Yes, they are aware that I use Linux and that I know how to write code using Java.

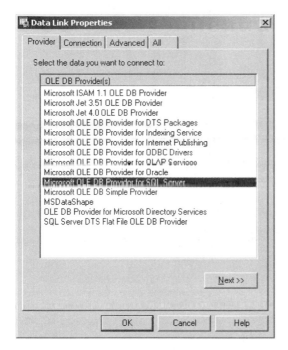

**Figure 10-2**   Ole DB provider selection screen.

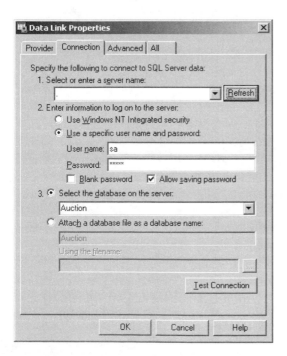

**Figure 10-3**   Connection setup for SQL Server/MSDE OLE DB provider.

the time April 2000 rolled around, this project had morphed into a toolkit. The toolkit received a lot of compliments and people started using it for real projects. During this same time, more SOAP toolkits appeared within Microsoft and elsewhere. Because of all the excitement, the COM version of the project was turned over to Microsoft's WebData group.[11] This group then went forward and made a more flexible, robust implementation of SOAP for the Microsoft platform. Version 1 saw its final release in December 2000. Version 2 debuted in beta on January 3, 2001.

Version 2 of the toolkit added a number of new features. The reason I chose it over Version 1 is that it supports WSDL instead of the proprietary Service Description Language (SDL). If a WSDL file exists, clients and servers can use that data to map calls to functions. For example, if the WSDL file specifies a function named `reverse` that takes a string and returns the string reversed, you can write VB code (or scripting code) that looks like this:

```
soapObj.mssoapinit "http://www.scottseely.com/someFile.wsdl"
reversedString = soapObj.reverse( "hello" )
```

To write the connector I had the following choices with the toolkit:

1.  I could write custom SOAP packets to the Apache Tomcat server.
2.  I could write my own WSDL file for use with the toolkit.

Because I knew that I would be giving examples of using the toolkit with WSDL examples, I decided that it would also be a good idea to show you how to build complex requests and read complex responses using the toolkit. You never know when you will need to talk to a SOAP server and have no access to a supporting WSDL file.

If no WSDL file exists, you can write a bunch of VB objects that understand how to read and write SOAP information. To do this, I wound up writing a mirror of the Java objects using VB. The `AuctionCustomer` COM library contains the following objects:

*   `Address`
*   `Customer`
*   `CustomerSOAP`
*   `PhoneNumber`

---

[11] As of this writing, independent implementations existed for .NET Web services, .NET remoting, ATL Server, BizTalk, and COM.

The library uses the Microsoft SOAP SDK v2 low-level API. The low-level API does not give you the niceties of the high-level one. Instead, this API allows you to compose and read SOAP messages at or just above the XML level.[12] This section shows how to read and write the return message shown in the Java Environment section of this chapter. To see how this works, let's trace the path of a customer record being saved and retrieved.

## Saving a Customer Record

When creating a customer, you need to set the customer's name as well as the following information:

- Shipping address
- Billing address
- Home phone number
- Work phone number
- Fax phone number

The previously mentioned VB classes (`Address`, `PhoneNumber`, etc.) all have a set of `get/let` methods that allow users of the classes to read and modify class properties. These classes also know how to read and write themselves to a SOAP message. As a result, the classes can take advantage of composition. The `Customer` class does not need to know how to read and write an `Address` or `PhoneNumber`—it just needs to know when to call on the other objects to do their thing. The methods that send and receive a customer object are `saveCustomer`, `lookupByID`, and `lookupByEmailAddress`. We will look at `saveCustomer` and `lookupByID`.

`saveCustomer` has a fairly simple implementation. It receives a `Customer`, sets up the SOAP call, serializes the `Customer`, and returns the `Customer ID`. This method does not worry about whether the customer is new or existing—that work is handled by the Java code. It looks like this:

```
Public Function saveCustomer(ByRef cust As Customer) As Long
    Dim theConnector As MSSOAPLib.SoapConnector
    Dim theSerializer As MSSOAPLib.SoapSerializer
    Dim reader As MSSOAPLib.SoapReader
    Dim numTries As Long
```

[12] The exact level of detail is open for debate. In the end, it all depends on your perspective. So, I choose to chicken out and sit on the fence.

```
Dim methodName As String

saveCustomer = False
methodName = "saveCustomer"

On Error GoTo alldone

' SOAP calls do not always go through on the first try.
' We'll try again if all else fails.
tryAgain:
    setupSOAPCall g_javaURL, g_NS, theConnector, theSerializer

    theSerializer.startElement methodName, _
        "urn:scottseely.com:CustomerSOAP", _
        "http://schemas.xmlsoap.org/soap/encoding/", "ns1"
    cust.Serialize theSerializer
    theSerializer.endElement
    theSerializer.endBody
    theSerializer.endEnvelope

    theConnector.EndMessage
    Set reader = New SoapReader

    reader.Load theConnector.OutputStream

    If Not reader.Fault Is Nothing Then
        saveCustomer = reader.faultstring.Text
    ElseIf Not (reader.Body Is Nothing) Then
        ' Update the ID
        cust.ID = CLng(reader.RPCResult.Text)
        saveCustomer = cust.ID
    End If

    Set reader = Nothing
    Set theConnector = Nothing
    Set theSerializer = Nothing
    Exit Function

alldone:
    If numTries < 15 Then
        numTries = numTries + 1
        ' Wait a little before trying again.
        Sleep g_SLEEP
        Resume tryAgain
    End If
```

```
   Set reader = Nothing
   Set theConnector = Nothing
   Set theSerializer = Nothing
End Function
```

The preceding code calls a function named `setupSOAPCall`. This function handles a bunch of code that I found myself typing in again and again. The code itself is specific to the Java server.

```
Public Sub setupSOAPCall(ByVal endPointURL As String, _
   ByVal theSoapAction As String, _
   ByRef theConnector As MSSOAPLib.SoapConnector, _
   ByRef theSerializer As MSSOAPLib.SoapSerializer, _
   Optional ByVal timeout As Long = 10)

   Set theConnector = New WinInetConnector
   Set theSerializer = New MSSOAPLib.SoapSerializer

   ' Set the destination of the message
   theConnector.Property("EndPointURL") = endPointURL
   theConnector.Connect Nothing
   theConnector.Property("SoapAction") = theSoapAction
   theConnector.Property("Timeout") = timeout

   ' Start the message
   theConnector.BeginMessage Nothing
   theSerializer.Init theConnector.InputStream
   theSerializer.startEnvelope , ""

   ' Setup the namespaces
   theSerializer.SoapNamespace "xsi", _
      "http://www.w3.org/1999/XMLSchema-instance"
   theSerializer.SoapNamespace "xsd", "http://www.w3.org/1999/XMLSchema"
   theSerializer.SoapNamespace "csoap", "urn:scottseely.com:CustomerSOAP"
   theSerializer.startBody ""

End Sub
```

In the function, you see a number of calls that set an empty string parameter. I started out by using a beta version of the Microsoft SOAP SDK v2 for this project and as a result, had to work around some issues. For example, the SDK takes a namespace name for a number of the elements you can insert. To have these insert nothing, I had to override the default value of an otherwise optional parameter. This should be resolved by the time that the toolkit is finally released. Other than that, you should just see a number of namespaces and the SOAP message itself being set up.

Another helper function in this COM library is addElement. I found that I was adding a lot of simple, individual elements to the SOAP message. Instead of writing the same four lines over and over again, I just wrote a simple function.

```
Public Sub addElement(ByRef theSerializer As_
  MSSOAPLib.SoapSerializer, _
  ByVal elemName As String, _
  ByVal theType As String, _
  ByVal value As String)

  theSerializer.startElement elemName, , ""
  theSerializer.SoapAttribute "type", , theType, "xsi"
  theSerializer.writeString value
  theSerializer.endElement
End Sub
```

Knowing all this, we can take a look at how we write out two parts of the message: the Customer and the related PhoneNumber records. Address serializes itself much the same as PhoneNumber, so we do not need to see it, too. All these objects have a method called Serialize. Customer's implementation looks like this:

```
Public Sub Serialize(ByRef theSerializer As MSSOAPLib.SoapSerializer)
  theSerializer.startElement "cust", , ""
  theSerializer.SoapAttribute "type", , "csoap:customer", "xsi"
  addElement theSerializer, "middleInitial", "xsd:string", middleInitial
  m_billingAddress.Serialize theSerializer
  addElement theSerializer, "emailAddress", "xsd:string", emailAddress
  m_defaultShippingAddress.Serialize theSerializer
  m_homePhone.Serialize theSerializer
  m_faxPhone.Serialize theSerializer
  m_businessPhone.Serialize theSerializer
  addElement theSerializer, "ID", "xsd:int", ID
  addElement theSerializer, "firstName", "xsd:string", firstName
  addElement theSerializer, "lastName", "xsd:string", lastName
  theSerializer.endElement
End Sub
```

Inside, you see calls to the various PhoneNumber and Address objects to serialize them as well. If the composition went deeper, you could continue serializing down through the layers. Here is how PhoneNumber serializes itself:

```
Public Const g_homePhone As String = "homePhone"
Public Const g_faxPhone As String = "faxPhone"
Public Const g_businessPhone As String = "businessPhone"

Public Sub Serialize(ByRef theSerializer As
MSSOAPLib.SoapSerializer)
  Dim elementName As String
  Select Case theType
    Case FAX
      elementName = g_faxPhone
    Case HOME
      elementName = g_homePhone
    Case BUSINESS
      elementName = g_businessPhone
  End Select
  theSerializer.startElement elementName, , ""
  theSerializer.SoapAttribute "type", , "csoap:phoneNumber", "xsi"
  addElement theSerializer, "ID", "xsd:int", ID
  addElement theSerializer, "areaCode", "xsd:string", areaCode
  addElement theSerializer, "prefix", "xsd:string", prefix
  addElement theSerializer, "suffix", "xsd:string", suffix
  theSerializer.endElement
End Sub
```

The enumeration containing FAX, HOME, and BUSINESS just states what type of phone number the object holds. To get the information from the SOAP message into the object, you just reverse the process. The reversal looks a lot different from the serialization. Again, all the objects have a common method, this time named Deserialize. The most complex decomposition happens in Customer because this object needs to know when to ask for help in deserializing.

```
Public Sub Deserialize(ByRef theNode As MSXML2.IXMLDOMElement)
  Dim aNode As Variant
  Dim i As Long
  Dim anotherNode As MSXML2.IXMLDOMElement
  Dim someNode As MSXML2.IXMLDOMNode
  Dim tempNode As MSXML2.IXMLDOMNode

  For Each aNode In theNode.childNodes
    Debug.Print aNode.baseName

    If (aNode.childNodes.length > 0) Then
      For i = 0 To aNode.childNodes.length - 1
        Set someNode = aNode.childNodes(i)
        If (someNode.childNodes.length = 1) Then
```

```
                         Set tempNode = someNode.childNodes(0)
                   End If

                   Select Case someNode.baseName
                     Case ""
                       ' Just to make the evaluation go quicker.
                       ' No short circuits in this world. :(
                     Case "middleInitial"
                       middleInitial = tempNode.nodeValue
                     Case "billingAddress"
                       m_billingAddress.Deserialize someNode
                     Case "emailAddress"
                       emailAddress = tempNode.nodeValue
                     Case "defaultShippingAddress"
                       m_defaultShippingAddress.Deserialize someNode
                     Case "homePhone"
                       m_homePhone.Deserialize someNode
                     Case "faxPhone"
                       m_faxPhone.Deserialize someNode
                     Case "businessPhone"
                       m_businessPhone.Deserialize someNode
                     Case "ID"
                       ID = tempNode.nodeValue
                     Case "firstName"
                       firstName = tempNode.nodeValue
                     Case "lastName"
                       lastName = tempNode.nodeValue
                   End Select
               Next i
           End If
       Next aNode

End Sub
```

The various `PhoneNumber` and `Address` members learn their type when
the `Customer` class gets initialized. This way, they always have the "right"
type all the time.

```
Private Sub Class_Initialize()
   m_businessPhone.theType = BUSINESS
   m_homePhone.theType = HOME
   m_faxPhone.theType = FAX
   m_billingAddress.theType = BILLING
   m_defaultShippingAddress.theType = SHIPPING
End Sub
```

Finally, here is how `PhoneNumber` transforms the XML in the SOAP message back into a VB object:

```
Public Sub Deserialize(ByRef theNode As MSXML2.IXMLDOMNode)
  Dim aNode As Variant
  Dim i As Long
  Dim anotherNode As MSXML2.IXMLDOMElement
  Dim someNode As MSXML2.IXMLDOMNode
  Dim tempNode As MSXML2.IXMLDOMNode

  For Each aNode In theNode.childNodes

    Select Case aNode.baseName
      Case ""
        ' Just to make the evaluation go quicker.
        ' No short circuits in this world. :(
      Case "ID"
        ID = aNode.nodeTypedValue
      Case "areaCode"
        areaCode = aNode.nodeTypedValue
      Case "prefix"
        prefix = aNode.nodeTypedValue
      Case "suffix"
        suffix = aNode.nodeTypedValue
    End Select
  Next aNode
End Sub
```

To see the rest of the code, just open up the `AuctionCustomer` project. If you do not own VB, you can view the files in any text editor. Let's finish up this phase by looking at the VB SOAP interface and how it is used in a few situations from the Web site.

## The VB Web Service

This Web service is exposed to the outside world. As a result, it needs to worry about things such as making sure that only authorized users are sending in requests. Most of the methods exposed by the service require the user's email address and a password. The two exceptions are when the bidder has forgotten his or her password or when the bidder wants to create a new account.

To help ensure some degree of security (limiting fake bids and the like), the service does not allow users to pick their first password. Instead, it generates a password for them. To understand how this looks, we look at the process of creating a new user starting at the top two layers of the application: the ASP page and the Web service. This Web service is described using WSDL and uses the high-level interface of the Microsoft SOAP SDK v2.

When coming into the Web site to add a new user, visitors first see the page shown in Figure 10–4. From this screen, the user can select "Create New User." This brings up the screen in Figure 10–5. The SOAP stuff starts happening when the user submits the request to the server. A page named updateCustomerData.asp actually processes the request. All of the pages that use SOAP include a page, loadWSDL.asp, that contains a function to initialize the SOAP connection and make sure that any external, essential SOAP connections are available.

```
Function soapInit( soapClient )
   Set soapClient = Nothing
   Set soapClient = Server.CreateObject( "MSSOAP.SoapClient" )
   On Error Resume Next

   ' Have this point to the location of the WSDL file on your machine.
```

**Figure 10–4**   Customer Account Management wecome page.

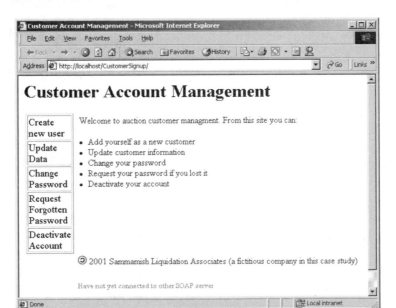

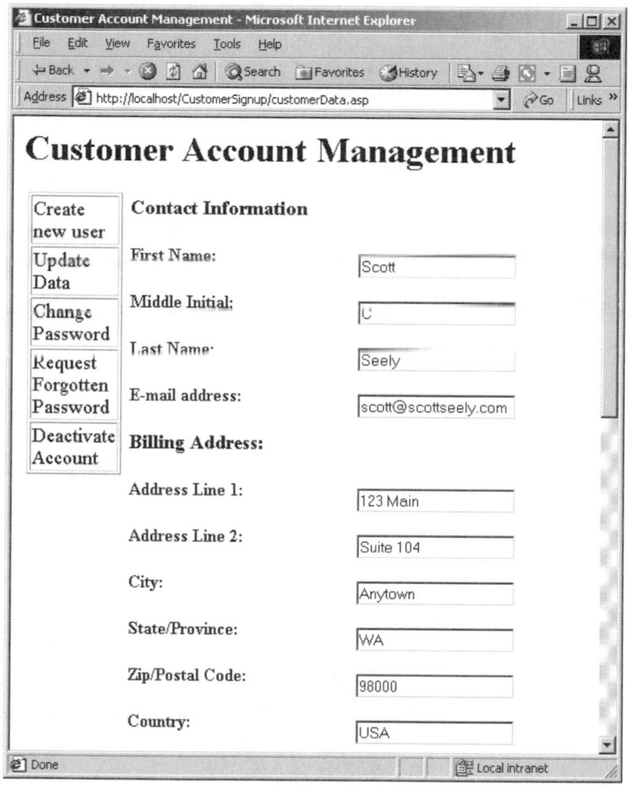

***Figure 10–5*** Create new customer page.

```
soapClient.mssoapinit _

  "G:\Inetpub\wwwroot\CustomerSignup\CustomerSignup.wsdl", _
  "CustomerSignup", "CustomerSignupPortType"

soapInit = True
If ( err.number <> 0 ) then
  If Not ( soapClient Is Nothing ) Then
    Response.Write "At least the soapClient inited.<br>"
  End If
  soapInit = False
  Response.Write err.number & "<BR>"
  Response.Write err.description & "<BR>"
ElseIf Application("Initialized") = False Then
  Application("Initialized") = _
      ( Len(soapClient.TestOtherConnections) > 0 )
End If

End Function
```

The `soapClient` variable comes in uninitialized and goes out referencing a fresh `MSSOAP.SoapClient` object. This function gets called before calling any other SOAP methods.

`updateCustomerData.asp` extracts all the information from the incoming HTTP request and then sends the request on to the SOAP object. It does this with the following function on the ASP:

```
Sub Main()
   Dim soapClient
   Dim firstName
   Dim middleInitial
   Dim lastName
   Dim emailAddress
   Dim homeAreaCode
   Dim homePrefix
   Dim homeSuffix
   Dim faxAreaCode
   Dim faxPrefix
   Dim faxSuffix
   Dim workAreaCode
   Dim workPrefix
   Dim workSuffix
   Dim billAddr1
   Dim billAddr2
   Dim billCity
   Dim billState
   Dim billZip
   Dim billCountry
   Dim shipAddr1
   Dim shipAddr2
   Dim shipCity
   Dim shipState
   Dim shipZip
   Dim shipCountry
   Dim bSuccess

   firstName = Request.Form("firstName")
   middleInitial = Request.Form("middleInitial")
   lastName = Request.Form("lastName")
   emailAddress = Request.Form("emailAddress")
   homeAreaCode = Request.Form("homeAreaCode")
   homePrefix = Request.Form("homePrefix")
   homeSuffix = Request.Form("homeSuffix")
   faxAreaCode = Request.Form("faxAreaCode")
   faxPrefix = Request.Form("faxPrefix")
   faxSuffix = Request.Form("faxSuffix")
```

```
workAreaCode = Request.Form("workAreaCode")
workPrefix = Request.Form("workPrefix")
workSuffix = Request.Form("workSuffix")
billAddr1 = Request.Form("billAddr1")
billAddr2 = Request.Form("billAddr2")
billCity = Request.Form("billCity")
billState = Request.Form("billState")
billZip = Request.Form("billZip")
billCountry = Request.Form("billCountry")
shipAddr1 = Request.Form("shipAddr1")
shipAddr2 = Request.Form("shipAddr2")
shipCity = Request.Form("shipCity")
shipState = Request.Form("shipState")
shipZip = Request.Form("shipZip")
shipCountry = Request.Form("shipCountry")


If ( soapInit( soapClient ) ) Then
  bSuccess = soapClient.CreateNewBidder( firstName, _
  middleInitial, lastName, emailAddress, homeAreaCode, _
  homePrefix, homeSuffix, faxAreaCode, faxPrefix, _
  faxSuffix, workAreaCode, workPrefix, workSuffix, _
  billAddr1, billAddr2, billCity, billState, _
  billZip, billCountry, shipAddr1, shipAddr2, _
  shipCity, shipState, shipZip, shipCountry )

  If ( Err.number <> 0 ) Then
    Response.Write "<BR>" & soapClient.faultstring
    bSuccess = False
  End If
  If ( bSuccess ) Then

    Response.Write "Successfully created a new bidder "&_
      "account " & _
      "for you. An e-mail message should be arriving "&_
      "shortly " & _
      "with your new password."
  Else
    Response.Write "Failed to create a new bidder account" & _
      "for " & _
      "you. You already have an account with us. You can" & _
      "get " & _
      "your existing password through the ""Request " & _
      "Forgotten " & _
      "Password"" option on the left."
  End If
End If
```

```
End Sub

' Actually do the work
Main
```

If the request fails, the code assumes that the call failed because another record with the same email address already exists. To do something more sophisticated, you would look at the fault*XXX* members of the soapClient instance. The preceding code calls into a function named Create NewBidder. CreateNewBidder is implemented in another VB COM library named auctionSOAP in the CustomerSignup object. The neat part about this function is that we have a Web service calling out to another Web service.

```
Public Function CreateNewBidder( _
  ByVal firstName As String, ByVal middleInitial As String, _
  ByVal lastName As String, ByVal emailAddress As String, _
  ByVal homeAreaCode As String, ByVal homePrefix As String, _
  ByVal homeSuffix As String, ByVal faxAreaCode As String, _
  ByVal faxPrefix As String, ByVal faxSuffix As String, _
  ByVal workAreaCode As String, ByVal workPrefix As String, _
  ByVal workSuffix As String, ByVal billAddressLine1 As String, _
  ByVal billAddressLine2 As String, ByVal billCity As String, _
  ByVal billState As String, ByVal billZipCode As String, _
  ByVal billCountry As String, ByVal shipAddressLine1 As String, _
  ByVal shipAddressLine2 As String, ByVal shipCity As String, _
  ByVal shipState As String, ByVal shipZipCode As String, _
  ByVal shipCountry As String) As Boolean

  CreateNewBidder = False

  Dim theCustomer As New AuctionCustomer.Customer
  Dim theSOAPObj As AuctionCustomer.CustomerSOAP
  Dim theBidder As New AuctionPersist.Bidder
  Dim newID As Long
  Dim theBody As String

  On Error Resume Next
  CreateNewBidder = False

  Err.Clear
  theBidder.Load emailAddress

  On Error GoTo 0
```

```
If (Len(theBidder.emailAddress) > 0) Then
   ' If we are creating, this user should not exist. Since it does,
   ' we failed. Return false.
   Exit Function
End If

' Fill in theCustomer
With theCustomer
   .firstName = firstName
   .middleInitial = middleInitial
   .lastName = lastName
   .emailAddress = emailAddress
   .ID = 0
End With

With theCustomer.homePhone
   .areaCode = homeAreaCode
   .prefix = homePrefix
   .suffix = homeSuffix
End With

With theCustomer.faxPhone
   .areaCode = faxAreaCode
   .prefix = faxPrefix
   .suffix = faxSuffix
End With

With theCustomer.businessPhone
   .areaCode = workAreaCode
   .prefix = workPrefix
   .suffix = workSuffix
End With

With theCustomer.billingAddress
   .addressLine1 = billAddressLine1
   .addressLine2 = billAddressLine2
   .city = billCity
   .state = billState
   .zipCode = billZipCode
   .country = billCountry
End With

With theCustomer.defaultShippingAddress
   .addressLine1 = shipAddressLine1
   .addressLine2 = shipAddressLine2
   .city = shipCity
   .state = shipState
```

```
     .zipCode = shipZipCode
     .country = shipCountry
  End With

  ' Instantiate the COM object that talks to the Java stuff.
  Set theSOAPObj = New AuctionCustomer.CustomerSOAP
  newID = theSOAPObj.saveCustomer(theCustomer)

  If (newID > 0) Then
     ' If the customer was successfully saved, we get its ID back.
     ' Save the new bidder
     Set theBidder = New AuctionPersist.Bidder
     With theBidder
       .emailAddress = theCustomer.emailAddress
       .ID = newID
       .Status = g_ACTIVE
       .password = generatePassword(10)

       .Save
       theBody = theCustomer.firstName & " " & theCustomer.lastName _
          & vbCrLf & "Your account has been created. " & _
          "Your new password is: " & .password
       sendEmail .emailAddress, theBody
     End With
     CreateNewBidder = True
  End If
  Set theSOAPObj = Nothing
End Function
```

One thing that may have just occurred to you is that this level does care about the fact that we are creating a new customer. Why? Well, we do not want to overwrite an existing record if someone tries to obliterate an existing record or update the customer's data. When a record is being created, we want a brand new customer ID. If a record is being updated, we want to reuse the same customer ID. We also want to authenticate the individual who is updating the data.

We also want to authenticate the user when he or she wants to change a password. Users will have a hard time remembering the one generated by generatePassword, a function that generates random passwords of a requested length. Figure 10–6 shows the Change Password ASP. If the email address and old password match, the old password is changed to the new one. Again, this is a simple task:

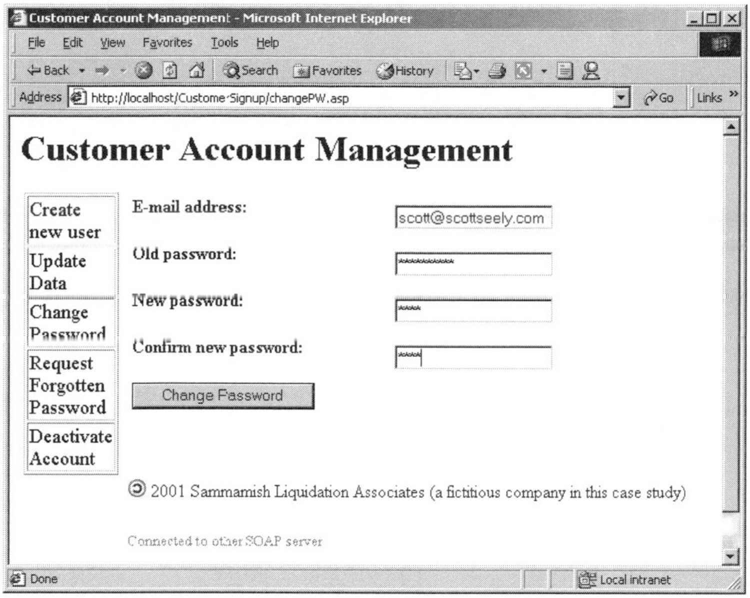

**Figure 10–6**  Change password page.

```
Public Function ChangePassword(ByVal emailAddress As String, _
  ByVal oldPassword As String, _
  ByVal newPassword As String) As Boolean

  Dim theCust As AuctionCustomer.Customer
  Dim theBidder As New AuctionPersist.Bidder
  Dim theBody As String
  ChangePassword = False

  On Error Resume Next
  With theBidder
    .Load emailAddress
    If (Err.Number <> 0) Or (.password <> oldPassword) Then
      ' We can't update a bidder whose password did not match or who
      ' does not exist.
      Exit Function
    End If

    .password = newPassword
    .Save
```

```
    theBody = "Your password was successfully changed to " & .password _
        & ". If this was done without your knowledge, contact us " & _
        "immediately."
    sendEmail .emailAddress, theBody
    ChangePassword = True
End With

End Function
```

The other functionality is handled in a similar fashion. We placed SOAP in between the ASP and the code that does the real work to help achieve some independence between the layers. This helps us get close to the ability to run virtually any auction where the Web services handle the business logic and the Web pages handle only the presentation logic.

# Summary

In this chapter we actually implemented the bidder enrollment subsystem. We got the Java and VB code to talk to each other using SOAP. The system also took a look at how to serialize and deserialize nontrivial objects if you have nothing to help you out. It's not the easiest thing you will ever have to do, it's also not one of the hardest.

If you want to extend this subsystem to make it ready for multiple auction sites and for this piece to only supply business logic, you should look at the following things:

1.  How do you differentiate users from different auctions? One solution might be to add an auction table and then identify users via auction ID, email address, and password.

2.  If you handle multiple auctions, should auction sites be allowed to log in on behalf of their users? If so, you will want to have the auction site log in on behalf of the user. You will also need to decide if auction sites have to authenticate themselves every hour and use a key for actions during that time or if they need to do a full authentication for every login.

3.  How will you audit usage? If you want to bill for the service, you will need to develop a way to figure out what went on when.

4.  Find some other features this piece might need to become a valuable service for those who want to run their own auctions. Now might be a good time to figure out how you would handle payment by check, credit card, or other means.

5.  Try writing a client for this service that uses something besides Microsoft's SOAP SDK v2.

I hope this list gives you some things to experiment with as you familiarize yourself with SOAP and the various tools out there. This should have shown you enough to feel comfortable with some of the more basic SOAP tools out there. The next chapter looks at this service from a seller's point of view. It also focuses on one of the newer technologies that has SOAP at its core: Microsoft's .NET computing environment. We see how different things can look when SOAP is a core enabling technology instead of an add-on.

# Chapter 11

# CATEGORY AND ITEM MANAGEMENT

The last chapter showed you how to use SOAP using two of the more popular tools from the first set of toolkits to appear. Between the two toolsets, Apache SOAP has the most to offer when it comes to sending complex objects over the wire. As I showed, you can send complex objects with either toolset, but Apache makes serialization a snap. After seeing how Apache works, I wondered if it could get any easier. My answer is a resounding "Yes." The easier way is to use .NET.[1] Unless you live under a rock, you should have heard of Microsoft's .NET initiative. .NET consists of a lot of components—servers,[2] operating system enhancements, and other items. Because so much of this seems like marketing speak and very little like a change in the way things are done, a lot of people have asked themselves if .NET is even real. It is real, very real. COM has evolved. The Java revolution took some ideas that lived in academia and proved that a number of them had commercial value. These ideas include the following:

- Garbage collection
- Reflection APIs (being able to extract metadata about the objects)
- Easy remoting of objects
- Virtual machines

[1] Pronounced "dot-net."

[2] Exchange, BizTalk, and SQL Server to name a few.

**283**

People wrote compilers that took various languages and compiled them into Java bytecodes.[3] It looks like Microsoft took a lot of these ideas and expanded on them. They borrowed from Java, Smalltalk, C++, and any other language they could find. In the end, they wound up with the next step in the evolution of COM. The part of .NET that embodies this change is the CLR. For SOAP developers, it makes Web service creation a snap. It will even create a WSDL file for you, complete with type information as well as SOAP and HTTP bindings.

The last chapter showed how you would expose existing COM objects via SOAP. It also showed how to act as a SOAP server for you Java developers out there. This chapter and the next one focus on what I feel is the best available SOAP development option. If you program for Windows, and at least 90% of all developers do, I recommend moving to .NET as soon as possible. Simply put, you can write network aware, distributed applications with very little effort.[4] Because of this, I focus on .NET for the rest of the case study. And yes, it all will run on one machine if needed. If you do not have a copy of Visual StudioNET, you should be able to run all of these examples using the .NET Framework SDK, available from *http://msdn.microsoft.com*.[5] Let's go back to SLA.

# General Implementation Rules

I took a look at how to segment the various pieces of the system and decided to put both the database access and the business logic into the Web service binary. This component's namespace is named `AuctionWS` for **A**uction **W**eb **S**ervice. I think that creating the customer management Web site as a separate virtual directory was a good idea. The other pieces in the system, category editor, item editor, and bidding system, should also be implemented as separate virtual directories off of the main Web site. This will enable the implementation of the various functions as separate but integrated applications.

---

[3] Bytecodes are understood by the virtual machine. As long as the virtual machine was ported correctly, the same compiled program should run the same regardless of operating system and processor.

[4] Yes, you can write stand-alone applications fairly easily, too.

[5] I can't give you the exact location on the Web site. Odds are pretty good that the location will change by the time you have this book in your hands.

# Category Management

Category management is a Web-based tool that will allow us to add, remove, and edit the auction categories. The view should allow users to see the complete category hierarchy. If the users click on a category name, it should bring them to a screen that will allow them to set the new category name and description. When the users submit a request, they should return to the main category view and see the new item as a subcategory of the category they originally clicked on. At this point in time, the page will not allow the user to drag and drop category subtrees between nodes of the tree. This might be a useful future enhancement.

This particular application should only be exposed to the intranet. In practice, a fairly small number of people in operations could add, edit, and remove categories. The virtual directory for this Web site will sit in the `CategoryEditor` virtual directory. The category editor is implemented by three separate elements:

1. The category data access component
2. The category Web service
3. The category editor

Let's see how the category editor was implemented.

## *Category Data Access*

All data access for manipulating categories happens in the `AuctionWS.Category` class. This class, like the other data access classes, defines all of the database column names and the table name in class constants. In the previous chapter, I put this information directly in the SQL queries. Both styles have their place. Putting the full SQL query in the text allows you to show the whole query at the expense of making column and table name typos easier to create. When building the query using named constants, readability can decline. So, what do you do to help increase readability? You could always do a `SELECT * FROM Table`, but the * can create maintenance issues when the table changes. You are usually better off when requesting the columns you want by name, even if you want all of them. I solve both problems by having each data access class define a constant named `ALL_FIELDS`. For the `Category` class, the constant declarations look like this:

```
public const string COL_ID = "ID";
public const string COL_NAME = "Name";
public const string COL_DESCRIPTION = "Description";
public const string COL_PARENT_CATEGORY = "ParentCategory";
public const string TABLE_NAME = "Category";
public const string ALL_FIELDS = COL_ID + ", " +
   COL_NAME + ", " + COL_DESCRIPTION + ", " +
   COL_PARENT_CATEGORY;
```

Using these variables, having the SQL load a given category by ID winds up being fairly readable:

```
public bool Load( long ID )
{
   string sql;
   Util util = new Util();
   DataSet dataSet;
   sql = "SELECT " + ALL_FIELDS + " FROM " + TABLE_NAME + " WHERE " +
      COL_ID + " = " + ID.ToString();
   dataSet = util.GetDataSet( sql );

   // We should only have one row with the given ID.
   // Fill it in.
   return Init( dataSet.Tables[0].Rows[0] );
}

public bool Init( DataRow aDataRow )
{
   bool retval = true;
   try
   {
     m_ID = Convert.ToInt32( aDataRow[COL_ID].ToString() );
     m_name = aDataRow[COL_NAME].ToString();
     m_description = aDataRow[COL_DESCRIPTION].ToString();
     m_parentCategoryID = Convert.ToInt32(
        aDataRow[COL_PARENT_CATEGORY].ToString() );
   }
   catch( Exception )
   {
     retval = false;
   }

   return retval;
}
```

You can be the judge on just how readable this code really is. The `Util` class used by this and other classes in the `AuctionWS` namespace contains some common code that provides some basic SQL functionality. The ADO.NET usage is extremely rudimentary in this case study and does not represent how to best use the technology. Rather, it shows how to get something working with the ADO.NET when you just want to get the code up and running. For example, this is the code in `Util` that returns the result of an SQL statement:

```
public DataSet GetDataSet( string sql )
{
  SqlDataAdapter sqlCommand;
  SqlConnection sqlConnection;
  DataSet dataSet = new DataSet();;
  sqlConnection = new SqlConnection(
    "server=localhost;uid=sa;pwd=;database=Auction");
  sqlConnection.Open();
  sqlCommand = new SqlDataAdapter( sql, sqlConnection );
  sqlCommand.Fill( dataSet );
  sqlConnection.Close();
  return dataSet;
}
```

I would advise against hard coding the database path in deployed applications. This works great for getting the prototype working. In production machines, you probably want your database and Web server running on separate machines. If nothing else, the separation makes it harder for crackers to get at your database.

When deleting a category, you do not want the delete to succeed when an `Item` references that `Category`. You can implement this rule via foreign key relationships and through checks within the database. The SQL creation script for the database does not implement the foreign key relationship. You can experiment with that and see what happens when you use it. For this implementation, we maintain the relationship only in code. You probably would want to handle the relationship in both locations. Checking for it in code works to avoid exceptions. Having the foreign key in the database would help catch bugs when new code or maintenance work stops making the checks.

We perform the delete via recursion. Why? If no items reference the current `Category` and all of its children can be deleted, then it can be deleted. This does mean that a delete can fail and still remove categories. It all depends on which categories are deleted first. You can prevent this behavior by using a transaction to wrap the entire action. `Category.Delete` looks like this:

```
public bool Delete()
{
  CategoryService itMng = new CategoryService();
  bool retval = true;
  Category[] categories = itMng.GetChildCategories( m_ID );
  foreach( Category category in categories )
  {
    if( !category.Delete() )
    {
      retval = false;
      break;
    }
  }

  // Now that all the child elements are gone, delete
  // myself
  if ( retval )
  {
    Util util = new Util();
    try
    {
      if ( util.GetCount( Item.TABLE_NAME, Item.COL_CATEGORY_ID
        + " = " + this.ID.ToString() ) < 1 )
      {
        // The category is not in use, so delete it.
        string sql = "DELETE FROM " + TABLE_NAME + " WHERE " + COL_ID
          + " = " + m_ID.ToString();
        util.GetDataSet( sql );
      }
      else
      {
        // This should prevent the cascading delete
        // from happening because this category is in use.
        retval = false;
      }
    }
    catch ( Exception e )
    {
      System.Console.WriteLine( e.Message );
      retval = false;
    }
  }
  return retval;
}
```

This function calls into the `CategoryService` Web Service to provide the immediate children of a given node. When called from the same library, all calls go straight through the CLR, completely avoiding SOAP. If you want to see more about how the data access layer is implemented, you can find the code in a file named `Category.cs`.

Before we leave this section, I want to touch on one of the nicer things C# did for instantiating getters and setters. Normally, you design `get` and `set` pairs for data access and hide all member variables from your public interface. This way, if a value ever becomes a derived value or needs extra data validation, you just change the way the accessor behaves, leaving users of the class unaffected. The biggest problem with this paradigm is the sheer number of ways different people like to do this. To see how C# handles this, let's take a look at how we set a `Category` name.

`Category` contains a private member variable named m_name. I named the accessor for this variable name. The code looks like this:

```
public string name
{
  get { return m_name; }
  set { m_name = value; }
}
```

Pretty simple, right? I expose the variable as a `string`, implement `get` and `set`, and I'm done. The name `value` is always set to the right hand side of an assignment. If I have the following code:

```
Category cat = new Category();
cat.name = "Some Category";
```

then `value` will be set to "Some Category" when in the `Category.name.set` operation. You will see `get` and `set` implemented this way for most of the code. We see how this benefits SOAP in the next section.

## Category Web Service

The category Web service exposes four methods via SOAP and HTTP:

1. **SaveCategory(Category cat):** Saves the given category to the database. Because the `Category` class knows how to differentiate between saved and unsaved categories, you only

need to call one function to do both. If you are updating an existing `Category`, make sure that the category ID is set before calling this method. When the ID is set to zero, the database component inserts a new record.

2. **`DeleteCategory(Category cat):`** Deletes the Category and its subcategories only if none of them are in use.

3. **`GetCategoryByID(long catID):`** Returns the Category with the given `catID`.

4. **`GetChildCategories(long parentCategoryID):`** Returns the immediate child categories whose parent is `parentCategoryID`.

`SaveCategory` and `DeleteCategory` simply call into the `Category` object.

```
[WebMethod]
public bool SaveCategory( Category cat )
{
   return cat.Save();
}

[WebMethod]
public bool DeleteCategory( Category cat )
{
   return cat.Delete();
}
```

The `WebMethod` attribute tells the compiler that these methods should expose themselves via SOAP. As you know, `Category` is a complex object. Until now, I have not discussed anything about how to serialize or deserialize a complex object with .NET. Unlike Java, where you have to specify a serialization mechanism, .NET makes things even easier. If you expose an object and it has public properties, .NET just serializes them for you. It also generates any WSDL files and proxy objects that you may need. `CategoryService` turns out to be a great place to discuss this: It has a few methods and only one complex datatype. The WSDL file for our service looks like this (for an exercise, see if you can decipher what all this means based on what you know about WSDL):

```
<?xml version="1.0"?>
<definitions xmlns:s="http://www.w3.org/2001/XMLSchema"
```

```
xmlns:http="http://schemas.xmlsoap.org/wsdl/http/"
xmlns:mime="http://schemas.xmlsoap.org/wsdl/mime/"
xmlns:urt="http://microsoft.com/urt/wsdl/text/"
xmlns:soap="http://schemas.xmlsoap.org/wsdl/soap/"
xmlns:soapenc="http://schemas.xmlsoap.org/soap/encoding/"
xmlns:s0="http://tempuri.org/"
targetNamespace="http://tempuri.org/"
xmlns="http://schemas.xmlsoap.org/wsdl/">
<types>
<s:schema attributeFormDefault="qualified" elementFormDefault="qualified"
   targetNamespace="http://tempuri.org/">
 <s:element name="GetChildCategories">
  <s:complexType>
   <s:sequence>
    <s:element name="parentCategoryID" type="s:long"/>
   </s:sequence>
  </s:complexType>
 </s:element>
 <s:complexType name="Category">
  <s:sequence>
   <s:element name="ID" type="s:long"/>
   <s:element name="parentCategoryID" type="s:long"/>
   <s:element name="name" nullable="true" type="s:string"/>
   <s:element name="description" nullable="true" type="s:string"/>
  </s:sequence>
 </s:complexType>
 <s:element name="GetChildCategoriesResponse">
  <s:complexType>
   <s:sequence>
    <s:element name="GetChildCategoriesResult" nullable="true">
     <s:complexType>
      <s:sequence>
       <s:element name="Category" nullable="true" type="s0:Category"
         minOccurs="0" maxOccurs="unbounded"/>
      </s:sequence>
     </s:complexType>
    </s:element>
   </s:sequence>
  </s:complexType>
 </s:element>
 <s:element name="SaveCategory">
  <s:complexType>
   <s:sequence>
    <s:element name="cat" nullable="true" type="s0:Category"/>
   </s:sequence>
  </s:complexType>
```

```
    </s:element>
    <s:element name="SaveCategoryResponse">
     <s:complexType>
      <s:sequence>
       <s:element name="SaveCategoryResult" type="s:boolean"/>
      </s:sequence>
     </s:complexType>
    </s:element>
    <s:element name="DeleteCategory">
     <s:complexType>
      <s:sequence>
       <s:element name="cat" nullable="true" type="s0:Category"/>
      </s:sequence>
     </s:complexType>
    </s:element>
    <s:element name="DeleteCategoryResponse">
     <s:complexType>
      <s:sequence>
       <s:element name="DeleteCategoryResult" type="s:boolean"/>
      </s:sequence>
     </s:complexType>
    </s:element>
    <s:element name="GetCategoryByID">
     <s:complexType>
      <s:sequence>
       <s:element name="catID" type="s:long"/>
      </s:sequence>
     </s:complexType>
    </s:element>
    <s:element name="GetCategoryByIDResponse">
     <s:complexType>
      <s:sequence>
       <s:element name="GetCategoryByIDResult"
         nullable="true" type="s0:Category"/>
      </s:sequence>
     </s:complexType>
    </s:element>
    <s:element name="ArrayOfCategory" nullable="true">
     <s:complexType>
      <s:sequence>
       <s:element name="Category" nullable="true"
         type="s0:Category" minOccurs="0" maxOccurs="unbounded"/>
      </s:sequence>
     </s:complexType>
    </s:element>
    <s:element name="Category" nullable="true" type="s0:Category"/>
```

```
      </s:schema>
    </types>
    <message name="GetChildCategoriesSoapIn">
      <part name="parameters" element="s0:GetChildCategories"/>
    </message>
    <message name="GetChildCategoriesSoapOut">
      <part name="parameters" element="s0:GetChildCategoriesResponse"/>
    </message>
    <message name="SaveCategorySoapIn">
      <part name="parameters" element="s0:SaveCategory"/>
    </message>
    <message name="SaveCategorySoapOut">
      <part name="parameters" element="s0:SaveCategoryResponse"/>
    </message>
    <message name="DeleteCategorySoapIn">
      <part name="parameters" element="s0:DeleteCategory"/>
    </message>
    <message name="DeleteCategorySoapOut">
      <part name="parameters" element="s0:DeleteCategoryResponse"/>
    </message>
    <message name="GetCategoryByIDSoapIn">
      <part name="parameters" element="s0:GetCategoryByID"/>
    </message>
    <message name="GetCategoryByIDSoapOut">
      <part name="parameters" element="s0:GetCategoryByIDResponse"/>
    </message>
    <message name="GetChildCategoriesHttpGetIn">
      <part name="parentCategoryID" type="s:string"/>
    </message>
    <message name="GetChildCategoriesHttpGetOut">
      <part name="Body" element="s0:ArrayOfCategory"/>
    </message>
    <message name="GetCategoryByIDHttpGetIn">
      <part name="catID" type="s:string"/>
    </message>
    <message name="GetCategoryByIDHttpGetOut">
      <part name="Body" element="s0:Category"/>
    </message>
    <message name="GetChildCategoriesHttpPostIn">
      <part name="parentCategoryID" type="s:string"/>
    </message>
    <message name="GetChildCategoriesHttpPostOut">
      <part name="Body" element="s0:ArrayOfCategory"/>
    </message>
    <message name="GetCategoryByIDHttpPostIn">
```

```
      <part name="catID" type="s:string"/>
    </message>
    <message name="GetCategoryByIDHttpPostOut">
     <part name="Body" element="s0:Category"/>
    </message>
    <portType name="CategoryServiceSoap">
     <operation name="GetChildCategories">
      <input message="s0:GetChildCategoriesSoapIn"/>
      <output message="s0:GetChildCategoriesSoapOut"/>
     </operation>
     <operation name="SaveCategory">
      <input message="s0:SaveCategorySoapIn"/>
      <output message="s0:SaveCategorySoapOut"/>
     </operation>
     <operation name="DeleteCategory">
      <input message="s0:DeleteCategorySoapIn"/>
      <output message="s0:DeleteCategorySoapOut"/>
     </operation>
     <operation name="GetCategoryByID">
      <input message="s0:GetCategoryByIDSoapIn"/>
      <output message="s0:GetCategoryByIDSoapOut"/>
     </operation>
    </portType>
    <portType name="CategoryServiceHttpGet">
     <operation name="GetChildCategories">
      <input message="s0:GetChildCategoriesHttpGetIn"/>
      <output message="s0:GetChildCategoriesHttpGetOut"/>
     </operation>
     <operation name="GetCategoryByID">
      <input message="s0:GetCategoryByIDHttpGetIn"/>
      <output message="s0:GetCategoryByIDHttpGetOut"/>
     </operation>
    </portType>
    <portType name="CategoryServiceHttpPost">
     <operation name="GetChildCategories">
      <input message="s0:GetChildCategoriesHttpPostIn"/>
      <output message="s0:GetChildCategoriesHttpPostOut"/>
     </operation>
     <operation name="GetCategoryByID">
      <input message="s0:GetCategoryByIDHttpPostIn"/>
      <output message="s0:GetCategoryByIDHttpPostOut"/>
     </operation>
    </portType>
    <binding name="CategoryServiceSoap"
   type="s0:CategoryServiceSoap">
```

```
<soap:binding transport="http://schemas.xmlsoap.org/soap/http"
   style="document"/>
<operation name="GetChildCategories">
 <soap:operation soapAction="http://tempuri.org/GetChildCategories"
   style="document"/>
 <input>
   <soap:body use="literal"/>
 </input>
 <output>
   <soap:body use="literal"/>
 </output>
</operation>
<operation name="SaveCategory">
 <soap:operation soapAction="http://tempuri.org/SaveCategory"
   style="document"/>
 <input>
   <soap:body use="literal"/>
 </input>
 <output>
   <soap:body use="literal"/>
 </output>
</operation>
<operation name="DeleteCategory">
 <soap:operation soapAction="http://tempuri.org/DeleteCategory"
   style="document"/>
 <input>
   <soap:body use="literal"/>
 </input>
 <output>
   <soap:body use="literal"/>
 </output>
</operation>
<operation name="GetCategoryByID">
 <soap:operation soapAction="http://tempuri.org/GetCategoryByID"
   style="document"/>
 <input>
   <soap:body use="literal"/>
 </input>
 <output>
   <soap:body use="literal"/>
 </output>
</operation>
</binding>
<binding name="CategoryServiceHttpGet" type="s0:CategoryServiceHttpGet">
 <http:binding verb="GET"/>
 <operation name="GetChildCategories">
```

```
  <http:operation location="/GetChildCategories"/>
  <input>
   <http:urlEncoded/>
  </input>
  <output>
   <mime:mimeXml part="Body"/>
  </output>
 </operation>
 <operation name="GetCategoryByID">
  <http:operation location="/GetCategoryByID"/>
  <input>
   <http:urlEncoded/>
  </input>
  <output>
   <mime:mimeXml part="Body"/>
  </output>
 </operation>
</binding>
<binding name="CategoryServiceHttpPost" type="s0:CategoryServiceHttpPost">
 <http:binding verb="POST"/>
 <operation name="GetChildCategories">
  <http:operation location="/GetChildCategories"/>
  <input>
   <mime:content type="application/x-www-form-urlencoded"/>
  </input>
  <output>
   <mime:mimeXml part="Body"/>
  </output>
 </operation>
 <operation name="GetCategoryByID">
  <http:operation location="/GetCategoryByID"/>
  <input>
   <mime:content type="application/x-www-form-urlencoded"/>
  </input>
  <output>
   <mime:mimeXml part="Body"/>
  </output>
 </operation>
</binding>
<service name="CategoryService">
 <port name="CategoryServiceSoap" binding="s0:CategoryServiceSoap">
  <soap:address location=
     "http://localhost/AuctionWS/CategoryService.asmx"/>
 </port>
 <port name="CategoryServiceHttpGet" binding="s0:CategoryServiceHttpGet">
  <http:address location=
```

```
      "http://localhost/AuctionWS/CategoryService.asmx"/>
  </port>
  <port name="CategoryServiceHttpPost" binding="s0:CategoryServiceHttpPost">
   <http:address location=
      "http://localhost/AuctionWS/CategoryService.asmx"/>
  </port>
 </service>
</definitions>
```

Yes, that is a lot of uncommented XML. It tells humans and machines exactly how to contact the service and what the interface looks like. Using this information, the WSDL.EXE utility in the .NET tools[6] generates the following proxy:

```
using System.Xml.Serialization;
using System;
using System.Web.Services.Protocols;
using System.Web.Services;


[System.Web.Services.WebServiceBindingAttribute(Name="CategoryServiceSoap",
  Namespace="http://tempuri.org/")]
public class CategoryService :
  System.Web.Services.Protocols.SoapHttpClientProtocol {

  public CategoryService() {
    this.Url = "http://localhost/AuctionWS/CategoryService.asmx";
  }

  [System.Web.Services.Protocols.SoapMethodAttribute(
    "http://tempuri.org/GetChildCategories",
    MessageStyle=System.Web.Services.Protocols.
      SoapMessageStyle.ParametersInDocument)]
  [return: System.Xml.Serialization.XmlArrayItemAttribute("Category",
    IsNullable=true)]
  public Category[] GetChildCategories(long parentItemManagementID) {
    object[] results = this.Invoke("GetChildCategories", new object[]
      {parentItemManagementID});
    return ((Category[])(results[0]));
  }

  public System.IAsyncResult BeginGetChildCategories(
    long parentItemManagementID,
```

---

[6] For those who hate command-line tools, this is exposed as a dialog in the Visual Studio IDE.

```
       System.AsyncCallback callback, object asyncState) {
       return this.BeginInvoke("GetChildCategories", new object[]
          {parentItemManagementID}, callback, asyncState);
    }

    public Category[] EndGetChildCategories(System.IAsyncResult asyncResult) {
       object[] results = this.EndInvoke(asyncResult);
       return ((Category[])(results[0]));
    }

    [System.Web.Services.Protocols.SoapMethodAttribute(
       "http://tempuri.org/SaveCategory", MessageStyle=System.Web.Services.
          Protocols.SoapMessageStyle.ParametersInDocument)]
    public bool SaveCategory(Category cat) {
       object[] results = this.Invoke("SaveCategory", new object[] {cat});
       return ((bool)(results[0]));
    }

    public System.IAsyncResult BeginSaveCategory(Category cat,
       System.AsyncCallback callback, object asyncState) {
       return this.BeginInvoke("SaveCategory", new object[]
          {cat}, callback, asyncState);
    }

    public bool EndSaveCategory(System.IAsyncResult asyncResult) {
       object[] results = this.EndInvoke(asyncResult);
       return ((bool)(results[0]));
    }

    [System.Web.Services.Protocols.SoapMethodAttribute(
       "http://tempuri.org/DeleteCategory",
       MessageStyle=System.Web.Services.Protocols.
          SoapMessageStyle.ParametersInDocument)]
    public bool DeleteCategory(Category cat) {
       object[] results = this.Invoke("DeleteCategory", new object[] {cat});
       return ((bool)(results[0]));
    }

    public System.IAsyncResult BeginDeleteCategory(Category cat,
       System.AsyncCallback callback, object asyncState) {
       return this.BeginInvoke("DeleteCategory",
          new object[] {cat}, callback, asyncState);
    }

    public bool EndDeleteCategory(System.IAsyncResult asyncResult) {
```

```
      object[] results = this.EndInvoke(asyncResult);
      return ((bool)(results[0]));
    }

    [System.Web.Services.Protocols.SoapMethodAttribute(
      "http://tempuri.org/GetCategoryByID",
      MessageStyle=System.Web.Services.Protocols.
        SoapMessageStyle.ParametersInDocument)]
    public Category GetCategoryByID(long catID) {
      object[] results = this.Invoke("GetCategoryByID",
        new object[] {catID});
      return ((Category)(results[0]));
    }

    public System.IAsyncResult BeginGetCategoryByID(long catID,
      System.AsyncCallback callback, object asyncState) {
      return this.BeginInvoke("GetCategoryByID",
        new object[] {catID}, callback, asyncState);
    }

    public Category EndGetCategoryByID(System.IAsyncResult asyncResult) {
      object[] results = this.EndInvoke(asyncResult);
      return ((Category)(results[0]));
    }
}

public class Category {

  public long ID;

  public long parentCategoryID;

  public string name;

  public string description;
}
```

This proxy was generated using the following command line:

```
wsdl http://localhost/AuctionWS/CategoryService.asmx?WSDL
```

Looking at that code and the proxy constructor, you might suppose that the proxy is bound to localhost. Nothing could be further from the truth! Assuming that you know the interface ahead of time and discover the location of the implementation via UDDI, a configuration file, or some other means, all you need to do is set the Url member variable prior to invoking any of the services exposed via the proxy. If the implementation exists on scottseely.com, I might set the URL to http://www.scottseely.com/ MyAuction/Category.asmx and the function would still work, assuming the site was up and running.

What does the SOAP look like when someone places a request? Let's see what they get when requesting the child items of the parent category.

Request

```xml
<?xml version="1.0" encoding="utf-8"?>
<soap:Envelope
   xmlns:soap="http://schemas.xmlsoap.org/soap/envelope/"
   xmlns:xsi="http://www.w3.org/2001/XMLSchema-instance"
   xmlns:xsd="http://www.w3.org/2001/XMLSchema">
  <soap:Body>
   <GetChildCategories xmlns="http://tempuri.org/">
     <parentItemManagementID>0</parentItemManagementID>
   </GetChildCategories>
  </soap:Body>
</soap:Envelope>
```

Response

```xml
<?xml version="1.0" encoding="utf-8"?>
<soap:Envelope
   xmlns:soap="http://schemas.xmlsoap.org/soap/envelope/"
   xmlns:xsi="http://www.w3.org/2000/10/XMLSchema-instance"
   xmlns:xsd="http://www.w3.org/2000/10/XMLSchema">
  <soap:Body>
   <GetChildCategoriesResponse xmlns="http://tempuri.org/">
    <GetChildCategoriesResult>
     <Category>
      <ID>12</ID>
      <parentCategoryID>0</parentCategoryID>
      <name>Home Appliances</name>
      <description>
        Stuff that you use in your kitchen or laundry room.
      </description>
     </Category>
     <Category>
      <ID>18</ID>
      <parentCategoryID>0</parentCategoryID>
```

```
      <name>Electronics</name>
      <description>TVs, stereos, and computers.</description>
    </Category>
    </GetChildCategoriesResult>
  </GetChildCategoriesResponse>
 </soap:Body>
</soap:Envelope>
```

In the preceding examples, you will have noticed that the URI `http://tempuri.org/` was used quite a bit. This URI is named in the WSDL 1.1 specification as a valid URI. You can use it when the WSDL file requires a temporary URI and that file will not contain references to other potentially conflicting objects. For example, you would not want to use this when mixing various street address type definitions. The namespaces would clash and create ambiguity in the WSDL, something a machine cannot handle.

This pretty much covers the SOAP side of things. We finish up by looking at how the Web interface uses all of this to communicate.

## Category Editor

The category view contains some basic HTML as well as a custom HTML control. The custom control displays the categories. Did I have to go this route? As we will see in Chapter 12, no I did not, but it does show some of the new things that ASP.NET has brought to Web page development. Without a doubt, the tools have become more sophisticated.

Figure 11–1 shows the category editor main page. The custom HTML control renders the content beneath "Categories." When someone says that a computer renders something, we mean that it draws it. For me, this usually brings up thoughts of executing code to draw lines and set pixels. When rendering to HTML, the drawing instructions are HTML tags and commands. The page that displays the content in Figure 11–1 is fairly short:

```
<%@ Page language="c#" Codebehind="default.aspx.cs"
  AutoEventWireup="false" Inherits="CategoryEditor.
    CategoryDisplay" %>
<%@ Register TagPrefix="Sammamish" Namespace="Sammamish"
  Assembly="CategoryEditor" %>

<HTML>
  <HEAD>
```

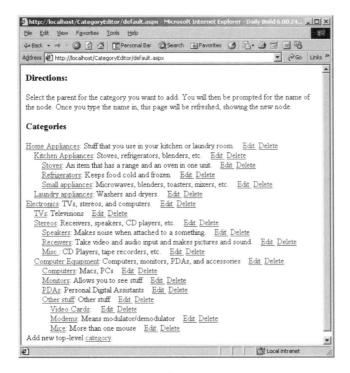

***Figure 11-1***   Catagory editor main page.

```
    <meta content="Internet Explorer 5.0" name=vs_targetSchema>
    <meta content="Microsoft Visual Studio 7.0" name=GENERATOR>
    <meta content=C# name=CODE_LANGUAGE>
    <meta http-equiv="EXPIRES" CONTENT="-1">
  </HEAD>
  <body>
    <h3>
      Directions:
    </h3>
    Select the parent for the category you want to add. You
    will then be prompted for the name of the node. Once
    you type the name in, this page will be refreshed,
    showing the new node.
    <br>
    <H3>
      Categories
    </H3>
    <Sammamish:CategoryView id="categoryView" runat=
        "server" />
  </body>
</HTML>
```

The part that displays the categories appears because of the two tags (in **bold**) on the page. The top of the page tells the Web server that the tags with the prefix `Sammamish` refer to HTML controls that live in an assembly named `CategoryEditor` within the `Sammamish` namespace. Whenever the server sees something with the prefix `Sammamish`, it will look inside the current application for an object with the same name as the suffix. In this case, it will look in the `Sammamish` namespace for an object named `CategoryView`.[7] So, what does this have to do with SOAP? Well, the `CategoryView` object calls the `CategoryService` Web service to display all of the categories when it is asked to render itself.

```
private void DisplayCategories( HtmlTextWriter output,
   int callDepth, long parentCategoryID )
{
  CategoryService catService = new CategoryService();

  // We can set the catService.Url member if we won't be using the
  // default as defined in the proxy constructor.

  Category[] categories = catService.GetChildCategories(parentCategoryID
       );
  string callDepthPrefix = GeneratePrefix( callDepth );
  bool bFoundOne = false;

  if ( categories != null )
  {
    foreach ( Category cat in categories )
    {
      // Display the active category
      output.WriteLine( callDepthPrefix
         + "<a href=\"addCategory.aspx?parentID="
         + cat.ID.ToString() + "\" >" + cat.name + "</a>: "
         + cat.description
         + "    "
         + "<a href=\"addCategory.aspx?ID=" + cat.ID.ToString()
         + "\">" + "Edit </a> <a href=\"deleteCategory.aspx?ID="
         + cat.ID.ToString() + "\">Delete</a><br>");

      // The below code works because we are creating a new int at call
      // time,so that the callDepth reference this function owns does
      // not get changed.
      DisplayCategories( output, callDepth + 1, cat.ID );
```

---

[7] This is not a typo. Namespace resolution within C#, the language used in these examples, resolves namespaces with a '.'. On the Web page, we see colons to resolve the namespaces.

```
        bFoundOne = true;
    }
  }

  // Check to see if we are at the top of the hierarchy
  if ( ( 0 == callDepth ) )
  {
    output.WriteLine( "Add new top-level <a href=\""
      + "addCategory.aspx?parentID=0\" >category</a>." );
  }
}

protected override void Render(HtmlTextWriter output)
{
  DisplayCategories( output, 0, 0 );
}
```

DisplayCategories is a recursive function that goes through the entire hierarchy until all elements are rendered on the screen. It generates three clickable elements. Users can click on the category name to add a child category. If they want to edit the category name and description, they can click on Edit. If they need to delete the element, they select Delete.

When users add or edit a category, they see the screen shown in Figure 11–2. Upon clicking Save, they return to the page shown in Figure 11–1. This uses a typical ASP setup where the user submits a form and the receiving

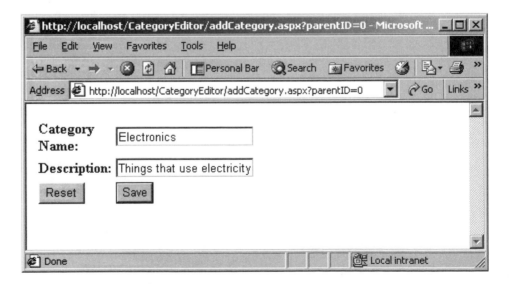

**Figure 11–2**   Add or edit a category.

page processes things. In ASP, you typically save all the data from the form as soon as the page loads. Microsoft implemented ASP.NET pages by using compiled code. The pages typically have a C# class associated with them that handles activities you would have normally performed within the ASP file. You do all of this through event handlers. One of the events you can respond to is `Page.Load`. To do this, you set up a chain of event handlers. In the page constructor, you set a handler for page initialization.

```
public CategoryDisplay()
{
   Page.Init += new System.EventHandler(Page_Init);
}
```

When `Page_Init` fires, it has one line that calls a private method: `InitializeComponent`. This method sets up the remaining event handlers.

```
private void InitializeComponent()
{
   this.Load += new System.EventHandler(this.Page_Load);
}
```

Event handlers always add methods using `+=`. You cannot set handlers using `=` or `+`. Why? Event handlers are chained, giving you the ability to have several functions respond to one event. This model works well and has been in use in other operating environments for many years.[8] When the page actually loads, we check to see if the users modified or edited a category. If they did, we save it.

```
private void Page_Load(object sender, System.EventArgs e)
{
   string parentID = Request.Form[ "parentID" ];
   string catID = Request.Form[ "catID" ];
   if ( parentID != null )
   {
     // Create a new category as a sub-category of the parent
     Category cat = new Category();
     cat.parentCategoryID = Convert.ToInt32( parentID );
     cat.description = Request.Form[ "desc" ];
     cat.name = Request.Form[ "name" ];

     if ( catID != null )
     {
```

[8] One example is X-Windows, a UNIX windowing environment.

```
      cat.ID = Convert.ToInt32( catID );
    }
    // Save the category to their service
    CategoryService catService = new CategoryService();
    catService.SaveCategory( cat ).ToString();
  }
  else
  {
    Response.Write( "<!-- ParentID didn't get through "
      + Request.Form[ "parentID" ] + "-->" );
  }
}
```

This is not the only way to save data. We look at another option in Chapter 12 when we look at saving bids.

The final thing we need to do is delete a category. When deleting a category, you get the screen shown in Figure 11–3. The code to delete executes within the .aspx page itself, not through the Page.Load event. ASP.NET added one other really neat enhancement. If you use regular ASP, you know that to control displaying text that differs depending on something like the success or failure of a method call, you need to use the Response object to write out the differing HTML. With ASP.NET, you can embed the conditional HTML within the else clauses and it just sort of works. Here is how we delete a category:

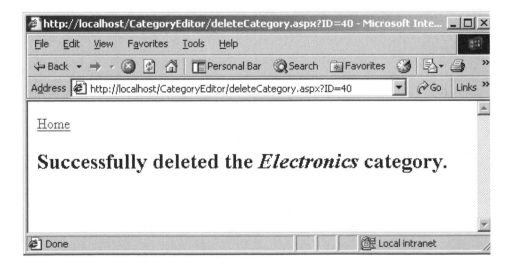

**Figure 11–3**  Successful deletion of a category.

```
<%@ Page language="c#" Codebehind="deleteCategory.aspx.cs"
   AutoEventWireup="false" Inherits="CategoryEditor.deleteCategory" %>

<HTML>
   <HEAD>
      <meta name=vs_targetSchema content="Internet Explorer 5.0">
      <meta name="GENERATOR" Content="Microsoft Visual Studio 7.0">
      <meta name="CODE_LANGUAGE" Content="C#">
   </HEAD>
   <body>
      <a href="default.aspx">Home</a>

<%
long catID = Convert.ToInt32( Request.QueryString["ID"] );
CategoryService categoryService = new CategoryService();
Category category = categoryService.GetCategoryByID( catID );

if ( categoryService.DeleteCategory( category ) ) {
%>
      <h2>
         Successfully deleted the <i><%=category.name%></i> 
         category.
      </h2>
<%
}
else
{
%>
      <h2>
         Failed to delete the category.
      </h2>
<%
}
%>

   </body>
</HTML>
```

One of the things you learn early on with the new .NET tools is that you always have a lot of ways to do something. With this, we have seen all of the category editing functionality. If you want to dig into how everything works, just take a look at the source code. Let's move on and take a look at the item editor.

# Item Management

As mentioned earlier, we want to allow sellers to come in and put up their own items for auction. An auction site could also perform this task for them as a value-added service. When adding an item, sellers will need to log in to prove they are who they claim and then let them add items. The proof of concept will use the query string to transfer the seller ID between pages. Before moving to production, you would need to come up with a better way to authenticate users.

When sellers come to the site, they will be able to do the following:

- Add items
- Edit items
- Delete items

They will only be able to edit and delete items if the auction has not yet begun. Once an auction starts, no changes are allowed. Item management consists of the following components:

1. Seller authentication
2. Item data access
3. Item Web service
4. Item editor

In our coverage, we skip over the item data access because it does nothing more than save, edit, and delete items. When deleting an item, it fails if the item has an existing bid or if the auction start date has already passed. If you are curious to see what the code looks like, you can see it in the `AuctionWS` project in the `Item.cs` file.

## *Seller Authentication*

The actual login screen has a fairly simple interface (shown in Figure 11–4). It just takes the seller's email address and password, then validates the seller. If the seller enters valid information, he or she goes to the page shown in Figure 11–5. Otherwise, the seller sees the page shown in Figure 11–6. The entire logon is performed with this snippet embedded in `itemMenu.aspx`:

**Figure 11-4**  Item editor login screen.

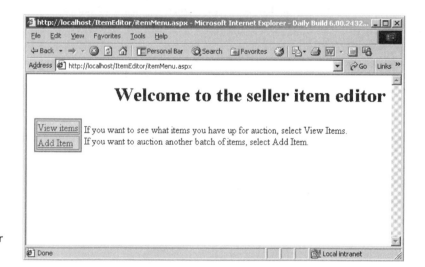

**Figure 11-5**  Item editor welcome page.

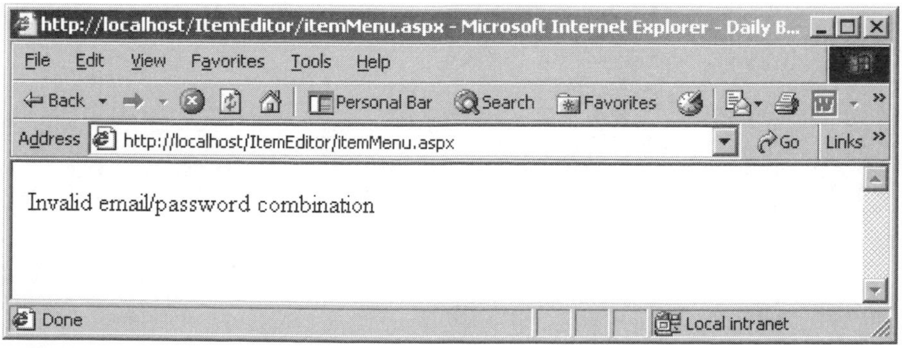

**Figure 11-6**  Invalid login to the item editor page.

```
Logon logon = new Logon();
long providerID;
string emailAddress = Request.Form["emailAddress"];

if ( null == emailAddress )
{
  providerID = Convert.ToInt32(
Request.QueryString["ID"].ToString() );
}
else
{
  providerID = logon.SellerLogon( emailAddress, Request.Form["password"] );
}
```

The Logon Web service provides similar functionality for bidders. The
Web service for logging in looks like this:

```
[WebMethod]
public long SellerLogon( string email, string password )
{
  long retval = -1;
  Util util = new Util();
  string sql = "SELECT ProviderID FROM Seller WHERE EmailAddress='" +
    util.SafeSQL( email ) + "' AND Password='" +
    util.SafeSQL( password ) + "'";

  try
  {
    DataSet dataSet = util.GetDataSet( sql );
    if ( dataSet.Tables.Count > 0 )
    {
      retval = Convert.ToInt32( dataSet.Tables[0].
        Rows[0]["ProviderID"].ToString() );
    }
  }
  catch( Exception e )
  {
    Object a = e.Message;
  }
  return retval;
}
```

Here is one instance in which I used straight SQL to get the information.
I did this only because the seller and bidder components were written using
VB and COM. Because I knew I would only use these tables here, I saw

little value in defining the various constants. If the `Seller` or `Bidder` table come into use again, I would recommend moving to constants instead of literal strings for composing the SQL.

## *Item Web Service*

The item Web service is used in both bidding and editing. In this chapter, we only cover the features needed to edit an item. These services are:

1. **DeleteItem( Item item ):** Deletes the Item if allowed.
2. **GetItemByID( long itemID ):** Returns an item given its ID.
3. **GetItemsByProvider( long providerID ):** Returns all items this seller has for auction.
4. **SaveItem( Item item ):** Saves the item to the database if allowed.

All of these except for `GetItemsByProvider` are trivial. The height of complexity comes when checking the time to make sure that the save or delete is allowed. For example, here is `SaveItem`:

```
[WebMethod]
public bool SaveItem( Item item )
{
  if ( item.ID > 0 )
  {
    // Check the item out and make sure
    // that the item in the database
    // agrees that we can change it.
    Item currentSavedItem = GetItemByID( item.ID );
    if ( currentSavedItem.auctionStartDate <
      System.DateTime.Now )
    {
      return false;
    }
  }
  return item.Save();
}
```

Even `GetItemsByProvider` winds up being fairly tiny. It calls a private function, `FillInArray`, which knows how to populate an array of `Items` given a `DataSet`.

```
[WebMethod]
public Item[] GetItemsByProvider( long providerID )
{
    string sql;
    Util util = new Util();

    sql = "SELECT " + Item.ALL_FIELDS
        + " FROM " + Item.TABLE_NAME
        + " WHERE " + Item.COL_PROVIDERID + " = " + providerID.ToString();

    return FillInArray( util.GetDataSet( sql ) );
}

private Item[] FillInArray ( DataSet dataSet )
{
    // We don't know how many matches we will have. No matches does
    // not mean failure, it just means no child elements.
    Item[] retval = new Item[dataSet.Tables[0].Rows.Count];
    long index = 0;

    foreach( DataRow dataRow in dataSet.Tables[0].Rows )
    {
        retval[index] = new Item();
        retval[index].Init( dataRow );
        ++index;
    }
    return retval;
}
```

An Item is defined by the proxy to have the following member variables:

```
public class Item {
    public long ID;
    public string name;
    public string description;
    public long quantity;
    public long providerID;
    public System.Double reservePrice;
    public long categoryID;
    public AuctionType eAuctionType;
    public System.DateTime auctionStartDate;
    public System.DateTime auctionEndDate;
    public System.Double approxWeight;
    public System.Double approxHeight;
    public System.Double approxWidth;
    public System.Double approxLength;
}
```

Using this structure, `Items` are sent between the Web service and the editor. Let's finish up by looking at the editor itself.

## Item Editor

The item editor provides the interface for adding, deleting, modifying, and viewing items available for auction. After logging in, sellers will see the page shown in Figure 11–5. If they want to add an item, they will click on Add Item and see the screen shown in Figure 11–7. The list of categories on the right also uses a custom HTML control with code similar, but not the same as, the code used to edit categories. From here, users can enter in all the details regarding an item. To set the item category, they simply click on one of the categories on the left to set that property. Figure 11–8 shows the form filled in to describe an oak rocking chair.

Once the user selects Save, the data is sent to the Web service. Assuming everything goes well, we will see the page shown in Figure 11–9. The page grabs all the data and shows a success message if everything went smoothly. If something went wrong, the seller is asked to contact the Web site administrator. This is all done within the body of the HTML page.

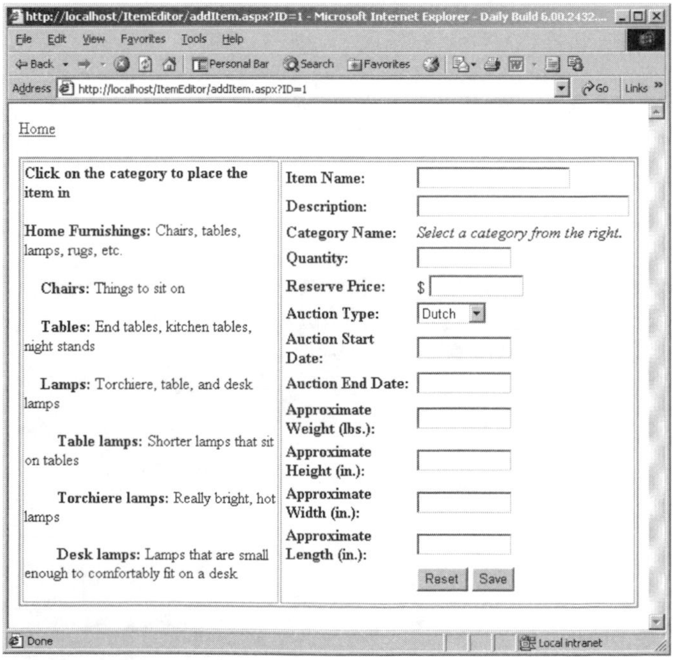

**Figure 11–7**  Adding an item to the system.

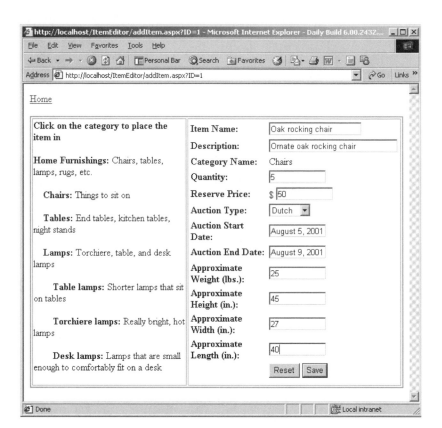

***Figure 11–8*** Auctioning an oak rocking chair.

```
    <body>
<%
Item item = new Item();
ItemService itemService = new ItemService();
string itemID = Request.Form["itemID"];

// Check to see if this was an add or an edit
if ( null != itemID )
{
      item.ID = Convert.ToInt32( itemID );
}

// Capture all of the data
item.approxHeight = Convert.ToDouble( Request.Form["itmHeight"] );
```

**Figure 11-9**  Saved items for auction system.

```
item.approxLength = Convert.ToDouble( Request.Form["itmLength"] );
item.approxWeight = Convert.ToDouble( Request.Form["itmWeight"] );
item.approxWidth = Convert.ToDouble( Request.Form["itmWidth"] );
item.auctionEndDate = Convert.ToDateTime( Request.Form["itmEndDate"] );
item.auctionStartDate = Convert.ToDateTime( Request.Form["itmStartDate"] );
item.categoryID = Convert.ToInt32( Request.Form["catID"] );
item.description = Request.Form["itmDescription"];

// Figure out the auction type.
if ( AuctionType.Yankee.ToString() == Request.Form["itmAuctionType"] )
{
  item.eAuctionType = AuctionType.Yankee;
}
else
{
  item.eAuctionType = AuctionType.Dutch;
}

item.name = Request.Form["itmName"];
item.providerID = Convert.ToInt32( Request.QueryString["ID"] );
item.quantity = Convert.ToInt32( Request.Form["itmQuantity"] );
item.reservePrice = Convert.ToDouble( Request.Form["itmReservePrice"] );

// Try to save the data
```

**Figure 11-10**   Items this user has for auction.

```
if ( itemService.SaveItem( item ) )
{
  // Emit the success message
%>
    <h2>
       Successfully saved your auction item:<%=item.name%>
    </h2>
<%
}
else{
  // Let the user know they should let us know that something is amiss.
%>
    <h2>
       Failed to save your auction item. Please contact 
       <a href="mailto:contact@foo.bar">us</a>.
    </h2>
<%}%>
    <a href="itemMenu.aspx?ID=<%=item.providerID%>">Home</a>
  </body>
```

Once the save is done, the user can choose to view the items he or she has for auction. The generated page is shown in Figure 11–10. From this screen, sellers can choose to edit or delete the item. If they choose to edit, the page shown in Figure 11–8 will appear again with all of the details filled in. If they choose to delete, the item will be removed and when they return to the view, it will contain no items.

# Summary

In Chapter 10, we saw that we needed to be conscious that SOAP provided the connection technology between our various components. Contrast that with what we saw in this chapter. We had to think about SOAP when deciding to expose a method as a Web service or knowing that we had to create a proxy. Thankfully we did not need to think about it when actually instantiating the proxies. Instead, we treated the objects as though they existed in our own project and the generated code took care of the magic. When looking at the file created by WSDL.EXE, we saw that the class was aware that SOAP is in use and that the protocol is asynchronous even though the proxy exhibits synchronous behavior. You can take the proxy and modify it to take advantage of asynchronous processing if that makes sense for your own application.

Because this is supposed to model the development of a proof of concept, not everything in the example should go forward for production. What things can you experiment with to learn how to use .NET to make this more solid and able to take on multiple auctions?

## *Things to Add to Category Management*

Category management is not ready to be sold as a Web service. It does not handle different accounts at all. First, you will want to add a table that uniquely identifies various auction accounts. This information can map back to a specific seller ID or to another table. You then want to add a column to the category table that identifies which Web Service user owns the category names.

You may want to add a screen that allows people running other auction sites to log in to manage their categories. This will help make sure that these people are editing their own information. Speaking of logging in, you should also investigate security. Would certificates be a better way of identifying customers? Would you want to integrate something like Microsoft's Passport?

Also, look for other things you want to see in this feature.

## *Things to Add to Item Management*

The provided source code does not perform parameter validation. .NET provides a number of options and we look at one of them in the next chapter. If you are going to provide all of this purely as a Web Service, you will need to do the validation at the service level as well as at the Web page level.

For entering dates, we have a fairly poor interface. It takes dates as strings. It is pretty easy for the user to enter something that is ambiguous or blatantly wrong. Look at how you would make this look better. The interface does not provide the ability for sellers to upload pictures of the items and the database does not provide storage for them. How would you implement the ability to associate pictures with items and send them back and forth?

# Chapter 12

# THE BIDDING SYSTEM

Finally, we are going to see this system actually take bids. If you have stuck with the case study this far, I hope you have taken some time along the way to play with and enhance the prototype. Maybe you even went off and experimented with some projects of your own. Regardless of how you got this far, I hope you have become excited about what SOAP can do for making applications talk to each other regardless of where they are located.

This chapter exists primarily to finish up the auction system. It shows that you can build a fairly complex system using SOAP as the cross-process communication mechanism. By the time this chapter is over, we will have completed the following pieces:

1. Java SOAP server and classes
2. Microsoft SOAP Toolkit v2 and classes
3. Customer sign-up Web site
4. Seller sign-up Web site
5. .NET Auction Web Services
6. Category editor
7. Item editor
8. Bidding system

All eight of these items communicate with each other using SOAP. This shows just what SOAP is capable of. Let's get moving now and finish up this proof of concept auction site.

When bidders come to the Web site, they are greeted with the page shown in Figure 12–1. We have already covered what many of the features do. Chapter 10 covers the creation of bidder accounts. The code that handles seller accounts looks more or less the same. Chapter 11 covered adding auction items. This chapter covers what happens when the user selects View Auction Items. We skip coverage of the data access components in this chapter. The Bid class just does not contain any interesting tricks. We focus on the following items:

- Bidding pages
- Bidding Web service

# Bidding Pages

## *Viewing the Selection By Category*

When bidders select View Auction Items, they see the page shown in Figure 12–2. This page shows what the user would see when viewing the chairs available for auction. We see that of the three items on this page, only

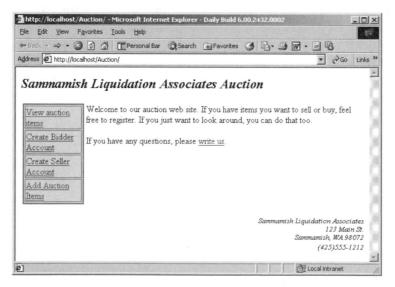

***Figure 12–1***   Auction site welcome page.

one is currently available for bidding. You should also notice that the page contains yet another category view. I mentioned that with .NET, you can always do the same thing several different ways. Before delving into the code, let's take a look at the HTML that allows this display to happen.

```
<table>
  <tr>
    <td id=categoryView width="33%">
      <asp:placeholder id=categoryPlaceHolder runat="server">
      </asp:placeholder>
    </td>
    <td valign="top">
      <table>
        <tr bgColor=greenyellow>
          <td>
            <STRONG>Name</STRONG>
          </td>
          <td>
            <STRONG>Number Available</STRONG>
          </td>
          <td>
            <STRONG>Reserve Price</STRONG>
```

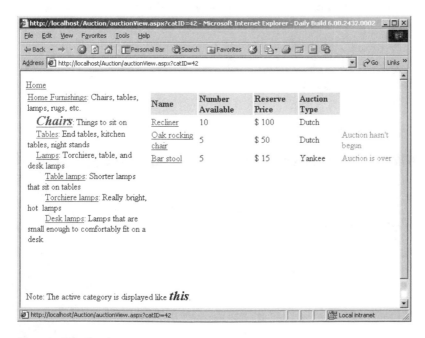

**Figure 12–2** Auction item view.

```
              </td>
              <td>
                <STRONG>Auction Type</STRONG>
              </td>
            </tr>
            <asp:placeholder id=itemPlaceHolder runat="server">
            </asp:placeholder>
          </table>
        </td>
      </tr>
</table>
```

The preceding HTML fragment contains two elements of the type `asp:placeholder`. The code behind this page uses these elements to indicate where to display the category and item information. The `Page.Load` event handler replaces these items with actual HTML. The category placeholder displays the categories with code very similar to the control shown in Chapter 11.

```
private string FillInCategories( long callDepth, long
parentCategoryID )
{
  string callDepthPrefix = GeneratePrefix( callDepth );
  string retval = "";
  try
  {
    CategoryService catService = new CategoryService();
    Category[] categories =
      catService.GetChildCategories( parentCategoryID );

    if ( categories != null )
    {
      foreach ( Category cat in categories )
      {
        retval += callDepthPrefix +
          "<a href=\"auctionView.aspx?catID=" +
          cat.ID.ToString() + "\" >";

        // If we are displaying the current category, display it
        // in big italics.
        if ( cat.ID == this.currentCategory )
        {
          retval += "<font size=5><b><i>" + cat.name +
            "</i></b></font>";
        }
```

```
        else
        {
           retval += cat.name;
        }
        retval += "</a>: " + cat.description + "<br>";

        retval += FillInCategories( callDepth + 1, cat.ID );
      }
    }
  }
  catch( System.NullReferenceException )
  {
     retval = "No categories defined.";
  }
  return retval;
}
```

We also want to display the various items in the category. For this purpose, the ItemService Web service exposes a method that retrieves items by category.

```
[WebMethod]
public Item[] GetItemsByCategory( long catID )
{
   string sql;
   Util util = new Util();

   sql = "SELECT " + Item.ALL_FIELDS
      + " FROM " + Item.TABLE_NAME
      + " WHERE " + Item.COL_CATEGORY_ID + " = " +
      catID.ToString();

   return FillInArray( util.GetDataSet( sql ) );
}
```

We call this function from the FillInItems method of the ASP.NET page.

```
private void FillInItems()
{
   ItemService itemService = new ItemService();
   string itemTable = "";
   try
   {
     // Get all the items in this category
     Item[] items = itemService.GetItemsByCategory( currentCategory );
```

```
foreach ( Item item in items )
{
  // Add a new table row
  itemTable += "<tr>";
  itemTable += "<td><a href=\"viewDetails.aspx?itemID=" +
  item.ID.ToString() + "\">" + item.name + "</a></td>";
  itemTable += "<td>" + item.quantity.ToString() + "</td>";
  itemTable += "<td>$ " + item.reservePrice.ToString() + "</td>";
  itemTable += "<td>" + item.eAuctionType.ToString() + "</td>";

  // Check to see if the auction has started or
      already
  // past and put up an appropriate warning.
  if ( item.auctionStartDate > System.DateTime.Now )
  {
   itemTable += "<td><font COLOR=\"RED\">" +
     "Auction hasn't begun</font></td>";
  }
  else if( item.auctionEndDate < System.DateTime.Now )
  {
     itemTable += "<td><font COLOR=\"RED\">" +
     "Auction is over</font></td>";
                }
  itemTable += "</tr>";
  }
}
```

This code fills in the rows of the table with details about the items within the category that are being auctioned. Within this page, bidders can see if any items spark their interest. If an item looks interesting, they can click on the item name to reveal the item detail view.

## Item Detail View

When bidders click on an item available for auction, we want to give them more detail about the item as well as what it will take to place a winning bid, so we show them all of the item details except for who is selling the item. Below the item details, we display any active bids for this item. Using this information, bidders can decide just how badly they want the item. It shows the public details of the bid: quantity, price, and comment. If the lowest bid exceeds what they want to pay, they can choose to continue looking at other items. Figure 12–3 shows the information we present to the user.

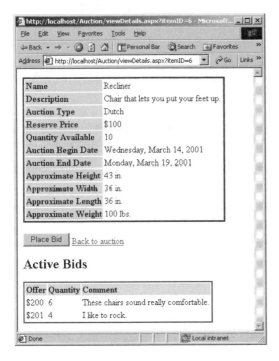

**Figure 12-3** Auction item detail view.

The tables are created using another new feature of ASP.NET. To display the items for auction by category, the code generated the raw HTML for the rows and cells. It then wrote the HTML out to the place-holder location. We could also use an ASP.NET `Table` object. These allow you to set up the layout at design time and run time. The code for this looks similar for the item details and the existing bids. Let's take a look at how the code calls out to the bid service. We cover the bid service itself in the second half of this chapter.

Like in the other ASP.NET pages, the `Page.Load` event handler loads up the dynamic contents of the page. To load up the bids, it calls `ViewDetails.DisplayActiveBids`. This function sets up the main table, then calls a helper function to fill in the details of the individual rows.

```
private void DisplayActiveBids()
{
  // Get the item being displayed
  long itemID = Convert.ToInt32(
      this.Request.QueryString["itemID"] );

  // Get all the active bids related to this item
  BidService bidService = new BidService();
  Bid[] bids = bidService.GetItemBids( itemID );
```

```
if ( bids == null )
{
  // If we do not have any bids, inform the user.
  this.activeBidPlaceHolder.Controls.Add(
    new LiteralControl( "<P><STRONG>No bids have been placed, "
    + "yet.</STRONG></P>" ) );
}
else
{
  // Bids exist for this item. Create a new table
  // and display the bid information.
  Table table = new Table();
  TableRow tableRow = new TableRow();

  // Create the cells for the header row.
  TableCell offerCell = new TableCell();
  TableCell quantityCell = new TableCell();
  TableCell commentCell = new TableCell();

  // Add the row to the table
  table.Rows.Add( tableRow );

  // Add the cells to the row.
  tableRow.Cells.Add( offerCell );
  tableRow.Cells.Add( quantityCell );
  tableRow.Cells.Add( commentCell );

  // Setup the display for the header row.
  tableRow.BackColor = System.Drawing.Color.Gold;
  table.BorderWidth = 2;
  table.BorderStyle = BorderStyle.Ridge;
  table.BorderColor = System.Drawing.Color.Crimson;
  offerCell.Text = "<STRONG>Offer</STRONG>";
  quantityCell.Text = "<STRONG>Quantity</STRONG>";
  commentCell.Text = "<STRONG>Comment</STRONG>";

  // Add the bids to the table.
  foreach ( Bid bid in bids )
  {
    table.Rows.Add( GetBidRow( bid ) );
  }

  // Insert the table at the location of the place
  // holder.
  this.activeBidPlaceHolder.Controls.Add( table );
```

```
      }
}
```

The helper function, ViewDetails.GetBidRow, simply takes a Bid and generates a TableRow for insertion into the table.

```
private TableRow GetBidRow( Bid bid )
{
   // Create a new row
   TableRow retval = new TableRow();

   // The cells that exist in the row
   TableCell offerCell = new TableCell();
   TableCell quantityCell = new TableCell();
   TableCell commentCell = new TableCell();

   // Setup the display text for the cells.
   offerCell.Text = "$" + bid.offer.ToString();
   quantityCell.Text = bid.quantity.ToString();
   commentCell.Text = bid.comment;

   // Add the cells to the row
   retval.Cells.Add( offerCell );
   retval.Cells.Add( quantityCell );
   retval.Cells.Add( commentCell );

   // Return the row
   return retval;
}
```

You may be worried that this code will produce incompatibilities for non-Microsoft browsers. The ASP.NET code for this fragment looks like this:

```
<asp:PlaceHolder id=activeBidPlaceHolder runat="server">
</asp:PlaceHolder>
```

By the time the code is done executing, the ASP.NET code is transformed into the following HTML:

```
<table bordercolor="Crimson" border="0"
   style=
"border-color:Crimson;border-width:2px;border-style:Ridge;">
   <tr style="background-color:Gold;">
     <td>
       <STRONG>Offer</STRONG>
```

```
    </td><td>
      <STRONG>Quantity</STRONG>
    </td><td>
      <STRONG>Comment</STRONG>
    </td>
  </tr>
  <tr>
    <td>
      $200
    </td><td>
      6
    </td><td>
      These chairs sound really comfortable.
    </td>
  </tr>
  <tr>
    <td>
      $201
    </td><td>
      4
    </td><td>
      I like to rock.
    </td>
  </tr>
</table>
```

Other than a potential problem with the embedded style, this should display on most browsers.

If users decide to place a bid, they can log in (Figure 12–4). Once they log in, they see the page shown in Figure 12–5. When the page loads, it requests the item from the `ItemService` and displays some of the basics to help remind users what they are bidding on.

The idea of reminding users what they are bidding on may strike you as odd, but I know it is something I have grown to appreciate. You see, I spent a little too much time on auction Web sites when I built my first dual-processor machine. I bought most of the parts through auctions.[1] I would review a large number of different components every day. More than once I started to place a bid and forgot what part I had just found. Nowadays, a typical auction will show you what you are bidding on.

---

[1] I purchased the motherboard, case, processor, and memory from a computer store. All too often, these parts went for retail cost, making the loss of warranty senseless.

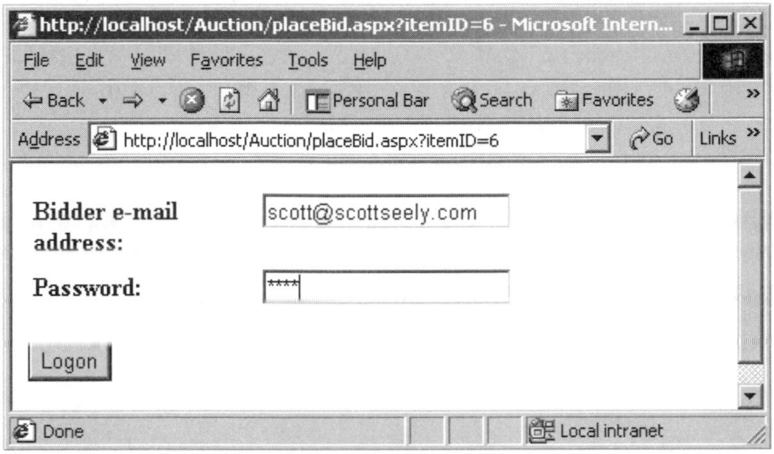

***Figure 12–4*** Bidder login screen.

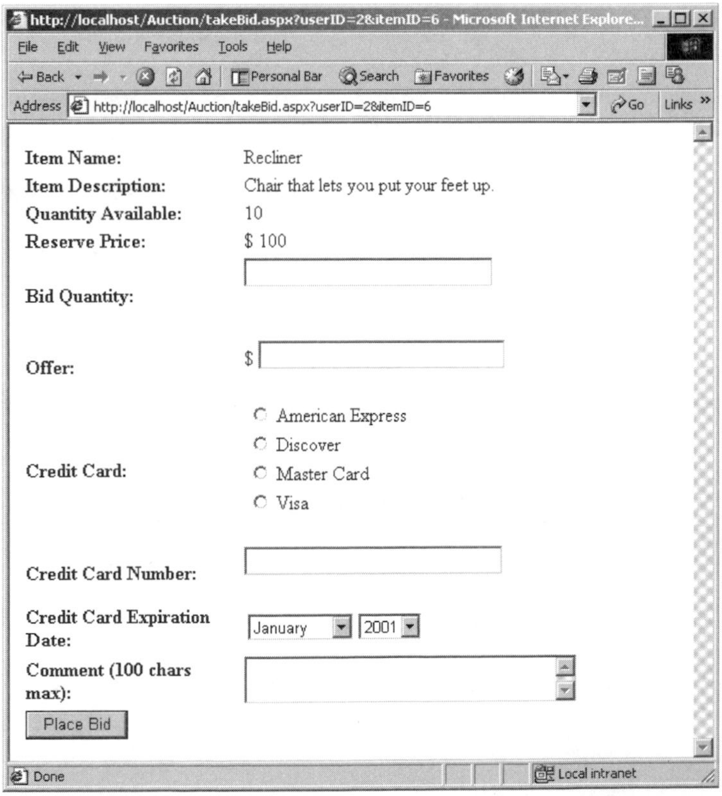

***Figure 12–5*** Bid placement page.

The system also allows bidders to enter a comment. Comments can range from anything like an innocent "I'm so excited that I finally found one of these" to a misleading "Retail cost is only $75. Don't overbid!" One of the more interesting things to do with the comments of the latter variety is to actually find out what retail is. I did this for a short time and discovered an even distribution of people overestimating and underestimating the real cost of items for auction. Regardless of the use of this field, it often proves entertaining for people reviewing the placed bids.

Once the bidder has filled in all of the information, he or she presses the Place Bid button. At this point, the form takes the data and validates it. The processing happens on the server in response to the button press.

```
protected void bidButton_Click(object sender,
System.EventArgs e)
{
  Bid bid = new Bid();
  BidService bidService = new BidService();

  // Capture the bid data
  bid.bidderID = Convert.ToInt32(
      Request.QueryString[USER_ID] );
  bid.comment = this.bidComment.Text;
  bid.creditCardExpirationDate = Convert.ToDateTime(
    this.expirationMonth.SelectedItem.Value + " " +
    this.expirationYear.SelectedItem.Text );
  bid.creditCardNumber = this.creditCardNumber.Text;
  bid.creditCardType = this.creditCardList.SelectedItem.Value;
  bid.itemID = Convert.ToInt32( Request.QueryString[ITEM_ID] );
  bid.offer = Convert.ToDouble( this.bidOffer.Text );
  bid.quantity = Convert.ToInt32( this.bidQuantity.Text );

  try
  {
    // Send the bid off to the server
    bidService.PlaceBid( bid );

    // The bid must have succeeded. Go to the
    // "accepted" page.
    Response.Redirect( "BidPlaced.aspx" );
  }
  catch (System.Web.Services.Protocols.SoapException excep )
  {
    this.outputLabel.Text = excep.ToString();
  }
}
```

**Figure 12–5** Bid placement page.

The code does no validation of the credit card details. Why? I do not want to hear of people putting in real information and exposing their credit card numbers to the world on unsecured development machines. Not only that, but I did not want to have to learn how to validate credit card numbers—that is a topic for another author of some other text. Assuming that everything goes well, the user sees the screen shown in Figure 12–6.

That is really all there is to see with respect to the user interface. We finish up by examining the BidService component.

# Bidding Web Service

The bidding Web service, AuctionWS.BidService, exposes two functions to the bidding logic.

1. **GetItemBids( long itemID ):** Retrieves all of the bids for a given item.
2. **PlaceBid( Bid bid ):** Takes a bid and checks to see if it has the possibility to win at the time of execution.

GetItemBids is the simpler of the two methods exposed by the Web service. It simply executes a query to get all bids with a given ItemID. It then takes the results of that query and returns an array of Bid objects.

```
[WebMethod]
public Bid[] GetBidderItems( long bidderID )
{
   return FillInArray( "SELECT " + Bid.ALL_FIELDS + " FROM "
      + Bid.TABLE_NAME + " WHERE "
      + Bid.COL_BIDDER_ID + " = "
      + bidderID.ToString() );
}

public Bid[] FillInArray( string sql )
{
   Util util = new Util();
   DataSet dataSet;
   int index;

   dataSet = util.GetDataSet( sql );

   // We don't know how many matches we will have. No matches does
   // not mean failure, it just means no bids.
   Bid[] retval = new Bid[dataSet.Tables[0].Rows.Count];
   index = 0;
   foreach( DataRow dataRow in dataSet.Tables[0].Rows )
   {
      retval[index] = new Bid();
      retval[index].Init( dataRow );
      ++index;
   }
   return retval;
}
```

The other method in the Web service is a little more complicated. This method needs to perform a lot more work and is the only method that explicitly throws SOAP exceptions. Why is this method more complicated? Most of the Web services deal with inserting, updating, and deleting data. Okay, so modifying and deleting bids is no great feat, but it took a while to get all the logic ironed out and working. The PlaceBid method has a set of comments that describe exactly what it is doing.

```
[WebMethod]
public bool PlaceBid( Bid bid )
{
   bool retval = false;
   // First, we need to go ahead and see if this bid can be placed.
   // Here is the general algorithm:
   // 1. Find out the number of items without existing bids.
```

```
// 2. If the number of items without bids is >= the
//    number requested by this bid, save it and we're done.
// 3. If the number of items without bids is less than the
//    number requested by this bid, get all bids where
//    the offer price is less than this one.
// 4. If we have enough to satisfy the demand, delete or
//    modify bids until enough free quantity works out.
//    Why? Because people who don't bid enough in an
//    auction lose.

// Load up the item in question.
Item item = new Item();
long quantityWithBids = GetQuantityWithBids( bid.itemID );
long quantityWithoutBids = 0;
long quantityBelowCurrentOffer = 0;

item.Load( bid.itemID );

// Let's do a quick sanity check and see if we have enough
// items to sell this person.
if ( item.quantity < bid.quantity )
{
  throw new SoapException(
    "This item does not have that many units available.",
    SoapException.ClientFaultCode );
}

quantityWithoutBids = item.quantity - quantityWithBids;

// See if we can just save the bid
if ( bid.quantity <= quantityWithoutBids )
{
  // easy case, we'll just save it
  retval = bid.Save();
}
else
{
  // Ok, someone is trying to win a bid. Let's get all the bids
  // below a certain price.
  quantityBelowCurrentOffer = GetQuantityBelowPrice(
    bid.itemID, bid.offer );

  if ( ( quantityBelowCurrentOffer + quantityWithoutBids ) <
    bid.quantity )
  {
    // We can't place a bid, so throw an exception.
```

```
    throw new SoapException(
        "The bid for this item needs to be higher " +
        "before it can be placed.",
        SoapException.ClientFaultCode );
}

// Get all the bids back. Order them by offer price
// ASCending.
string sql = "SELECT " + Bid.ALL_FIELDS
    + " FROM " + Bid.TABLE_NAME
    + " WHERE " + Bid.COL_ITEM_ID + " = " + bid.itemID.ToString()
    + " AND " + Bid.COL_OFFER + " < " + bid.offer.ToString()
    + " ORDER BY " + Bid.COL_OFFER + " ASC";

Bid[] lowBids = FillInArray( sql );

// If we got this far, we can place a bid, so let's make some losers
long quantityAllocatedForBid = quantityWithoutBids;
foreach( Bid placedBid in lowBids )
{
    // How much do we need?
    long quantityNeeded = bid.quantity - quantityAllocatedForBid;

    // See if this bid has enough to satisfy the amount needed
    if ( placedBid.quantity >= quantityNeeded )
    {
        placedBid.quantity -= quantityNeeded;
        /*throw new SoapException ( "bid.quantity = "
            + placedBid.quantity.ToString(),
            SoapException.ServerFaultCode );*/
        if ( placedBid.quantity == 0 )
        {
            // They lost the bid, so delete the bid
            retval = placedBid.Delete();
        }
        else
        {
            // The original bid is lower now because the
            // bidder lost some of the items they bid for,
            // but they still have a winning bid.
            retval = placedBid.Save();
        }
        if ( retval )
        {
            retval = bid.Save();

            // We discovered enough quantity, so leave.
```

```
        break;
      }
    }
    else
    {
      if ( placedBid.Delete() )
      {
        quantityAllocatedForBid += placedBid.quantity;
      }
      else
      {
        throw new SoapException(
          "Failed to delete a losing bid.",
          SoapException.ServerFaultCode );
      }
    }
  }
}
return retval;
}
```

One of the first things this function does is check to see how many items have bids by calling `GetQuantityWithBids`. This helper method simply sums up the `Quantity` column for all bids on the given `itemID`.

```
private long GetQuantityWithBids( long itemID )

{
  long retval = 0;
  string sql;
  const string COL_SUM = "theSum";
  Util util = new Util();

  // Find out how many of the items have bids.
  sql = "SELECT SUM(" + Bid.COL_QUANTITY + ") as " + COL_SUM +
    " FROM " + Bid.TABLE_NAME +
    " WHERE " + Bid.COL_ITEM_ID + " = " + itemID.ToString();

  sql = util.GetDataSet( sql
      ).Tables[0].Rows[0][COL_SUM].ToString();

  if ( sql.Length > 0 )
  {
    retval = Convert.ToInt32( sql );
  }
  return retval;
}
```

GetQuantityBelowPrice, the other helper method called by PlaceBid, returns the quantity of the item with bids that are below the current offer.

```
private long GetQuantityBelowPrice( long itemID, double price )
{
  long retval = 0;
  string sql;
  const string COL_SUM = "theSum";
  Util util = new Util();

  // Count up the number of items with bids
  // that are below the bid price.
  sql = "SELECT SUM(" + Bid.COL_QUANTITY + ") as " + COL_SUM +
    " FROM " + Bid.TABLE_NAME +
    " WHERE " + Bid.COL_ITEM_ID + " = " + itemID.ToString() +
    " AND " + Bid.COL_OFFER + " < " + price.ToString();
  sql = util.GetDataSet( sql
      ).Tables[0].Rows[0][COL_SUM].ToString();

  if ( sql.Length > 0 )
  {
    retval = Convert.ToInt32( sql );
  }
  return retval;
}
```

That is all there is to the bid service. The proof of concept is complete.

## Summary

There we go: We have a fully functional auction system, but there still is a lot of work to be done. The user interface is fairly rough, it does not handle concurrency well, and it does not always take advantage of reducing common code. What happens when two people place a bid on the same item at the same time? How could we share the code for displaying categories? These are just some of the things for you to consider as you work with the supplied code and improve on it.

# Chapter 13

## CASE STUDY SUMMARY

The auction system is made up of several interrelated parts. When going over the code, the places where SOAP provides the communication mechanism do not always stand out and shout "This is SOAP!!!" After going over the case study, we know that objects communicate through several different technologies:

- Java virtual machine
- SOAP
- COM
- The .NET Universal Run Time (URT)

The auction application itself is composed of several subsystems:

- Customer sign-up
- Seller sign-up
- Customer interface (the excuse to use Apache SOAP)
- Category editor
- Item editor
- Auction Web service
- Auction site

The logical view of the application contains four areas of functionality:

1.  Client management (sellers and buyers). Implementation is covered in Chapter 10.
2.  Category management. Implementation is covered in Chapter 11.
3.  Item management. Implementation is covered in Chapter 11.
4.  Auctioning items. Implementation is covered in Chapter 12.

For all of these items, general overviews of the functionality are provided in Chapter 9. This chapter serves to review how each of these areas work and the technologies they use to communicate internally. All of the subsystems communicate with each other through their effects on the shared databases. For example, if the item management subsystem adds an item to the database, it appears in the auction subsystem.

# Client Management

Client management provides the ability to manage both bidders and sellers. Bidders and sellers are allowed to add themselves to the system by providing their email address as well as various telephone numbers and postal mail addresses. In a real-world situation, you would want to provide a mechanism to verify these contacts before allowing businesses or individuals to post items for sale. We made verification a future feature and left it out of the proof of concept.

The client management piece contains the customer and seller sign-up and customer interface subsystems. From the perspective of the customer interface subsystem, customers (i. e., bidders) and sellers are all customers of SLA. Figure 13–1 shows the technologies in use within and between the Java, customer sign-up, and seller sign-up subsystems. The classes in the Java subsystem all belong to the com.scottseely.auction namespace. Those in the VB side all belong to different COM libraries. To help you make sense of everything, I appended the library names to the VB class names so you can look up the code as needed.

Take another look at Figure 13–1. Notice that the connections between the user interface pieces communicate only via SOAP. This satisfies one of the

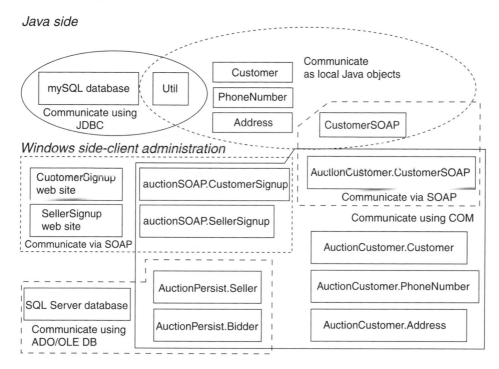

*Figure 13–1* Object communication within the client management subsystem.

primary design constraints—provide a Web service that permits other entities to use our databases to auction items. The current implementation only handles one customer, us. We still wanted to prove to ourselves that the user interface could act as a SOAP client without direct access to the databases.

# Category Management

Category management allows site administrators to add, modify, and delete categories from the auction system. The categories allow sellers to specify the types of items they are trying to sell. Bidders can then browse items based on category. Currently, we only want to give the ability to manage categories to the auction site administrators. This puts the onus of avoiding category duplication on them. Because of the small size of this group with respect to the

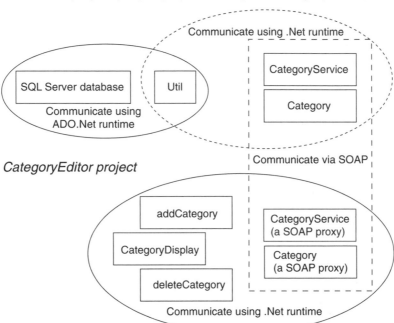

**Figure 13–2**   Object communcation within category management subsystem.

potential number of sellers, the smaller group should be more familiar with what categories do and do not exist. As owners of the site, they have a vested interest in keeping the categories well managed. Because of this self-imposed limitation, sellers must send requests to add or change categories to the site administrators.

The various pieces of the category management system communicate with each other in different ways. Figure 13–2 shows the various mechanisms in use. Again, you will see that the user interface talks to the back end only through SOAP. This means that we could later switch the user interface to Java Server Pages, PHP, Zope, or some other technology without needing to update the back-end processes. Likewise, we can move the back-end to Java, Perl, or anything else that makes sense without impacting established user interfaces. SOAP provides a great abstraction layer because it requires that both sides write to an interface. Interface-based programming allows radical changes to happen on either side of the interface as long as the interface itself remains static.

# Item Management

We allow sellers to manage the items they have for sale. A few rules exist for modifying these items:

- New items cannot have auction start dates before today.
- Existing items cannot be modified if the auction is in progress or has happened in the past.

We enforce these rules in the code. Like all of the other subsystems, the business objects only communicate with the user interface through SOAP. Figure 13–3 shows the objects in use by this subsystem as well as their communication mechanisms.

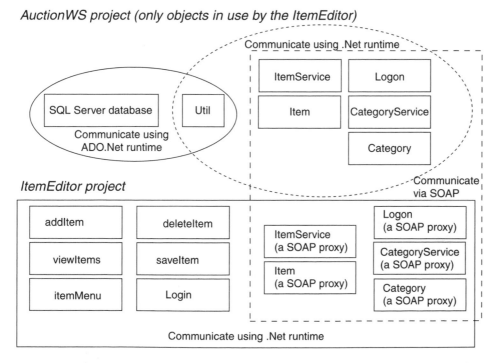

**Figure 13–3**  Object communcation within item management subsystem.

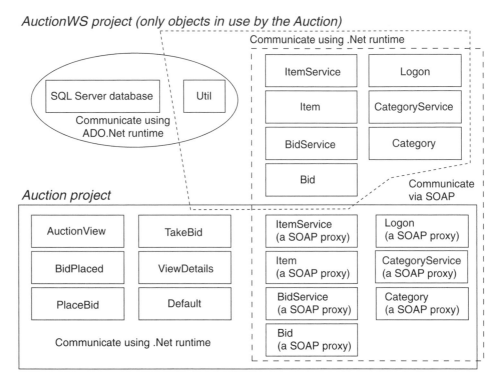

**Figure 13-4**  Object communcation within auction subsystem.

# Auction

Finally, we have the auction part of the application. This part deals with the bids. In particular it allows the user to do the following:

- See the items for sale
- See bids on active items
- Place bids on active items
- Remove bids when a bid is no longer a "winner"

This subsystem did not implement the billing functions. In particular, it does not decide what bidders will be charged based on the auction format (Dutch or Yankee, as described in Chapter 8). This is an exercise left for the reader to handle while experimenting with the tools.

In a final, multiple auction site version of the product, this subsystem would be responsible for hosting auctions for several providers. Our system would provide the billing functionality while sending information on winning bids (i.e., item, bidder, billing, and shipping information). On a number of the sites, we might simply provide the user interfaces to add items, edit categories, and add sellers. The two pieces that businesses subscribing to our Web service would want to customize are the bidder registration and auction user interfaces. These user interfaces might come from SOAP-aware Web sites, C++ binaries, or Perl scripts. Figure 13–4 shows the objects in use by this subsystem as well as their communication mechanisms.

# Summary

In this chapter, I tried to briefly explain the various pieces of the system and give detailed views of how the subsystems communicate internally. This chapter exists because my reviewers asked for it after reading Chapters 8-12. I hope you found this case study summary helpful. Its biggest benefit is the addition of diagrams explaining how the subsystems communicate internally and with each other.

# Appendix

## Quick Start Guide with SOAP and SOAP::Lite

SOAP (Simple Object Access Protocol) is a way for you to remotely make method calls upon classes and objects that exist on a remote server. It's the latest in a long series of similar projects like CORBA, DCOM, and XML-RPC.

SOAP specifies a standard way to encode parameters and return values in XML, and standard ways to pass them over some common network protocols like HTTP (web) and SMTP (email). This guide is not about those meaty technical aspects of SOAP, though, it's a very quick introduction in writing SOAP servers and clients. We will hardly scratch the surface of what's possible.

All examples will use **SOAP::Lite module**. Don't be misled by the 'Lite' suffix—this refers to the effort it takes to use the module, not its capabilities.

## *Writing a CGI-based Server*

Here's a simple CGI-based SOAP server:

1.a.server

```perl
#!perl -w

use SOAP::Transport::HTTP;

SOAP::Transport::HTTP::CGI
  -> dispatch_to('Demo')
  -> handle;

package Demo;

sub hi {
  return "hello, world";
}

sub bye {
  return "goodbye, cruel world";
}
```

There are basically two parts to this: the first four lines set up a SOAP wrapper around a class. Everything from 'package Demo' onward is the class being wrapped.

In the previous version of the SOAP specification (1.0), SOAP over HTTP was supposed to use a new HTTP method, M-POST. In practice, there are many web servers that don't understand the M-POST method so this requirement was weakened and now it's common to try a normal POST first and then use M-POST if the server needs it. If you don't understand POST and M-POST, don't worry, you don't need to know all about it to use the module.

## *Client*

This program prints the results of the `hi()` method call:

1.a.client

```perl
#!perl -w

use SOAP::Lite;
```

```
print SOAP::Lite
  -> uri('http://www.soaplite.com/Demo')
  -> proxy('http://services.soaplite.com/hibye.cgi')
  -> hi()
  -> result;
```

The uri() identifies the class on the server, and the proxy() identifies the CGI script that provides access to the class. Since both look like URLs, I'll take a minute to explain the difference, as it's quite important.

**proxy()**    proxy() is simply the address of the server to contact that provides the methods. You can use http:, mailto:, even ftp: URLs here.

**uri()**    Each server can offer many different services through the one proxy() URL. Each service has a unique URI-like identifier, which you specify to SOAP::Lite through the uri() method. If you get caught up in the gripping saga of the SOAP documentation, the 'namespace' corresponds to the uri() method.

Run your client and you should see:

1.a.result

```
hello, world
```

That's it (assuming you're connected to the Internet).

If your method returns multiple values:

1.b.server

```
#!perl -w

use SOAP::Transport::HTTP;

SOAP::Transport::HTTP::CGI
  -> dispatch_to('Demo')
  -> handle;

package Demo;

sub hi {
  return "hello, world";
}

sub bye {
  return "goodbye, cruel world";
}
```

```
sub languages {
  return ("Perl", "C", "sh");
}
```

Then the `result()` method will only return the first. To access the rest, use the `paramsout()` method:

1.b.client

```
#!perl -w

use SOAP::Lite;

$soap_response = SOAP::Lite
  -> uri('http://www.soaplite.com/Demo')
  -> proxy('http://services.soaplite.com/hibye.cgi')
  -> languages();

@res = $soap_response->paramsout;

$res = $soap_response->result;
print "Result is $res, outparams are @res\n";
```

This code will produce:

1.b.result

```
Result is Perl, outparams are C sh
```

## *Passing Values*

Methods can take arguments. Here's a SOAP server that translates between Fahrenheit and Celsius:

2.a.server

```
#!perl -w

use SOAP::Transport::HTTP;

SOAP::Transport::HTTP::CGI
  -> dispatch_to('Temperatures')
  -> handle;
```

```
package Temperatures;

sub f2c {
    my ($class, $f) = @_;
    return 5/9*($f-32);
}

sub c2f {
    my ($class, $c) = @_;
    return 32+$c*9/5;
}
```

And here's a sample query:

2.a.client

```
#!perl -w

use SOAP::Lite;

print SOAP::Lite
   -> uri('http://www.soaplite.com/Temperatures')
   -> proxy('http://services.soaplite.com/temper.cgi')
   -> c2f(37.5)
   -> result;
```

You can also create an object representing the remote class, and then make method calls on it:

2.b.client

```
#!perl -w

use SOAP::Lite;

my $soap = SOAP::Lite
   -> uri('http://www.soaplite.com/Temperatures')
   -> proxy('http://services.soaplite.com/temper.cgi');

print $soap
   -> c2f(37.5)
   -> result;
```

Check your math, it should give you:

2.result

```
99.5
```

## *Autodispatching*

This being Perl, there's more than one way to do it:

2.c.client

```
#!perl -w

use SOAP::Lite +autodispatch =&gt;

  uri => 'http://www.soaplite.com/Temperatures',
  proxy => 'http://services.soaplite.com/temper.cgi';

print c2f(37.5);
```

After you specify the uri and proxy parameters, you are able to call remote functions with the same syntax as local ones (e.g., c2f). This is done with UNIVERSAL::AUTOLOAD, which catches all unknown method calls. Be warned that all calls to undefined methods will result in an attempt to use SOAP.

## *Objects access (it's 'simple OBJECT access protocol', isn't it?)*

Methods can also return real objects. Let's extend our Temperatures class with an object-oriented interface.

2.b.server

```
#!perl -w

use SOAP::Transport::HTTP;

SOAP::Transport::HTTP::CGI
  -> dispatch_to('Temperatures')
  -> handle;
```

```perl
package Temperatures;

sub f2c {
    my ($class, $f) = @_;
    return 5/9*($f-32);
}

sub c2f {
    my ($class, $c) = @_;
    return 32+$c*9/5;
}

sub new {
    my $self = shift;
    my $class = ref($self) || $self;
    bless {_temperature => shift} => $class;
}

sub as_fahrenheit {
    return shift->{_temperature};
}

sub as_celsius {
    return 5/9*(shift->{_temperature}-32);
}
```

Here is a client to access this class:

2.d.client

```perl
#!perl -w

use SOAP::Lite;

my $soap = SOAP::Lite
  -> uri('http://www.soaplite.com/Temperatures')
  -> proxy('http://services.soaplite.com/temper.cgi');

my $temperatures = $soap
  -> call(new => 100) # accept Fahrenheits
  -> result;

print $soap
  -> as_celsius($temperatures)
  -> result;
```

Similar code with autodispatch is shorter and easier to read.

2.e.client

```
#!perl -w

use SOAP::Lite +autodispatch =>
  uri => 'http://www.soaplite.com/Temperatures',
  proxy => 'http://services.soaplite.com/temper.cgi';

my $temperatures = Temperatures->new(100);
print $temperatures->as_fahrenheit;
```

# Error Handling

A SOAP call may fail for numerous reasons, such as: transport error, incorrect parameters, an error on the server. Transport errors (which may occur if, for example, there is a network break between the client and the server) are dealt with below. All other errors are indicated by the `fault()` method:

2.f.client

```
#!perl -w

use SOAP::Lite;

my $soap = SOAP::Lite
  -> uri('http://www.soaplite.com/Temperatures')
  -> proxy('http://services.soaplite.com/temper.cgi');

my $result = $soap->c2f(37.5);

unless ($result->fault) {
  print $result->result();
} else {
  print join ', ',
    $result->faultcode,
    $result->faultstring,
    $result->faultdetail;
}
```

`faultcode()` gives you information about the main reason for the error. Possible values may be:

### Client: you provided incorrect information in the request.

This error may occur when parameters for remote call are incorrect, for example, for service that returns name of a state in the U.S. based on number of this state you provide negative or too big number. Or type of parameter is incorrect (specified `int` instead of `string`), or likewise.

### Server: something is wrong on the server side.

This means that provided information is correct, but server couldn't handle the request because of temporary difficulties, for example, unavailable database.

### MustUnderstand: Header element has mustUnderstand attribute, but wasn't understood by server.

Basically that means that the server was able to parse the request but that the client is requesting functionality that can't be provided. For example, request requires execution of SQL statement and client wants to be sure that several requests will be executed in one transaction. It could be implemented as three differents calls with common TransactionID.

In this case, the SOAP header may be extended with a new header element 'TransactionID' which carries the transaction ID across the 3 separate invocations. However, the server may not understand what a 'TransactionID' is. If the server does not have this understanding and tries to process the request anyway, problems may arise if there is a problem with processing the 3 invocations together, as the server will not maintain transactional integrity across the group of 3. To guard against this, the client may indicate that the server 'mustUnderstand' the element 'TransactionID'. If the server sees this and does NOT understand the meaning of the element, it will not try and process the requests in the first place.

This functionality makes services more reliable and distributed system more robust.

### VersionMismatch: the server can't understand the version of SOAP used by the client.

This is provided for (possible) future extensions, when new versions of SOAP will have different functionality and only clients that are knowledgeable about it will be able to use it.

### Other errors

The server is allowed to create its own errors, like **Client.Authentication**.

`faultstring()` provides a readable explanation, whereas `faultdetail()` gives access to more detailed information, which may be a string, object, or more complex structure. For example, if you change **uri** to something else (let's try with 'Test' instead of 'Temperatures'), this code will generate:

2.f.result

```
Client, Bad Class Name, Failed to access class (Test)
```

By default client will **die with diagnostic** on *transport errors* and **do nothing** for *faulted calls*, so, you'll be able to get fault info from result. You can alter this behavior with `on_fault()` handler either per object (will die on both transport errors and SOAP faults):

2.g.client

```perl
#!perl -w

use SOAP::Lite;

my $soap = SOAP::Lite
  -> uri('http://www.soaplite.com/Temperatures')
  -> proxy('http://services.soaplite.com/temper.cgi')

-> on_fault(sub { my($soap, $res) = @_;
    die ref $res ? $res->faultdetail : $soap->transport->status, "/n";
  });
```

or globally:

2.h.client

```perl
#!perl -w

use SOAP::Lite

 on_fault => sub { my($soap, $res) = @_;
   die ref $res ? $res->faultdetail : $soap->transport->status, "/n";
 };

my $soap = SOAP::Lite
```

```
-> uri('http://www.soaplite.com/Temperatures')
-> proxy('http://services.soaplite.com/temper.cgi');
```

Now you wrap your SOAP call into `eval {}` block and catch both transport errors and SOAP faults:

2.j.client

```perl
#!perl -w

use SOAP::Lite

   on_fault => sub { my($soap, $res) = @_;
     die ref $res ? $res->faultdetail : $soap->transport->status, "/n";
   };

my $soap = SOAP::Lite
   -> uri('http://www.soaplite.com/Temperatures')
   -> proxy('http://services.soaplite.com/temper.cgi');

eval {
   print $soap->c2f(37.5)->result;
1 } or die;
```

You may also consider this variant that will return `undef` and setup `$!` on failure, just like many Perl functions do:

2.k.client

```perl
#!perl -w

use SOAP::Lite
   on_fault => sub { my($soap, $res) = @_;
     eval { die ref $res ? $res->faultdetail : $soap->transport->status };
     return ref $res ? $res : new SOAP::SOM;
   };

my $soap = SOAP::Lite
   -> uri('http://www.soaplite.com/Temperatures')
   -> proxy('http://services.soaplite.com/temper.cgi');

defined (my $temp = $soap->c2f(37.5)->result) or die;

print $temp;
```

And finally, if you want to ignore errors (however, you can still check for them with the `fault()` method call):

2.fragment

```
use SOAP::Lite
  on_fault => sub {};
```

or

2.fragment

```
my $soap = SOAP::Lite
  -> on_fault(sub{})
  ..... other parameters
```

# Service Dispatch (different services on one server)

So far our CGI programs have had a single class to handle incoming SOAP calls. But we might have one CGI program that dispatches SOAP calls to many classes. This section shows you how to do that.

Static dispatch is when you hard-code the name of the module that the SOAP requests go to. That module can be defined by your program or loaded when needed.

First, what is this **dispatch**? When server gets SOAP request it binds it to class specified in request. This class could be already loaded on server side (on server startup or as result of previous calls) or will be loaded on demand according to server configuration. Dispatch is the process of determining what class should handle this request and loading of this class. **Static** means that name of the class is specified in configuration and **dynamic** means that only directory is specified and **any** class from this particular directory can be accessed.

Now imagine you want to give access to two different classes on server side, and want to provide the same address for both. What should you do? Several options are available (surprised?):

## Static internal

That is something you already are familiar with:

3.a.server (Static internal)

```perl
#!perl -w

use SOAP::Transport::HTTP;

SOAP::Transport::HTTP::CGI
  -> dispatch_to('Demo')
  -> handle;

package Demo;

sub hi {
  return "hello, world";
}

sub bye {
  return "goodbye, cruel world";
}

1;
```

## Static external

Similar to `Static internal`, but module is somewhere outside of server code:

3.b.server (Static external)

```perl
#!perl -w

use SOAP::Transport::HTTP;

use Demo;

SOAP::Transport::HTTP::CGI
  -> dispatch_to('Demo')
  -> handle;
```

Following file should be somewhere in @INC directory:

3.b.module (Static external)

```
package Demo;

sub hi {
  return "hello, world";
}

sub bye {
  return "goodbye, cruel world";
}

1;
```

## Dynamic

As you can see in both Static internal and Static external modes the name of the module is hardcoded in the server's code. But what if you want to be able to add new modules dynamically without changing the code? Dynamic dispatch allows you to do that. Specify the directory and any module in this directory becomes available for dispatching:

3.c.server (Dynamic)

```
#!perl -w

use SOAP::Transport::HTTP;

SOAP::Transport::HTTP::CGI

   -> dispatch_to('/home/soaplite/modules')

   -> handle;
```

Then put Demo.pm in /home/soaplite/modules directory:

3.c.module (Dynamic)

```
  package Demo;

sub hi {
```

```
  return "hello, world";
}

sub bye {
  return "goodbye, cruel world";
}

1;
```

That's it. The **any** module you put in */home/soaplite/modules* is now available, but don't forget that the URI on the client side should match the module/class name you want to dispatch your call to.

## Mixed

Why do we need this? Unfortunately, both dynamic and static dispatch have disadvantages. During dynamic dispatch access to @INC is disabled (due to security reasons) and static dispatch loads modules on startup, but this may not be what we want if we have a bunch of modules we want to access. To avoid this, you can combine the dynamic and static approaches.

Let's assume you have 10 modules in /home/soaplite/modules directory, and want to provide access, but don't want to load all of them on startup. All you need to do is this:

3.d.server (Mixed)

```
#!perl -w

use SOAP::Transport::HTTP;

SOAP::Transport::HTTP::CGI

  -> dispatch_to('/home/soaplite/modules', 'Demo', 'Demo1',
'Demo2')

  -> handle;
```

Now access to all of these modules is enabled and they'll be loaded on a demand basis, only when needed. And, more importantly, **all these modules now have access to @INC array**, so can do any use they want.

# Types and Names

Since Perl is a typeless language (in the sense that there is no difference between an integer 123 and a string '123') the transformation process from a SOAP message to Perl data is very simple. For most simple types we can just ignore types during this stage. However there are drawbacks also: we need to provide additional information during the generation of our SOAP message, because another side (server) may expect to get type information. SOAP::Lite tries hard to do this job for you and doesn't force you to type every parameter explicitly. It tries to guess the datatype based on the actual value stored in the variable, and behave appropriately (according to another Perl motto, DWIM, 'Do What I Mean').

For example, the variable that has value 123 becomes element with type int in the SOAP message, and a variable that has value 'abc' gets type string. There are several more complex cases. For example, a variable that has a value with binary zeroes "\0" will be encoded with type base64 and objects (blessed references) will have type and name (unless specified) according to their types.

It may not work in all cases though. There is no way to make (by default) element with type string or type long from value 123, because autotyping will always make type int for this variable.

You may alter this behavior in several ways. You may disable it completely (with autotype(0)), you may change autotyping for different types, or you may explicitly specify type for your variable:

```
my $var = SOAP::Data->type(string => 123);
```

$var is encoded as an element with type string and value 123. You may use this variable in ANY place where you use usual variables in SOAP calls. You may also provide not only specific **data types**, but also **name** and **attributes**.

Since many services count on **names** of parameters (instead of **positions**) you may specify the name for your parameters through the same syntax. To specify the name for the $var variable you may use $var->name('myvar'), or make it in one line:

```
my $var = SOAP::Data->type(string => 123)->name('myvar');

# - OR -
```

```
my $var = SOAP::Data->type('string')->name(myvar => 123);

# - OR -
my $var = SOAP::Data->type('string')->name('myvar')->value(123);
```

You may always get/set the value of this variable with the value() method:

```
$var->value(321);              # set new value
my $realvalue = $var->value; # store it in variable
```

# More Complex Server (daemon, mod_perl and mod_soap)

You shouldn't have many problems with the CGI-based SOAP server you created; however, performance could be significantly better. The next logical step might be to implement SOAP services using accelerators (like PerlEx or VelociGen) or persistent technologies (like mod_perl). Another lightweight solution might be to implement the SOAP service as an HTTP daemon; in that case you don't need to use a separate web server. This might be useful in a situation where a client application accepts SOAP calls, or for internal usage.

## *HTTP daemon*

For HTTP daemon implementation you may write this code:

4.a.server(HTTP daemon)

```
#!perl -w

use SOAP::Transport::HTTP;

use Demo;

# don't want to die on 'Broken pipe' or Ctrl-C
$SIG{PIPE} = $SIG{INT} = 'IGNORE';

SOAP::Transport::HTTP::CGI
   -> new (LocalPort => 80)
```

```
   -> dispatch_to('/home/soaplite/modules')
;

print "Contact to SOAP server at ", $daemon->url, "\n";
$daemon->handle;
```

Not much difference from the CGI server (Dynamic), huh? And it makes the same interface accessible, only through the different endpoint. This code is all you need to run the SOAP server on your computer without anything else.

## HTTP daemon in VBScript

Similar code in VBScript may look like:

4.b.server (HTTP daemon,VBScript)

```
call CreateObject("SOAP.Lite") _
  .server("SOAP::Transport::HTTP::Daemon", _
    "LocalPort", 80) _
  .dispatch_to("/home/soaplite/modules") _
  .handle
```

That is all that you need to run SOAP server on Microsoft platform (and it will run on Win9x/Me/NT/2K as soon as you register Lite.dll with `regsvr32 Lite.dll`).

## ASP/VB

ASP server could be created with VBScript or PerlScript code:

4.c.server(ASP server,VBScript)

```
<%
  Response.ContentType = "text/xml"
  Response.Write(Server.CreateObject"SOAP.Lite") _
    .server("SOAP::Server") _
    .dispatch_to("/home/soaplite/modules") _
    .handle(Request.BinaryRead(Request.TotalBytes)) _
  )
%>
```

## Apache::Registry

One of the easiest ways to significantly speed up your CGI-based SOAP server is to wrap it with mod_perl Apache::Registry module. You need to configure it in httpd.conf file:

4.d.server (Apache::Registry, httpd.conf)

```
Alias /mod_perl/ "/Apache/mod_perl/"
<Location /mod_perl>
  SetHandler perl-script
  PerlHandler Apache::Registry
  PerlSendHeader On
  Options +ExecCGI
</Location>
```

Put CGI script `soap.mod_cgi` in */Apache/mod_perl/* directory mentioned above:

4.d.server (Apache::Registry, soap.mod_cgi)

```
use SOAP::Transport::HTTP;

SOAP::Transport::HTTP::CGI
  -> dispatch_to('/home/soaplite/modules')
  -> handle
;
```

## mod_perl

Let's consider mod_perl-based server now. To run it as a server you'll need to put SOAP::Apache module (*Apache.pm*) in any directory from `@INC`:

4.e.server (mod_perl, Apache.pm)

```
package SOAP::Apache;

use SOAP::Transport::HTTP;

my $server = SOAP::Transport::HTTP::Apache
  -> dispatch_to('/home/soaplite/modules')
```

```
sub handler { $server->handler(@_) }

1;
```

Then modify your httpd.conf file:

4.e.server (mod_perl, httpd.conf)

```
<Location /soap>
  SetHandler perl-script
  PerlHandler SOAP::Apache
</Location>
```

## *mod_soap*

mod_soap allows you to create a SOAP server by simply configuring the httpd.conf or .htaccess file.

4.f.server (mod_soap, httpd.conf)

```
# directory-based access
<Location /mod_soap>
  SetHandler perl-script
  PerlHandler Apache::SOAP
  PerlSetVar dispatch_to "/home/soaplite/modules"
  PerlSetVar options "compress_threshold => 10000"
</Location>

# file-based access
<FilesMatch "\.soap">
  SetHandler perl-script
  PerlHandler Apache::SOAP
  PerlSetVar dispatch_to "/home/soaplite/modules"
  PerlSetVar options "compress_threshold => 10000"
</FilesMatch>
```

Directory-based access turns a directory into a SOAP endpoint. For example, you may point your request to *http://localhost/mod_soap* (there is no need to create this directory).

File-based access turns a file with a specified name (or mask) into a SOAP endpoint. For example, *http://localhost/somewhere/endpoint.soap*.

Alternatively, you may turn an existing directory into a SOAP server if you put `.htaccess` file inside it:

4.g.server (mod_soap, .htaccess)

```
SetHandler perl-script
PerlHandler Apache::SOAP
PerlSetVar dispatch_to "/home/soaplite/modules"
PerlSetVar options "compress_threshold => 10000"
```

# Access to Remote Services

It's time now to reuse what has already been done and to try and call services available on the Internet. After all, the most interesting part in SOAP is inter operability between systems where communicating parts are created in different languages, running on different platforms or in different environments, and providing interfaces with service descriptions or documentation. XMethods.net can be a perfect starting point

### Name of state based on state's number (in alphabetical order)

Frontier's implementation has a test server that returns the name of a state based upon a number you provide. By default, SOAP::Lite generates a SOAPAction header with the structure of `[URI]#[method]`. Frontier, however, expects SOAPAction to be just the URI, so we have to use on_action to modify it. In our example we specify `on_action(sub { sprintf '"%s"', shift })`, so the resulting SOAPAction will contain only the URI (and don't forget double quotes there).

5.a.client

```
#!perl -w

use SOAP::Lite;

# Frontier http://www.userland.com/

$s = SOAP::Lite
  -> uri('/examples')
```

```
   -> on_action(sub { sprintf '"%s"', shift })
   -> proxy('http://superhonker.userland.com/')
;

print $s->getStateName(25)->result;
```

You should get the output:

5.a.result

```
Missouri
```

## *Whois*

We will target services with different implementations and this service is running on the Windows platform:

5.b.client

```
#!perl -w

use SOAP::Lite;

# 4s4c (aka Simon's SOAP Server Services For COM) http://www.4s4c.com/

print SOAP::Lite
   -> uri('http://www.pocketsoap.com/whois')
   -> proxy('http://soap.4s4c.com/whois/soap.asp')
   -> whois(SOAP::Data->name('name' => 'yahoo'))
   -> result;
```

Nothing fancy here, 'name' is the name of the field and 'yahoo' is the value. That should give you the output:

5.b.result

```
The Data in Network Solutions' WHOIS database is provided
by Network Solutions for information purposes, and to
assist persons in obtaining information about or related
to a domain name registration record. Network Solutions
does not guarantee its accuracy. By submitting a WHOIS
query, you agree that you will use this Data only for law-
ful purposes and that, under no circumstances will you use
```

this Data to: (1) allow, enable, or otherwise support the transmission of mass unsolicited, commercial advertising or solicitations via e-mail (spam); or (2) enable high volume, automated, electronic processes that apply to Network Solutions (or its systems). Network Solutions reserves the right to modify these terms at any time. By submitting this query, you agree to abide by this policy.

```
Yahoo (YAHOO-DOM)                                  YAHOO.COM
Yahoo Inc. (YAHOO27-DOM)                           YAHOO.ORG
Yahoo! Inc. (YAHOO4-DOM)                           YAHOO.NET
```

To single out one record, look it up with "!xxx," where xxx is the handle, shown in parentheses following the name, which comes first.

## *Book price based on ISBN*

In many cases the SOAP interface is just a frontend that requests information, parses the response and formats it and returns according to your request. It may not be doing that much, but it saves you time on the client side and fixes this interface, so you don't need to update it every time your service provider changes format or content. In addition to that, the major players are moving quickly toward XML; for example, Google already has an XML-based interface for their search engine. Here is the service that returns book price based on ISBN:

5.c.client

```perl
#!perl -w

use SOAP::Lite;

# Apache SOAP http://xml.apache.org/soap/ (running on
XMethods.net)

$s = SOAP::Lite
  -> uri('urn:xmethods-BNPriceCheck')
  -> proxy('http://services.xmethods.net/soap/servlet/rpcrouter');

my $isbn = '0596000278'; # Programming Perl, 3rd Edition
print $s->getPrice(SOAP::Data->type(string => $isbn))->result;
```

Here is the result for *Programming Perl, 3rd Edition*:

5.c.result

```
39.96
```

Note that we explicitly specified 'string' type, because ISBN looks like a number and will be serialized by default as a number, but the SOAP server we work with requires it to be a string.

## Currency Exchange rates

This service returns a value of 1 unit of country1's currency converted into country2's currency:

5.d.client

```
#!perl -w

use SOAP::Lite;

# GLUE http://www.themindelectric.com/ (running on
XMethods.net)

my $s = SOAP::Lite
  -> uri('urn:xmethods-CurrencyExchange')
  -> proxy('http://services.xmethods.net/soap');

my $r = $s->getRate(SOAP::Data->name(country1 => 'England'),
                SOAP::Data->name(country2 => 'Japan'))
        ->result;
print "Currency rate for England/Japan is $r\n";
```

Which gives you (as of 2001/03/11):

5.d.result

```
Currency rate for England/Japan is 175.4608
```

## NASDAQ quotes

This service returns a delayed stock quote based on a stock symbol:

5.e.client

```perl
#!perl -w

use SOAP::Lite;

# GLUE http://www.themindelectric.com/ (running on
XMethods.net)

my $s = SOAP::Lite
   -> uri('urn:xmethods-delayed-quotes')
   -> proxy('http://services.xmethods.net/soap');

my $symbol = 'AMZN';
my $r = $s->getQuote($symbol)->result;
print "Quote for $symbol symbol is $r\n";
```

It may (or may not, depending on how Amazon is doing) give you:

5.e.result

```
Quote for AMZN symbol is 12.25
```

## *Access with service description (WSDL)*

Although support for WSDL 1.1 is limited in SOAP::Lite for now (service description may work in some cases, but hasn't been extensively tested), you can access services that don't have complex types in their description:

6.a.client

```perl
#!perl -w

use SOAP::Lite;

print SOAP::Lite
   -> service('http://www.xmethods.net/sd/StockQuoteService.wsdl')
   -> getQuote('MSFT');
```

If we take a look under the hood we'll find that SOAP::Lite makes the request for service description, parses it, builds the stub (object that make available the same methods as remote service) and returns it to you. As the result, you can run several requests using the same service description:

6.b.client

```perl
#!perl -w

use SOAP::Lite;


my $service = SOAP::Lite
  -> service('http://www.xmethods.net/sd/StockQuoteService.wsdl');

print 'MSFT + ORCL = ',
      $service->getQuote('MSFT') + $service->getQuote('ORCL');
```

The service description doesn't need to be on the Internet, you can access it from your local drive also:

6.c.client

```perl
use SOAP::Lite
  service => 'http://www.xmethods.net/sd/StockQuoteService.wsdl',
  # service => 'file:/your/local/path/StockQuoteService.wsdl',
  # service => 'file:./StockQuoteService.wsdl',
;

print getQuote('MSFT'), "\n";
```

This code works in a similar way to the previous example (in OO style), but loads description and imports all methods, so you can use the function interface.

And finally, a couple of one-liners for those who like to do something short and simple (albeit useful and powerful):

6.d.client

```perl
# following command is splitted for readability
perl "MSOAP::Lite
service=>'http://www.xmethods.net/sd/StockQuoteService.wsdl'"
      -le "print getQuote('MSFT')"

perl "-MSOAP::Lite service=>'file:./quote.wsdl'" -le "print getQuote('MSFT')"
```

Last example (marked line) seems to be the shortest SOAP method invocation.

# Security
# (SSL, basic/digest authentication, cookie-based authentication, ticket-based authentication, access control)

Though SOAP itself doesn't impose any security mechanisms (unless you count SOAP Security Extensions: Digital Signature specification), the extensibility of protocol allows you to leverage many security methods that are available for different protocols, like SSL over HTTP or S/MIME. We'll consider how SOAP can be used together with SSL, basic authentication, cookie-based authorization, and access control.

## SSL

Let's start with **SSL**. Surprisingly there is nothing SOAP-specific you need to do on the server side, and there is only a minor modification on the client side: just specify `https:` instead of `http:` as the protocol for your endpoint and everything else will be done for you. Obviously, endpoint should support this functionality and server should be properly configured.

7.a.client

```perl
#!perl -w

use SOAP::Lite +autodispatch =>
  uri => 'http://www.soaplite.com/My/Examples',

  proxy => 'https://localhost/cgi-bin/soap.cgi',

  on_fault => sub { my($soap, $res) = @_;
    die ref $res ? $res->faultdetail : $soap->transport->status, "\n";
  }
;

print getStateName(21);
```

## *Basic authentication*

The situation gets even more interesting with **authentication**. Consider this code that accesses an endpoint that requires authentication.

7.b.client

```
#!perl -w

use SOAP::Lite +autodispatch =>
  uri => 'http://www.soaplite.com/My/Examples',
  proxy => 'http://services.soaplite.com/auth/examples.cgi',
  on_fault => sub { my($soap, $res) = @_;
    die ref $res ? $res->faultdetail : $soap->transport->status, "\n";
  }
;

print getStateName(21);
```

Keep in mind that the password will be in clear text during the transfer (not exactly in clear text; it will be base64 encoded, but that's almost the same) unless the user uses https (i.e., authentication doesn't mean encryption).

The server configuration (for an Apache webserver) with authentication may look like this (can be specified in .conf or in .htaccess file):

7.b.server(.htaccess)

```
AuthUserFile /path/to/users/file/created/with/htpasswd
AuthType Basic
AuthName "SOAP::Lite authentication tests"
require valid-user
```

If you run example 7.b against this endpoint, you'll probably get error like this:

7.b.result

```
401 Authorization Required
```

You may provide required credentials on client side (user `soaplite`, and password `authtest`) overriding function `get_basic_credentials()` in class SOAP::Transport::HTTP::Client:

7.c.client

```perl
#!perl -w

use SOAP::Lite +autodispatch =>
  uri => 'http://www.soaplite.com/My/Examples',
  proxy => 'http://services.soaplite.com/auth/examples.cgi',
  on_fault => sub { my($soap, $res) = @_;
    die ref $res ? $res->faultdetail : $soap->transport->
status, "\n";
  }
;

sub SOAP::Transport::HTTP::Client::get_basic_credentials {
  return 'soaplite' => 'authtest';
}

print getStateName(21);
```

That gives you the correct result:

7.c.result

```
Massachusetts
```

Alternatively you may provide this information with `credentials()` functions, but you need to specify host and realm also:

7.d.client

```perl
#!perl -w

use SOAP::Lite +autodispatch =>
  uri => 'http://www.soaplite.com/My/Examples',

  proxy => [
    'http://services.soaplite.com/auth/examples.cgi',
    credentials => [
      'services.soaplite.com:80',            # host:port
      'SOAP::Lite authentication tests', # realm
      'soaplite' => 'authtest',              # user, password
    ]
  ],

  on_fault => sub { my($soap, $res) = @_;
```

```
      die ref $res ? $res->faultdetail : $soap->transport->status, "\n";
   }
;

print getStateName(21);
```

The simplest and most convenient way would probably be to provide the user and password embedded in a URL. Surprisingly, this works:

7.e.client

```
#!perl -w

use SOAP::Lite;

print SOAP::Lite
   -> uri('http://www.soaplite.com/My/Examples')

   ->
proxy('http://soaplite:authtest@services.soaplite.com/auth/
examples.cgi')

   -> getStateName(21)
   -> result;
```

## Cookie-based authentication

**Cookie-based authentication** also doesn't require a lot of work on the client side. Usually, it means that you need to provide credentials in some way, and if everything is OK, the server will return a cookie on success, then will check it for all subsequent requests. Using available functionality you may not only support this behavior on the client side in one session, but even store cookies in a file and use the same server session for several runs. All you need to do is:

7.f.client

```
#!perl -w

use SOAP::Lite;
use HTTP::Cookies;

my $soap = SOAP::Lite
```

```
    -> uri('urn:xmethodsInterop')

    ->
proxy('http://services.xmethods.net/soap/servlet/rpcrouter',
            cookie_jar => HTTP::Cookies->new(ignore_discard => 1));

print $soap->echoString('Hello')->result;
```

All the magic is in the cookie jar :). You may even add or delete cookies between calls, but the underlying module does everything you need by default. Add `file => 'filename'` option to `new()` method to save/restore cookies between sessions. Not much work, huh? Kudos to Gisle Aas on that!

## Ticket-based authentication

**Ticket-based authentication** is a little bit more complex. The logic is similar to cookie-based authentication, but it is executed on the application level, instead of at the transport level. The advantage is that it works for any SOAP transport (not only for HTTP) and gives you a little bit more flexibility. As a result, you won't get support from a webserver and you'll have to do everything manually. No big deal, right?

First step is ticket generation. We'll build a ticket that contains email, time, and signature.

7.g.server(TicketAuth)

```
package TicketAuth;

# we will need to manage Header information to get a ticket
@TicketAuth::ISA = qw(SOAP::Server::Parameters);

# _____
# private functions
# _____

use Digest::MD5 qw(md5);

my $calculateAuthInfo = sub {
  return md5(join '', 'something unique for your implementation', @_);
};

my $checkAuthInfo = sub {
```

```
  my $authInfo = shift;
  my $signature = $calculateAuthInfo->(@{$authInfo}{qw(email time)});
  die "Authentication information is not valid\n"
    if $signature ne $authInfo->signature};
  die "Authentication information is expired\n"
    if time() > $authInfo->(time};
  return $authInfo->{email};
};

my $makeAuthInfo = sub {
  my $email = shift;
  my $time = time()+20*60; # signature will be valid for 20
minutes
  my $signature = $calculateAuthInfo->($email, $time);
  return +{time => $time, email => $email, signature =>
$signature};
};

# ----------------------------------------------------------
# public functions
# ----------------------------------------------------------

sub login {
  my $self = shift;

  pop; # last parameter is envelope, don't count it
  die "Wrong parameter(s): login(email, password)\n" unless @_ == 2;
  my($email, $password) = @_;

  # check credentials, write your own is_valid() function
  die "Credentials are wrong\n" unless is_valid($email, $password);

  # create and return ticket if everything is ok
  return $makeAuthInfo->($email);

}

sub protected {
  my $self = shift;

  # authInfo is passed inside the header
  my $email = $checkAuthInfo->(pop->valueof('//authInfo'));

  # do something, user is already authenticated
  return;
}
```

It would be very careless (and insecure) to create `calculateAuthInfo()` as a normal, exposed function because then the client could invoke it and generate a valid ticket without providing valid credentials (unless you forbid it in the SOAP server configuration, but we'll show another way). We will create `calculateAuthInfo()`, `checkAuthInfo()` and `makeAuthInfo()` as 'private' functions, so only other functions inside the same file may access it. It effectively prevents clients from accessing them directly.

The `login()` function returns hash that has email and time inside as well as an MD5 signature that disallows the user from altering this information. Since the server used a secret string during signature generation, the user is not able to tamper with the resulting signature. To access protected methods, client has to provide the obtained ticket in the header:

7.g.fragment

```
# login
my $authInfo = login(email => 'password');

# convert it into the Header
$authInfo = SOAP::Header->name(authInfo => $authInfo);

# invoke protected method
protected($authInfo, 'parameters');
```

This is just a fragment, but it should give you some ideas on how to implement ticket-based authentication on application level. You MAY even get the ticket in one place (via HTTP for example) and then access SOAP server via SMTP providing this ticket (ideally you should use PKI [public key infrastructure] for that matter).

## Access control

Why would you need **access control**? Imagine that you have a class and want to give access to it selectively, for example, read access to one person and read/write access to another person (or list of persons). At a low level, read and write access means access to specific functions/methods in class.

You may put this check in at the application level (for example with ticket-based authentication), or you may split your class into two different classes and give one person access only to one of them, but it's not an optimal solution. We consider a different approach, where you create two different endpoints that refer to the same class on the server side, but have different access options.

7.e.server (first endpoint)

```
use SOAP::Transport::HTTP;

use Protected;
SOAP::Transport::HTTP::CGI
  -> dispatch_to('Protected::readonly')
  -> handle
;
```

This endpoint will have access only to `readonly()` method in the `Protected` class.

7.e.server (second endpoint)

```
use SOAP::Transport::HTTP;

use Protected;
SOAP::Transport::HTTP::CGI
  -> dispatch_to('Protected')
  -> handle
;
```

This endpoint will have unrestricted access to all methods/functions in the `Protected` class. Now you may put it under basic, digest or some other kind of authentication preventing access to it.

Thus, by combining the capabilities of webserver with the SOAP server you can create an application that best suits your needs.

## *Handling LoLs (List of Lists, Structs, Objects, or something else)*

Processing of complex data structures isn't different in any aspect from usual processing in your programming language. The general rule is simple: **'Treat the result of SOAP call as variable of specified type'**.

The next example shows service that works with array of structs:

8.a.client

```perl
#!perl -w

use SOAP::Lite;

my $result = SOAP::Lite
      -> uri('urn:xmethodsServicesManager')
      ->
proxy('http://www.xmethods.net/soap/servlet/rpcrouter')
      -> getAllSOAPServices();

if ($result->fault) {
  print $result->faultcode, " ", $result->faultstring, "\n";
} else {
  # reference to array of structs is returned
  my @listings = @{$result->result};

  # @listings is the array of structs
  foreach my $listing (@listings) {
    print "————————————————————-\n";
    # print description for every listing
    foreach my $key (keys %{$listing}) {
      print $key, ": ", $listing->{$key} || '', "\n";
    }
  }

}
```

Exactly the same thing is true about structs inside of other structs, list of objects, objects that have lists inside, etc. 'What you return on server side is what you get on client side, and let me know if you get something else.'

(OK, not always. You **MAY** get a blessed array even when you return a simple array on the other side and you **MAY** get a blessed hash when you return a simple one, but it won't change anything in your code, just access it as you usually do.)

# COPYRIGHT

## Author and Contributors

Paul Kulchenko (paulclinger@yahoo.com)

## Major contributors

### Nathan Torkington

Basically started this work and pushed the whole process.

### Tony Hong

Invaluable comments, fixes and input help me keep this material correct, fresh and simple.

# Index

## A

Abacus, 4–6
Access control
    security, 377–378
Accessor
    SOAP rules, 47
Accessor names
    unique, 61
Activation, 45
Active Server Page (ASP). *See* ASP
Active template library (ATL), 230
Active X data objects (ADO), 259
Actor attribute, 70
Add method's implementation, 151–153
ADO, 259
Apache, 210–211
Apache http server, 210–211

Apache module
    Perl, 363–364
    SOAP, 364–365
Apache registry, 363
Apache tcl, 211
Apache xml project, 210–211
ARPANET, 10
Array of bytes, 52
Arrays, 58–60
    SOAP rules, 47
ASP, 12
ASP server
    created
        Perl script, 362
        VB script, 362
ASP/VB, 362
ATL, 230
Attributes

declared, 38
format, 40
keywords, 38–39
SOAP root, 62
XML, 37–41
Attribute type, 38–39
full syntax, 39
Auction
case study summary, 342
object communication, 342–343
Auction item detail view, 325
Auction item view, 321
Auction system
case study, 221–228
design, 229–242
proof of concept, 229
Auto dispatching
Perl, 350

**B**

Babbage, Charles, 7–9
Basic authentication
security, 372–374
Batching of messages, 44
Berners-Lee, Tim, 19
Bet item bids
bidding web service, 331–336
Bid
placement page, 329, 331
placing, 240–241
Bidders
enrollment and management, 243–281
example, 223–224, 231–234
logging in, 240
login screen, 329
Bidding
item web service, 311
pages, 320–334
item detail view, 320–331
viewing selection by category, 320–324
web service, 331–336
Bidding system, 238–241, 319–336
example, 225–226

use cases, 238–241
Binary data
attach
SOAP, 45
Binding
WSDL, 173–174, 180–181
documents, 165
SOAP, 182–184
xsd, 167
Binding key
UDDI, 203
Binding template
UDDI, 203
BizTalk, 45
Body
SOAP message, 75–76
Bounds, 32
Browse patterns
UDDI, 205–206
Business entity element
UDDI, 201–203
Business service
UDDI, 203

**C**

Calculators, 6–7
Cardinality, 32
Case study
summary, 337–343
Category, 285–307
add new, 235
add or edit, 304
delete, 236, 287–289
deletion, 306
edit, 236
Category data access
category management, 285–289
Category editor, 234, 285
category management, 301–307
main page, 302
Category management, 235
case study summary, 339–340
object communication, 340
things to add, 317
use cases, 235–236

Category service
    WSDL file, 290
        code, 290–299
Category web service
    category management, 289–301
Cell directory service, 13
CGI-based SOAP server, 346
Class relationships
    on client, 94
    on server, 93
Client
    error handling, 353
    SOAP application, 76–77
    SOAP lite, 346–348
Client interface, 156
Client management
    case study summary, 338–339
    object communication, 339
CLR, 213
COBRA, 16–20
COLOSSUS, 10
COM, 19
Combined with schemas
    namespaces, 37
Common language runtime (CLR), 213
Common object request broker architec-
    ture (CORBA), 12
Component object model (COM), 19
Compound type
    SOAP rules, 47
Compound value
    representation, 54–56
    SOAP rules, 47
Cookie-based authentication
    security, 374–375
(CORBA), 12
Create
    customer, 233
    delete, 233–234
    edit
        information, 233
    get, 233
Credit card verification services, 199
Currency exchange rates, 368
Customer

account management, 272–274
create, 233
database table relationships, 232
record
    saving, 265–271
SOAP, 250
use cases, 233
Custom marshaler, 14

**D**

Data access layer, 259–262
Database connection
    using JDBC, 246
Database intermediaries, 246
Data link properties, 263
Data types, 34
    attribute, 39
    SOAP, 360
DCE, 12–16
    services needed
        distributed computing secure and
            reliable, 13
DCE security, 13
DCOM, 12, 16–20
Debugging
    RPC, 15–16
Default value
    attribute, 39
Default values, 61–62
Definitions
    WSDL xsd, 167
Delete category
    category Web service, 290
Delete item
    item web service, 311
Detail
    SOAP message, 75–76
Develop Mentor, 88
Dim connector
    soap connector, 155
Dispatch, 356
Display active bids, 235–237
Distributed component object model
    (DCOM). *See* DCOM
Distributed computing, 10–12

challenges, 19
Distributed computing environment
    (DCE). *See* DCE
Distributed garbage collection, 44
Distributed time service, 13
Documentation
    WSDL xsd, 167
Document type declaration (DTD), 28
Dot net. *See* Net
Drill-down pattern
    UDDI, 206
DTD, 28
Duration, 33
Dynamic, 356
    service dispatch, 358–359

**E**

Editing
    item web service, 311
Electronic computers, 9–10
Element
    SSL, 94–100
        element, 96–100
E-mail, 20
Embedded element
    SOAP encoding rules, 48
Encode fault
    SOAP message, 123
Encode method call
    SOAP message, 122
Encode method response
    SOAP message, 123
Encoding, 33
Encoding type information
    WSDL, 174–175
Encoding types
    XML
        rules, 46–49
Endian format, 13–16
ENIAC, 10
Enumerations, 33, 51
Envelope
    SOAP message, 66–67
Equal, 31

Error handling, 352–356
Ethernet, 10
Execute SQL, 261
Extensibility elements, 173–174
    location meaning and use, 174
Extensible markup language (XML), 23–
    42

**F**

Facets, 31–34
    types, 31
Fault
    SSL, 126–128
        code, 127–128
    WSDL xsd, 167
Fault actor
    SOAP message, 75
Fault code, 77
    SOAP message, 75
Fault string, 77
    SOAP message, 75
File transfer protocol (FTP), 20, 25, 79–80
Fill in categories
    bidding system, 322–323
Fill in items method
    ASP.NET page, 323–324
Flagging
    data, 41
Format
    attribute, 40
Forte, 230
FTP, 20, 25, 79–80
Fundamental facet, 31–32

**G**

Galileo, 6
Generate password, 278
Generic compound types, 60–61
Get category by ID
    category Web service, 290
Get child categories
    category Web service, 290
Get item by ID

item web service, 311
Get items by provider
    item web service, 311
Goldfarb, Charles F., 42
Gopher, 25

# H

Handling LoLs, 378–379
Headers
    SOAP message, 67–69
Host, 25
Hosting redirectory
    UDDI, 203
HTML, 26
HTTP, 12–13, 25
    address, 190
    binding, 190
    daemon, 361–362
        in VB script, 362
    encoding, 190–191
    extension framework, 82–83
    get, 187–190
    operation, 190
    specific functionality, 141–146
    url replacement, 191
    using SOAP, 79–80
Hypertext markup language (HTML), 26
Hypertext transfer protocol (HTTP). See
    HTTP

# I

IDE, 230
IDL, 13
IdooXoap, 211
IIOP, 20
Independent element
    SOAP encoding rules, 48
Input
    WSDL xsd, 167
Integrated development environment
    (IDE), 230
Interface definition language (IDL), 13
Intermediary
    SOAP message, 70–74

Internet
    protocols, 44
Internet inter-ORB protocol (IIOP), 20
Interop stack, 200
Invocation pattern
    UDDI, 206
Iona, 212
Iona iPortal SOAP adapter, 212
Iona orbix ORB layering model, 213
IPortal, 212
ISBN
    book price, 367–368
Italics
    purpose, 36
Item, 308
    add, 237
    adding, 313
    delete, 237
    edit, 237
    saved
        for auction system, 315
Item detail view
    bidding system, 324–331
Item editor, 234, 313–316
    login screen, 309
    welcome page, 309
Item enrollment and management
    example, 224–228, 234–247
Item management, 308–318
    case study summary, 341–342
    object communication, 341
    use cases, 237
Item web service, 311–313

# J

Jakarta, 210–211
Java apache, 211
Java data access layer
    coding, 245–250
Java environment, 244–256
    access layer, 245–250
    setting up, 244–245
Java interface
    and SOAP, 250
Java Server Page (JSP), 12

JDBC driver, 230
JSP, 12

**L**

Language binding, 173–174
Language extensibility, 173–174
Languages
    things in common, 46
Length, 32–34
Lesser GNU public license, 89
Library design, 88–90
List of lists, 378–379
Locally scoped
    SOAP encoding rules, 48
Logging in
    bidders, 240

**M**

Mail to, 25
Managing bidders, 259
Max exclusive, 33
Max inclusive, 33
Max length, 33
Message
    WSDL documents, 165
    WSDL xsd, 167
Message definition
    WSDL xsd, 175–176
Message processor
    building, 147–149
Microsoft
    SOAP implementation, 213–215
Microsoft Data Engine (MSDE), 230
Microsoft's .Net initiative, 283
Microsoft SOAP Toolkit v2, 154
Microsoft transaction server (MTS), 19
MIME, 45
    URI and definition, 166
MIME binding, 191–195
MIME content element, 194
MIME-MIME Xml element, 195
MIME multipart related element, 195
Min exclusive, 33

Mini length, 33
Min inclusive, 33
Mixed
    service dispatch, 359
Mod perl, 211
MSDE, 230
MTS, 19
Multidimensional arrays, 59
Multipurpose internet mail extensions
    (MIME). *See* MIME
Multireference values, 56–57
Must understand
    error handling, 353
    SOAP application, 76

**N**

Namespace
    attribute, 39
    combined with schemas, 37
    purpose, 34–35
    specific string, 26
    XML, 34–37
Namespace ID, 26
Napier, John, 6
Napier's Bones, 6
NASDAQ quotes, 368–369
Net, 283
Net Framework SDK, 284
Network news transport protocol
    (Usenet), 79–80
News, 25
Nntp, 25
Null values, 54
Numeric, 32

**O**

Object-by-reference, 45
Object communication
    auction, 342–343
    category management, 340
    client management, 339
    item management, 341
Object creator

SSL, 102–104
Object-oriented interface, 350
Object request broker (ORB), 16
Objects access, 350–352
Ole DB provider selection screen, 263
Open software foundation (OSF), 12
Operation
    WSDL documents, 165
    WSDL xsd, 167
ORB, 16
Orbix 2000, 213
Order, 32
OSF, 12
Oughtred, William, 6
Output
    WSDL xsd, 167

**P**

Packaging model, 43
Parameter order attribute
    WSDL, 176
Parse
    SSL, 129–139
        code, 129–133
Parse message, 139
Parser, 90
Partially transmitted arrays, 59–60
Pascal, Blaise, 7
Passing values
    SOAP, 348–350
Password, 25, 278
    change, 234
Password page
    change, 279
Pattern, 33
Period, 34
Perl
    auto dispatching, 350
PerlEx, 361
PHP, 211
Place bid
    bidding web service, 331–336
Placing bid, 240–241
Plietz, Jasen, 91

Pocket SOAP, 215
Polymorphic accessor, 52–54
Ports, 25
    WSDL, 181–182
    WSDL documents, 165
    WSDL xsd, 167
Port types
    WSDL, 176
    WSDL documents, 165
    WSDL xsd, 167
POST binding, 187–190
Post Office Protocol 3, 79–80
Precision, 33
Prescod, Paul, 42
Processing requirements
    SOAP application, 78
Programmable machines, 7–9
Programmer's API
    UDDI specification, 204–206
Prospero, 25
Protocol layering
    SOAP, 80

**Q**

Query patterns
    UDDI, 205–206
Question element, 55–56

**R**

References, 56–57
Register objects, 147–148
Remote procedure call (RPC). *See* RPC
Remote services
    access, 365–367
Request for Comments (RFC). *See* RFC
Required
    attribute, 39
Reverse
    method implementation, 151–153
RFC 1738, 24–25
RFC 1808, 24–25
RFC 2141, 26
RFC 2617, 257

Rogue wave, 215–216
Rogue wave XML link
    with SOAP, 216
RPC, 12, 13
    block diagram
        basic client/server, 14
    debugging, 15–16
    mechanism, 43
    problems with, 17–20
    SOAP body, 84–85
    using SOAP, 83–84

## S

Sample value representation, 50–54
Save category
    category Web service, 289–290
Save item
    item web service, 311
Scale, 33
Schemas
    SOAP specification, 49
    XML, 28–34
Scheme syntax
    parts, 25
Schickard, Wilhelm, 7
Scoping rules
    XML, 36
Secure sockets layer (SSL), 257, 258, 371
Security, 371–379
    UDDI, 205
Self-documenting XML, 36
Seller authentication
    item management, 308–314
Serialization mechanism, 43
Serialize data
    SOAP specification, 49–54
Server
    error handling, 353
    SOAP application, 77
Service
    WSDL, 181–182
    WSDL documents, 165
    WSDL xsd, 167
Service description
    access

        WSDL, 369–370
Service dispatch, 356–359
Service key
    UDDI, 203
SGML, 26
Share obj, 260
Shipping
    example, 227–228
Shrikumar, Hariharasubrahmanian, 18
Simple mail transport protocol (SMTP), 20
Simple Object Access Protocol (SOAP).
    *See* SOAP
Simple SOAP client, 156–159
Simple SOAP library
    architecture, 91
    SSL, 92–135
Simple SOAP server, 146–156
Simple type
    SOAP rules, 47
Simple value
    SOAP rules, 47
Single-dimensional arrays, 58–59
Singleton class, 106
Singleton pattern, 106
Site displays items
    in category, 239
Slide rule, 6
SMTP, 20
SOAP, 3
    body, 75–76
    design goal, 44
    fault, 75–76
    payload, 75–76
    specification, 43–85
    v1.1 protocol, 43–85
SOAP address
    WSDL binding, 187
SOAP attribute
    SSL
        code, 101–102
SOAP binding
    WSDL, 182–184
    WSDL binding, 184–185
SOAP body
    element, 195

RPC, 84–85
WSDL binding, 185–186
SOAP client, 274–276
SOAP connector
dim connector, 155
SOAP dispatcher, 147–148
SSL, 105–112
code, 107–111
SOAP element, 94–100
code, 96–100
SOAP ENC
URI, 46
SOAP encoder
SSL, 112–124
code, 114–122
SOAP ENC root, 62–63
SOAP ENV
actor, 70–74
must understand, 69–70
URI, 45
SOAP envelope, 43, 66–67
XML document, 64–65
SOAP fault
SSL, 126–128
code, 127–128
WSDL binding, 186–187
SOAP header, 67–69
WSDL binding, 187
SOAP HTTP request, 80–81
SOAP HTTP response, 81–82
SOAP implementations, 209–218
SOAP interface
writing, 250–256
SOAP library, 88–90
SOAP lite, 217
quick start guide, 345–352
SOAP messages, 209
block diagram, 67
body, 75–76
example, 63–64
exchange model, 63–66
processing, 78
scenario, 71–74
structure, 66–74
SOAP method, 124–128
SSL, 124–126

code, 124–126
SOAP network library, 139–146
classes, 139
SOAP object
creator
SSL, 102–104
SSL, 104–105
SOAP on HTTP, 141–146
SOAP on protocol, 139–141
SOAP operation
WSDL binding, 185
SOAP parser
SSL, 129–139
code, 129–133
SOAP requests
responding, 150–155
SOAP root
attribute, 62
SOAP RPC representation, 43
SOAP Toolkit, 213–215
SOAP Toolkit v2, 214
Social engineering, 257
Socket library, 90–91
Sparse arrays, 60
Specification
SOAP, 43–85
SQL, 260–262
SSL, 257, 258, 371
Standard generalized markup language
(SGML), 26
Static, 356
Static external
service dispatch, 357–358
Static internal
service dispatch, 357
Std list
SSL, 95
Std map
SSL, 95
Std vector
SSL, 95
Strings, 51
Structs, 378–379
SOAP rules, 47

# T

TCP/IP, 10
TCP server, 91–92
    library, 147–149
Telnet, 25
Thirteen-column abacus, 4
Threads, 13
Ticket-based authentication
    security, 375–377
Tmodel
    UDDI, 199–200
        element, 203
Tns
    URI and definition, 166
Tomcat, 250
Transmission control protocol/internet
    protocol (TCP/IP), 10. *See also* TCP
Transmission primitive
    WSDL
        notification operation, 179–180
        one-way, 177
        request-response, 178
        solicit-response, 178–179
Two-dimensional array, 59
Type model, 199
Types
    service dispatch, 360–361
    WSDL documents, 165

# U

UDDI, 197–207
    basics, 198
    enables Web services, 200
    information model, 202
    information types, 201–203
    invocation model, 204
    registry, 163
    registry's inquiry API, 204
    schema
        information needed, 201
    specification
        programmer's API, 204–206
    tmodels, 199–200
    usage scenario, 199

UML, 201
Unified modeling language (UML), 201
Uniform resource identifiers (URIs), 24
Uniform resource locator (URL). *See* URL
Uniform resource names (URNs), 25–26
Unique
    accessor names, 61
    methods, 61
Universal description discovery and inte-
    gration (UDDI). *See* UDDI
Universally scoped
    SOAP encoding rules, 48
URIs, 24
URL, 24–25
    path, 25
    schemes, 25
URNs, 25–26
Usenet, 79–80
User, 25
User selects item, 239–240
User selects view items
    for auction, 239
UUDI, 66

# V

Value
    SOAP rules, 47
Value representation, 50
Value space, 31
Value type
    determining, 50
VB application, 154
VB environment, 259–280
VB script
    http daemon, 362
VB to Java connection, 262–271
VB web server, 271–380
VelociGen, 361
Versioning
    UDDI, 205
Version mismatch
    error handling, 353
    SOAP application, 76
Visual basic (VB) application. *See* VB ap-

plication
Visual Studio Net, 214, 284

## W

Wais, 25
WAN, 198
Web method attribute, 290
Web servers
    world's smallest, 18
Web service
    defining, 167–173
    securing access, 256–259
Web services description language (WS-DL). *See* WSDL
Web site
    entrance to, 238
White mesa, 217
Wide area network (WAN), 198
Windows shell programming, 28
WSDL, 163–196
    URI and definition, 166
WSDL document
    layout, 168–171
WSDL file
    category service
        code, 290–299
WSDL 1.1 specification
    prefixes used, 166

## X

Xerces parser, 88
X Link, 41
XML, 23–42
    attributes, 37–41
    basics, 26–28
    namespaces, 34–37
    query language, 41
    schema data types, 34
    schemas, 28–34
    scoping rules, 36
XML-DB link, 215–216
*XML Developers Toolkit*, 42
XML documents
    using Microsoft Internet Explored

    to view, 40
*XML Handbook*, 42
XML schema documents (XSD), 163
XML services framework, 215–216
XML style language (XSL), 41
XML style sheet (XSLT), 209
X Path, 41
X Pointer, 41
XSD, 163
    URI, 46
    URI and definition, 166
Xsi type
    attribute, 39
    URI, 46
Xsi values, 39
XSL, 41
XSLT, 209

## Z

Zope, 218

## LICENSE AGREEMENT AND LIMITED WARRANTY

READ THE FOLLOWING TERMS AND CONDITIONS CAREFULLY BEFORE OPENING THIS DISK PACKAGE. THIS LEGAL DOCUMENT IS AN AGREEMENT BETWEEN YOU AND PRENTICE-HALL, INC. (THE "COMPANY"). BY OPENING THIS SEALED DISK PACKAGE, YOU ARE AGREEING TO BE BOUND BY THESE TERMS AND CONDITIONS. IF YOU DO NOT AGREE WITH THESE TERMS AND CONDITIONS, DO NOT OPEN THE DISK PACKAGE. PROMPTLY RETURN THE UNOPENED DISK PACKAGE AND ALL ACCOMPANYING ITEMS TO THE PLACE YOU OBTAINED THEM FOR A FULL REFUND OF ANY SUMS YOU HAVE PAID.

1. **GRANT OF LICENSE:** In consideration of your payment of the license fee, which is part of the price you paid for this product, and your agreement to abide by the terms and conditions of this Agreement, the Company grants to you a nonexclusive right to use and display the copy of the enclosed software program (hereinafter the "SOFTWARE") on a single computer (i.e., with a single CPU) at a single location so long as you comply with the terms of this Agreement. The Company reserves all rights not expressly granted to you under this Agreement.

2. **OWNERSHIP OF SOFTWARE:** You own only the magnetic or physical media (the enclosed disks) on which the SOFTWARE is recorded or fixed, but the Company retains all the rights, title, and ownership to the SOFTWARE recorded on the original disk copy(ies) and all subsequent copies of the SOFTWARE, regardless of the form or media on which the original or other copies may exist. This license is not a sale of the original SOFTWARE or any copy to you.

3. **COPY RESTRICTIONS:** This SOFTWARE and the accompanying printed materials and user manual (the "Documentation") are the subject of copyright. You may not copy the Documentation or the SOFTWARE, except that you may make a single copy of the SOFTWARE for backup or archival purposes only. You may be held legally responsible for any copying or copyright infringement which is caused or encouraged by your failure to abide by the terms of this restriction.

4. **USE RESTRICTIONS:** You may not network the SOFTWARE or otherwise use it on more than one computer or computer terminal at the same time. You may physically transfer the SOFTWARE from one computer to another provided that the SOFTWARE is used on only one computer at a time. You may not distribute copies of the SOFTWARE or Documentation to others. You may not reverse engineer, disassemble, decompile, modify, adapt, translate, or create derivative works based on the SOFTWARE or the Documentation without the prior written consent of the Company.

5. **TRANSFER RESTRICTIONS:** The enclosed SOFTWARE is licensed only to you and may not be transferred to any one else without the prior written consent of the Company. Any unauthorized transfer of the SOFTWARE shall result in the immediate termination of this Agreement.

6. **TERMINATION:** This license is effective until terminated. This license will terminate automatically without notice from the Company and become null and void if you fail to comply with any provisions or limitations of this license. Upon termination, you shall destroy the Documentation and all copies of the SOFTWARE. All provisions of this Agreement as to warranties, limitation of liability, remedies or damages, and our ownership rights shall survive termination.

7. **MISCELLANEOUS:** This Agreement shall be construed in accordance with the laws of the United States of America and the State of New York and shall benefit the Company, its affiliates, and assignees.

8. **LIMITED WARRANTY AND DISCLAIMER OF WARRANTY:** The Company warrants that the SOFTWARE, when properly used in accordance with the Documentation, will operate in substantial conformity with the description of the SOFTWARE set forth in the Documentation. The Company does not warrant that the SOFTWARE will meet your requirements or that the operation of the SOFTWARE will be uninterrupted or error-free. The Company warrants that the media on which the SOFTWARE is delivered shall be free from defects in materials and workmanship under normal use for a period of thirty (30) days from the date of your purchase. Your only remedy and the Company's only obligation under these limited warranties is, at the Company's option, return of the warranted item for a refund of any amounts paid by you or replacement of the item. Any replacement of SOFTWARE or media under the warranties shall not extend the original warranty period. The limited warranty set forth above shall not apply to any SOFTWARE which the Company determines in good faith has been subject to misuse, neglect, improper installation, repair, alteration, or damage by you. EXCEPT FOR THE EXPRESSED WARRANTIES SET FORTH ABOVE, THE COMPANY DISCLAIMS ALL WARRANTIES, EXPRESS OR IMPLIED, INCLUDING WITHOUT LIMITATION, THE IMPLIED WARRANTIES OF MERCHANTABILITY AND FITNESS FOR A PARTICULAR PURPOSE. EXCEPT FOR THE EXPRESS WARRANTY SET FORTH ABOVE, THE COMPANY DOES NOT WARRANT, GUARANTEE, OR MAKE ANY REPRESENTATION REGARDING THE USE OR THE RESULTS OF THE USE OF THE SOFTWARE IN TERMS OF ITS CORRECTNESS, ACCURACY, RELIABILITY, CURRENTNESS, OR OTHERWISE.

IN NO EVENT, SHALL THE COMPANY OR ITS EMPLOYEES, AGENTS, SUPPLIERS, OR CONTRACTORS BE LIABLE FOR ANY INCIDENTAL, INDIRECT, SPECIAL, OR CONSEQUENTIAL DAMAGES ARISING OUT OF OR IN CONNECTION WITH THE LICENSE GRANTED UNDER THIS AGREEMENT, OR FOR LOSS OF USE, LOSS OF DATA, LOSS OF INCOME OR PROFIT, OR OTHER LOSSES, SUSTAINED AS A RESULT OF INJURY TO ANY PERSON, OR LOSS OF OR DAMAGE TO PROPERTY, OR CLAIMS OF THIRD PARTIES, EVEN IF THE COMPANY OR AN AUTHORIZED REPRESENTATIVE OF THE COMPANY HAS BEEN ADVISED OF THE POSSIBILITY OF SUCH DAMAGES. IN NO EVENT SHALL LIABILITY OF THE COMPANY FOR DAMAGES WITH RESPECT TO THE SOFTWARE EXCEED THE AMOUNTS ACTUALLY PAID BY YOU, IF ANY, FOR THE SOFTWARE.

SOME JURISDICTIONS DO NOT ALLOW THE LIMITATION OF IMPLIED WARRANTIES OR LIABILITY FOR INCIDENTAL, INDIRECT, SPECIAL, OR CONSEQUENTIAL DAMAGES, SO THE ABOVE LIMITATIONS MAY NOT ALWAYS APPLY. THE WARRANTIES IN THIS AGREEMENT GIVE YOU SPECIFIC LEGAL RIGHTS AND YOU MAY ALSO HAVE OTHER RIGHTS WHICH VARY IN ACCORDANCE WITH LOCAL LAW.

### ACKNOWLEDGMENT

YOU ACKNOWLEDGE THAT YOU HAVE READ THIS AGREEMENT, UNDERSTAND IT, AND AGREE TO BE BOUND BY ITS TERMS AND CONDITIONS. YOU ALSO AGREE THAT THIS AGREEMENT IS THE COMPLETE AND EXCLUSIVE STATEMENT OF THE AGREEMENT BETWEEN YOU AND THE COMPANY AND SUPERSEDES ALL PROPOSALS OR PRIOR AGREEMENTS, ORAL, OR WRITTEN, AND ANY OTHER COMMUNICATIONS BETWEEN YOU AND THE COMPANY OR ANY REPRESENTATIVE OF THE COMPANY RELATING TO THE SUBJECT MATTER OF THIS AGREEMENT.

Should you have any questions concerning this Agreement or if you wish to contact the Company for any reason, please contact in writing at the address below.

Robin Short
Prentice Hall PTR
One Lake Street, Upper Saddle River, New Jersey 07458